Race, Self-employment,
and Upward Mobility

Race, Self-employment, and Upward Mobility

An Illusive American Dream

TIMOTHY BATES

THE WOODROW WILSON CENTER PRESS
Washington, D.C.

THE JOHNS HOPKINS UNIVERSITY PRESS
Baltimore and London

EDITORIAL OFFICES:

The Woodrow Wilson Center Press
370 L'Enfant Promenade, S.W., Suite 704
Washington, D.C. 20024-2518
Telephone 202-287-3000, ext. 218

ORDER FROM:

The Johns Hopkins University Press
Hampden Station
Baltimore, Maryland 21211
Telephone 1-800-537-5487

2 4 6 8 9 7 5 3 1

Library of Congress Cataloging-in-Publication Data

Bates, Timothy Mason.
    Race, self-employment, and upward mobility : an illusive American
dream / Timothy Bates.
        p.   cm.
    Includes bibliographical references and index.
    ISBN 0-8018-5798-8 (alk. paper). — ISBN 0-8018-5799-6 (pbk. :
alk. paper)
    1. Self-employed Afro-Americans.   2. Self-employed Asian
Americans.   3. Occupational mobility—United States.   I. Title.
HD8037.U5B384   1997
331.6'3'0973—dc21   97-17782
                                                                    CIP

Contents

Acknowledgments ix

CHAPTER ONE
Entrepreneurship and Upward Mobility
among Asian Immigrants and African Americans 1

CHAPTER TWO
Class Resources and Self-employment
Entry and Exit Patterns 24

CHAPTER THREE
Social Resources Generated by Group Support Networks: Do They
Benefit Asian-Immigrant-Owned Small Businesses? 50

CHAPTER FOUR
Escaping from Self-Employment:
An Analysis of Asian-Immigrant-Owned Small Businesses 77

CHAPTER FIVE
Explaining the Self-employment Patterns of
Asian Immigrants in the United States 97

CHAPTER SIX
Financing Small-Business Creation:
The Case of Chinese and Korean Entrepreneurs 121

CHAPTER SEVEN
Traditional and Emerging Lines of
Black-Owned Small Businesses 142

CHAPTER EIGHT
The Owner's Human Capital and Market
Accessibility: Factors Shaping the Black
Business Community 163

CHAPTER NINE
Access to Financial Capital: Factors Shaping
the Black Business Community 189

CHAPTER TEN
Entrepreneurship as a Route to Upward
Mobility among the Disadvantaged 207

CHAPTER ELEVEN
Government's Role in Assisting
Minority-Owned Businesses 225

CHAPTER TWELVE
The Meaning of Small-Business Success 248

Appendix: Databases and Variable Definitions 261

References 275

Index 285

Acknowledgments

Most of the research reported in this book was undertaken during the term of my fellowship appointment at the Woodrow Wilson International Center for Scholars in 1994. The supportive staff and the inspiring environment at the Woodrow Wilson Center added significantly to my research endeavors. My analysis of government preferential procurement programs seeking to assist minority-owned businesses (chapter 11) was supported by the Minority Business Development Agency (MBDA), U.S. Department of Commerce.

Darrell Williams helped me conduct the analysis of preferential procurement's impact upon minority-owned businesses, as did the staff of the Joint Center for Political and Economic Studies (Washington, D.C.), particularly Margaret Simms. Constance Dunham worked extensively with me to produce the analyses (chapters 2 and 9) that are based upon the Census Bureau's Survey of Income and Program Participation (SIPP) database. The comprehensiveness of the analyses reported in this book reflects their expert assistance. At various stages of writing, I benefited greatly from the comments, criticisms, and suggestions of Darrell Williams, Roger Waldinger, Harriet Duleep, Nathan Glazer, Margaret Simms, Robert McGuckin, Alfred Nucci, Cordelia Reimers, Richard Stevens, and Stanley Tucker.

Perhaps my greatest debt is to several pioneers in the federal government who fought long and hard to create sophisticated databases describing small businesses and their owners. Every chapter in this volume draws upon the Census Bureau's Characteristics of Business Owners (CBO) database, the nation's premier small business database. Richard Stevens (MBDA) is most responsible for the creation of the CBO data, and he was assisted by Bruce Phillips of the U.S. Small Business Administration.

Much of our supposed knowledge of the role of small business in the U.S. economy is, in fact, a mix of folklore and dogma. Because of the efforts of Stevens, Phillips, and others, I have been provided with the hard data to challenge some of this dogma. Much of their work to bring sophistication to small-business analysis is now being swept away as the federal government contracts. The CBO database itself is headed for oblivion after being in existence for only a decade. My hope is that Stevens and Phillips, as they read this book, will realize again how important their efforts have been to bring self-employment and small-business research out of the closet.

My thanks, finally, are owed to the U.S. Bureau of the Census Center for Economic Studies (CES). Under the directorship of Robert McGuckin, the CES has made huge strides forward in providing access for researchers to the various business databases compiled by the Census Bureau. Most of the data analyses reported in this book were conducted at the CES, which serves as a vehicle for permitting researchers to access classified business data. Alfred Nucci is the resident CES expert on small-business data files; I have benefited extensively from his generous assistance.

Earlier versions of several chapters of this book have appeared in scholarly journals, including *Social Forces*, the *Journal of Business Venturing*, *Urban Affairs Quarterly*, and the *Journal of Urban Affairs*.

Race, Self-employment, and Upward Mobility

Entrepreneurship and Upward Mobility among Asian Immigrants and African Americans

The immigrant experience is often put forth as a parable of economic opportunity in the United States. Successive waves of immigrants have arrived in this country and successfully placed themselves on the economic mobility escalator. Small-business creation and operation have played a prominent role in the efforts of immigrant groups to achieve upward mobility. Is the self-employment element of the immigrant success parable an accurate representation of recent experience? In fact, the ingredients for success in self-employment vary little between immigrants and nonimmigrants or across racial-ethnic groups in contemporary America. People most likely to pursue self-employment are highly educated and skilled, often possessing significant personal financial resources. Likewise, those lacking the requisite skills and capital, whether immigrant or otherwise, are unlikely to start small businesses. Among people who choose self-employment without appropriate education, skills, and financial resources, business failure and self-employment exit rates are high. These patterns typify black, Asian, and white Americans, men and women, immigrants and the native born.

Dinesh D'Souza states that "blacks have done very poorly in small business, a vital source of American jobs and upward mobility" (1995, 33). Such statements reflect widely held perceptions about small business that are poorly grounded in fact. A paucity of empirical data coexists with numerous stereotypes about self-employment patterns, particularly regarding the experiences of Asian immigrants who create small businesses in the United States. "Asian immigrants were poor and visibly non-European and were subject to racial discrimination on that account. These very qualities tended to force the Chinese and Japanese into the classic small business occupations with which they have now become identified in the popular mind" (Light 1972, 5–6). While this depiction may accurately characterize Asian self-employment patterns in California a century ago, its applicability to contemporary America is nil.

The urban Korean grocer exemplifies the belief that small-business ownership is a route to upward mobility in America for those who work hard and live frugally. If this latter-day Horatio Alger, "famous neo-conservative icon" (Kutter 1994, 8) flourishes selling groceries in America's poorest urban areas, then why don't local residents (including African Americans) take advantage of these business opportunities? What about the local poor, the unemployed, and the welfare recipients: why do they not seize the opportunities exploited by the Koreans? Is it because of aversion to hard work, lack of initiative, or related cultural deficiencies? Alternatively, is it because the local poor often lack college educations, white-collar work experience, and the financial resources possessed by many of the Korean immigrant entrepreneurs?

OVERVIEW

Racial and ethnic groups do pursue different self-employment and small-business ownership strategies in their attempts to get ahead in American society. This study focuses primarily on the approaches of two groups—African Americans and Asian-immigrant Americans, both of whom have made substantial progress in small business over the past two decades.

Widely varying and inconsistent interpretations of performance in self-employment typify these groups: Asian immigrants are seen as the classic small-business success story, while scholars and journalists often address black entrepreneurship by asking, "What's wrong with blacks?" In actuality there is really very little consensus, much less hard evidence, as to why Asians might be successful and African Americans lag behind in self-employment. This book concentrates on the hard evidence.

Influential qualitative studies of minority entrepreneurship often focus on immigrants operating businesses in a specific location—Koreans in Los Angeles (Bonacich and Light 1988) or Chinese in New York (Waldinger 1986). These studies are often provocative and interesting, yet generalizing their results is difficult because they rarely use sophisticated statistical methods to sort out and establish cause-and-effect relationships regarding business outcomes. These studies, however, tend to be downright substantive relative to quantitative studies using databases that are not suited for small-business analysis. For example, decennial census of population data are often used to investigate self-employment dynamics (Light and Rosenstein 1995). Yet since these studies lack essential data on the amount of financial capital invested in the firm by its owner, the size of the firm (neither gross revenues nor number of employees), the nature of the market in which the firm competes, and so forth, conclusions are hard to draw (see, for example, Boyd 1990a; Borjas 1986; Portes and Zhou 1996).

The comprehensiveness of this study is made possible by a major breakthrough in the quality of small-business data. The Characteristics of Business Owners (CBO) survey, compiled by the U.S. Bureau of the Census in 1992, produced the first national database that describes self-employed people as individuals and characterizes the traits of the businesses they own, such as volume of sales, amount of financial capital invested in the firm, number of employees, nature of the markets served, profits, and so forth. The owners of nearly 90,000 small businesses were surveyed to create the CBO database, and minority owners were very heavily oversampled. The outcome is a database of small businesses that is representative of all firms owned by Asians, blacks, and whites (among others) for which small-business federal income-tax returns were filed in 1987. The firms were then traced to late 1991 to delineate those still operating from those that had gone out of business (see the appendix, "Databases and Variable Definitions"). Although I analyze data on self-employment from several sources, I focus heavily on 25,337 firms in the CBO database that began operation between 1979 and 1987. The relevant data on the characteristics of firms and owners for these firms were provided by owners' responses to Census Bureau survey questionnaires (see the appendix, "Databases and Variable Definitions"). Table 1.1 describes traits of these 25,337 firms and their owners. I use the nonminority-owned firms as a comparison group: they are the small-business norm in the United States, and they highlight how blacks and Asian immigrants deviate from that norm.

Table 1.1

Traits of Firms Nationwide Formed 1979–1987

	Asian Immigrant	African American	Nonminority
Firm's traits (mean values)			
Gross sales, 1987	$121,596	$64,526	$154,274
Total financial capital*	$53,550	$14,226	$31,939
Equity capital*	$26,838	$7,010	$14,195
Debt capital*	$26,711	$7,216	$17,744
Percent started with			
zero financial capital	16.2%	28.9%	23.7%
Percent still operating			
in 1991	81.2%	73.6%	76.9%
Owner's traits (mean values)			
Percent college graduates	57.8%	30.2%	37.7%
Annual owner-labor input			
in hours	2,064	1,803	1,960

Note: Variables are defined in the appendix, "Databases and Variable Definitions," pp. 270–3.

Source: U.S. Bureau of the Census, Characteristics of Business Owners (CBO) database, 1992.

*At date of entry into self-employment.

This study concludes that successful small businesses tend to be those created with a substantial investment of the owner's financial capital, along with the strong educational credentials of business owners. Table 1.1 shows that 57.8 percent of Asian entrepreneurs were college graduates versus 30.2 percent of black and 37.7 percent of the non-minority business owners. Table 1.1 also shows that the average financial capital invested at business start-up was $53,550 among the Asian immigrants versus $14,226 among blacks and $31,939 among non-minorities. The owner's equity investment—derived almost entirely from household wealth—averaged $26,838 among Asian immigrants, 383 percent higher than the $7,010 averaged among African Americans. The stereotype of the poor immigrant starting a business on a shoestring is inconsistent with the data on Asian-immigrant start-up capital in table 1.1. Of the Asian start-ups, 16.2 percent had no financial capital whatsoever to work with, but groups other than Asian immigrants more frequently start out with no capital. Asian immigrants who become self-employed are outstanding as a group for the tremendous amount of human and financial capital they invest in their new small businesses.

TRADITIONAL VERSUS EMERGING
LINES OF MINORITY ENTERPRISE

Theorists like to stress personal preferences, talents, and personality traits that delineate dynamic, innovative, risk-taking entrepreneurs from wage and salary earners. Kihlstrom and Laffont (1979) depict the decision to become an entrepreneur in terms of choosing the risky return of self-employment over the less risky return of wage and salary work. Lucas (1978) portrays entrepreneurial ability as a seemingly innate trait: some have what it takes to be an entrepreneur and some do not. An unsettling aspect of the Lucas approach is its limited insight into the causes of the huge differences in self-employment rates across the racial, ethnic, and gender subgroups. Do the low self-employment rates typifying African Americans reflect their relative lack of the necessary abilities and inclinations? Further, are such abilities and personality traits somehow historically contingent on the prevailing social, economic, and political circumstances, or are they ahistoric, innate characteristics? Lucas's work suggests the latter; my work suggests the former.

Scholars who study the development of the minority small-business community in the United States are unanimous on at least one issue: minority self-employment patterns only make sense in the context of prevailing constraints and opportunities (Waldinger, Aldrich, and Ward 1990). Changes in these constraints and opportunities transform self-employment entry, types of business opportunities, and so forth. Changes in constraints and opportunities, in fact, have profoundly altered the minority business community in the United States in recent decades.

Forty years ago minority entrepreneurship was not a major route to upward mobility in the United States. Numbers of small businesses were declining nationwide, and traditional minority business strongholds in small-scale retailing were under particular pressure. Minority business owners—whether black or Asian—commonly struggled to make a living running marginal enterprises. The typical firm in the black community was the mom-and-pop food store, the small restaurant, the beauty parlor, and the barber shop. These tiny firms, concentrated in black residential areas and serving a local clientele, had been in a state of decline since the 1930s. The traditional Asian small-business sector exhibited even less diversity than the black business community. Three lines of small-scale enterprise—laundries, restaurants, and food stores—made up the bulk of Asian-owned firms. Census data indicate that self-employed minorities nationwide had, on average, 7.6 years of education in 1960 and mean self-employment earnings of $1,812 in 1959. Their earnings lagged behind those of all minorities working as employees (Bates 1987).

Distinct traces of a racial caste system shaped the minority business community during the first six decades of the twentieth century. Highly educated members of minority groups were particularly trapped. Difficulties facing the Asian American educated elite were spelled out clearly in 1932 by an official of Stanford University: "It is almost impossible to place a Chinese or Japanese of either the first or the second generation in any kind of position, engineering, manufacturing, or business. Most firms have general regulations against employing them; others object to them on the grounds that the other men employed by the firms do not care to work with them" (Ichihashi 1932, in Bonacich and Modell 1981, 86). Denied access to most managerial and professional jobs, self-employment was a common refuge for Asian college graduates. Unlike laundries and restaurants—which often catered to whites—self-employed Asian professionals were restricted to serving Asian clients.

Well into the twentieth century, African Americans who attended college were hemmed in by social attitudes about which occupations were appropriate for blacks. Between 1912 and 1938, 73 percent of black college graduates nationwide became either teachers or preachers (Holsey 1938). The few entering professions—law, medicine, dentistry—served an all-black clientele. Shoeshiners, caterers—even barbers—might serve a white clientele, but black college graduates did not. This sort of hemming in is what shaped and narrowed Asian as well as African American small business: a few doors were held open but many were closed. White attitudes about appropriate roles for self-employed minorities shaped the opportunities. Merit still mattered in this caste system, but the range of alternatives people entering careers faced was greatly narrowed. Thus, the size of the middle class was artificially restricted, and the nature of the resultant small-business community was severely circumscribed.

The Chinese, according to Ivan Light, did not by nature gravitate toward laundries and restaurants. Yet by 1920 over 50 percent of all Chinese in the United States were employed or self-employed in these businesses: "Obtaining a livelihood was a question of scraping the bottom of the barrel after whites had helped themselves" (Light 1972, 7).

Chinese-owned manufacturing firms of this era were pressured not to compete with white firms. Whites "raised no barrier to Chinese in the laundry trade, since this occupation was not one in which white males cared to engage. Chinese-owned restaurants were also tolerated" (Light 1972, 7).

Japanese self-employment in early twentieth century America was heavily concentrated in vegetable farming, particularly in California. When the Japanese began to buy and lease agricultural land to establish independent farms, California growers turned to state government to combat this unwanted competition. Japanese Americans farmed 4,698 acres of California land in 1900 and 281,687 acres in 1913 (Ichihashi 1932, in Bonacich and Modell 1981), but Alien Land Laws, first passed in California in 1913, prevented Japanese farmers from acquiring additional agricultural land. A wave of these laws, passed by California and other western states, halted the growth of Japanese farming. Driven increasingly into urban areas by such laws, the Japanese were restricted to menial wage employment. Self-employment was an attractive alternative. Among all employed Japanese men living in Los Angeles in 1941, Bloom and Riemer found that 47 percent were self-employed (cited in Bonacich and Modell 1981).

The Japanese, indeed, may have been particularly entrepreneurial by nature, but the presence or absence of entrepreneurial personality traits was overshadowed by the fact that they were "pushed into small business by the surrounding society, rather than by forces internal to the group" (Bonacich and Modell 1981, 61). In a similar vein, Ivan Light notes, "Since World War II, salaried white-collar jobs have become increasingly available to college-educated Chinese Americans, who prefer these jobs to self-employment in restaurants, curio stores, or laundries" (1972, 8).

Minority entrepreneurs have often catered to a clientele of fellow ethnic-group members, but when they ventured into the broader marketplace, opportunities were limited to those that white society felt were appropriate to their inferior status. Traditional service occupations—ironing shirts, shining shoes, preparing and serving meals—were commonly found suitable by the dominant society. Minority entrepreneurs providing such services to whites were acting the way minorities were supposed to act. This sentiment was still profoundly shaping the nature of the minority business community in 1960. This is why college-educated blacks avoided self-employment, and this is why college-educated Asian Americans left self-employment in the post–World War II years as options for salaried employment began to expand. The traditional minority business community entered the 1960s as a fading relic of a declining era. In fact, a new age was dawning. Years of great growth were about to begin for minority entrepreneurship in America.

The nature of the minority business community is profoundly different in the 1990s than it was in the 1960s. As size and scope have expanded, business diversity has flourished. The growing lines of minority businesses are dominated today by large-scale firms serving a racially diverse clientele. These operations are commonly run by college-educated entrepreneurs. Areas of particularly rapid growth include skill-intensive services: finance and business and various professional services. Such growth sectors are commonly called "emerging" lines of minority enterprise because minority ownership in these areas has heretofore been minimal. This all-important transformation—away from declining traditional fields, toward the emerging lines of minority entrepreneurship—is actually much more pronounced in the black business community than in its Asian counterpart.

Since the 1960s, the African American business community has started to diversify and expand in response to an influx of entrepreneurial talent and financial capital. Aggregate figures on black-owned businesses understate this progress because they fail to identify two divergent trends: absolute decline in many traditional lines of business and real progress in emerging fields. Why the decline in the traditional strongholds? The large traditional sector of the black business community developed under pervasive racial segregation. Partial desegregation in housing, the workplace, commercial establishments, and public accommodations contributed to the decline of these firms: desegregation widened the range of retail and service markets accessible to black consumers. Desegregation did not, however, lead to whites patronizing black-owned businesses in significant numbers. And many of the traditional black firms were ill-equipped to exploit the new opportunities desegregation offered.

Constraints that shaped the traditional African American business community—limited access to capital, barriers to education and training, limited markets, and so forth—have changed substantially since the 1960s. The availability of government loans guaranteed against default, in conjunction with pressure generated by the 1977 Community Reinvestment Act, induced many banks in the late 1960s and 1970s to extend business loans to African Americans, thus eroding a tradition of minimal contact between blacks and the commercial lenders (Bates and Bradford 1979). In addition, college enrollment by black students has increased dramatically since the 1960s, especially in business-related fields.

Gains in higher education typify how reductions in discriminatory barriers are translated into significant progress in the minority business community. Fewer than 300,000 African Americans were enrolled nationwide in colleges and universities in 1965. By 1980, that number had risen to 1,107,000. Whereas African Americans receiving bachelor's degrees in 1965 were concentrated in education departments, by the mid-1970s business had become the most popular major among black male graduates. Although education remained the most common major among black women, less than half of the recipients of bachelor's degrees in 1976 were education majors. Selected figures cited below (table 1.2) demonstrate that this transformation in the educational pursuits of black college graduates continued throughout the 1980s: teaching gave way to business and technical fields (Carter and Wilson 1992; Carter and Wilson 1995).

In less than one generation, college enrollment nearly quadrupled, and the fields of concentration pursued by African American college students shifted dramatically. The educational gains that took place a

Table 1.2

Bachelor's Degrees Awarded Nationwide to African Americans

		1976	1992	Percentage Change, 1976–92
Education	Men	3,700	1,266	
	Women	10,509	3,960	
	Total	14,209	5,226	−63.2
Business	Men	5,877	7,167	
	Women	3,612	11,137	
	Total	9,489	18,304	+92.9
Engineering	Men	1,303	2,583	
	Women	67	997	
	Total	1,370	3,580	+161.3

Source: Carter and Wilson 1992; 1995.

generation ago are particularly relevant to comprehending present-day trends in black business. Self-employment is rarely pursued full-time by recent college graduates; entry into small business is most wide-spread among people in their late thirties and forties with fifteen to twenty years of work experience (Bates 1995c). Thus, the full impact of the educational gains of the late 1960s and 1970s is reflected in the number and nature of the business start-ups of African Americans in the 1980s and 1990s.

College enrollment among Asian Americans has grown even faster than it has among blacks, particularly in recent years. Black enrollment grew explosively from 1965 to 1975, rising from 274,000 to 948,000, but that growth rate has since slowed: college enrollments nationwide among African Americans rose from 1,107,000 in 1980 to only 1,410,000 in 1993. Enrollments among Asian Americans, however, have risen very rapidly, from 286,000 nationwide in 1980 to 724,000 in 1993. Immigration drives much of this enrollment growth, making direct comparisons with African Americans difficult to interpret. But one trend is clear: the shift in field of concentration typifying black college students applies to Asian Americans as well (table 1.3).

For black and Asian American college graduates, business and tech-nical degrees awarded have outdistanced overall enrollment growth. For both groups, bachelor's degrees in business are more numerous

Table 1.3
Bachelor's Degrees Awarded Nationwide to Asian Americans

		1976	1992	Percentage Change, 1976–92
Education	Men	292	246	
	Women	484	731	
	Total	776	977	25.9%
Business	Men	1,297	4,761	
	Women	532	5,831	
	Total	1,829	10,592	+479.1%
Engineering	Men	924	5,881	
	Women	47	1,300	
	Total	971	7,181	+639.5%

Source: Carter and Wilson 1992; 1995.

than degrees in any other field, and technical degrees exhibit the most rapid growth rates. Educational gains stand out as a major cause of the ongoing transformation of the minority business community: high growth fields for small business are those in which college-graduate small-business owners are most numerous.

Emerging firms have also benefited from the erosion of discrimination, which has allowed them to penetrate traditionally inaccessible markets. Since the 1970s, large corporations in consumer products businesses have steadily increased their purchases from minority-owned businesses. Government procurement opportunities have also expanded, although the experiences of minority vendors serving government clients have been mixed (chapter 11).

Growing numbers of experienced, financially sophisticated black entrepreneurs are thrusting some enterprises into the mainstream of corporate America. In 1987, Reginald Lewis completed the largest transaction ever negotiated by an African American when he purchased the International Foods Division of Beatrice, Inc., with annual sales of $1.8 billion. J. Bruce Llewellyn and Julius Erving own the Philadelphia Coca-Cola Bottling Company (Jaynes and Williams 1989). The largest of the black-owned businesses today compete in the open marketplace: they do not typically target a minority clientele. In contrast, the largest black-owned enterprises of the mid-twentieth century catered exclusively to minority clients. These giants of an earlier era flourished in market niches that were generally overlooked by corporate America. Black-owned businesses reliant upon these traditional markets have experienced growing competition from mainstream corporate America since the 1960s. Their changing fortunes are a reflection of the same social forces that have permitted emerging black-owned firms to compete successfully in the nonminority marketplace.

Black Enterprise magazine first published a list of the top one hundred black-owned firms—ranked by sales revenue—in 1972. Total sales for those one hundred firms were $473 million (Jaynes and Williams 1989, 181). By 1995, corresponding total sales for the largest one hundred black-owned firms had grown to $7.4 billion. In the 1970s, the largest one hundred black enterprises were dominated by firms catering to black households; of the top one hundred in 1976, forty-three were retailers and only two were in business services. By 1995, few of the top one hundred black-owned businesses were in retailing: twenty-five were in manufacturing, and twenty-seven were in business services. Business services, in turn, were dominated by computer software firms, whose clients were commonly other businesses or government agencies, not black consumers.

The nature of the black business community has changed profoundly since the 1960s. A key factor responsible for the growth of black enterprises is the rising incidence of highly educated entrepreneurs in nontraditional lines of business. The shift in the composition of the black business community—away from traditional personal services and mom-and-pop retail stores, toward high-yield businesses—has resulted in entrepreneurship increasingly leading to upward mobility. In stark contrast, Asian self-employment rates, which have consistently been higher than rates for whites, continue to rise, both because of progress in more rewarding lines of business and because of continued heavy concentration in the lower-yielding traditional fields. In fact, immigrant Asian entrepreneurs are responsible for the continuing high rate of growth in traditional minority enterprises. Highly educated Asian immigrants to the United States continue to start small-scale restaurants, grocery stores, and laundries that yield low profits to their owners and often degenerate into underemployment.

The crowding of Asian immigrants into fields such as small-scale retailing has often been misinterpreted as evidence of success (Bonacich and Light 1988). Why have Asian Americans, including highly educated individuals, clung to traditional retail ventures, such as food stores and restaurants, while blacks as well as whites have moved away from mom-and-pop retail and personal-service firms? The behavior of college-educated Asian immigrants entering traditional self-employment fields reflects declining opportunities for salaried employment rather than attractive self-employment options (Borjas 1994).

Educated Asian immigrants are often blocked from occupying professional or managerial jobs in the United States commensurate with their work experience and skills because of language barriers or employer hesitation to recognize foreign credentials. Small businesses are an alternative.

Properly viewed, self-employment is often a temporary expedient for immigrant households that are establishing themselves economically and socially in the United States. If the returns are low and the hours are long, that period of hardship represents part of the price of admission to the new homeland. However painful, the costs of transition will be borne in hopes that the decision to immigrate will pay off in the long run. Once well-educated Asian small-business owners acquire the English-language skills and the connections they need, they move out of marginal firms into jobs that use their professional skills more directly. Barring successful transition out of traditional lines of self-employment, they nonetheless encourage their children to enter the mainstream economy.

The recognition that African Americans—after controlling for human and financial capital investments—earn higher self-employment returns than Asian-immigrant grocery store owners puts the issue of black business viability in a different light. College-educated African Americans tend to avoid such businesses because they can earn higher returns elsewhere. Running a small retail store in the ghetto, bluntly, is a waste of their time. The circumstances that made traditional self-employment ventures a rational choice are unique to the immigrant experience: indigenous minorities, whether college graduates or high-school dropouts, would find nothing useful to emulate if they were contemplating self-employment, because their opportunities and barriers are fundamentally unlike those of immigrant business owners.

MAINSTREAM EXPLANATIONS OF SMALL-BUSINESS CREATION AND OPERATION

Different ethnic groups in the United States exhibit widely varying self-employment rates. Among adults nationwide reporting a single dominant ancestry in the 1980 census data, Fratoe (1986) calculated self-employment rates for selected groups as follows:

Lebanese	10.7 %
Norwegian	8.8 %
Korean	6.9 %
English	6.0 %
Filipino	2.2 %
Mexican	1.9 %
Puerto Rican	1.1 %

Looking solely at people migrating to the United States between 1970 and 1980, Koreans ranked first in self-employment, at 11.5 percent. In contrast, less than 2 percent of Mexican immigrants to the United States in that period worked for themselves (Waldinger, Aldrich, and Ward 1990).

Why do self-employment rates vary so widely across groups defined by race and ethnicity? Regarding immigrants, the dominant view is this: the incidence of self-employment reflects the interplay between characteristics of the immigrant group and opportunity structures (Waldinger, Aldrich, and Ward 1990). Relevant group characteristics include class resources (such as education and wealth), cultural norms, and various social resources forthcoming from the broader community of fellow ethnic-group members. Applicable opportunity structures include situational constraints limiting employment and factors that shape access to small-business ownership.

It is fashionable to use complicated theories stressing interactions among multiple causes to explain self-employment patterns. The purpose of this book is not to refute such theories but to make sense out of them. As opposed to presenting a list of possible causes, chapters 2 though 6 present and test empirically a well-articulated theory of entrepreneurship. The primary self-employment theories I examine in this book are sketched out below.

Resources Shaping Self-employment Patterns

Human and financial capital (class resources) help aspiring entrepreneurs overcome barriers to starting a small business. The bedrock of small-firm creation is the owner's human capital, that is, the founder's education, training, work experience, and skills. In the rapidly growing skill-intensive services, for example, most firms are created by individuals with graduate training (Bates 1995c). Those lacking such human capital have low self-employment rates. When they do start their own firms, they concentrate in low-yielding fields—small-scale retailing, for example.

In many lines of business, appropriate human capital must be matched by substantial financial investment if the firm is to survive. Manufacturing is the most capital-intensive small-business field, followed by wholesaling and large-scale retailing. The trait that most accurately predicts self-employment entry into financially intensive fields is a household net worth of over $100,000 (chapter 2). Evans and Leighton (1989) have shown that people with a high net worth are much more likely to become self-employed than others. Evans and Jovanovic (1989) argue that the need for financial capital effectively kills the plans of numerous potential entrepreneurs, whose firms never get off the ground. Of course, some individuals who lack the requisite financial capital nonetheless become self-employed, even in manufacturing, but they are usually relegated to small-scale niches, such as rural sawmills and urban garment factories.

Human and financial capital are properly thought of as prerequisites for success in most lines of self-employment: for persons lacking the requisite skills and capital, self-employment entry rates are low; for those lacking appropriate human and financial capital who nonetheless start a small business, business failure and self-employment exit rates are high (Bates 1990b). Thus, the limited ability to compete that typifies weak small businesses combines with entry barriers to keep many potential entrepreneurs on the sidelines: low human- and financial-capital endowments translate into low self-employment rates.

Social Resources Shaping Self-employment Patterns

Class resources are the endowments of individual entrepreneurs and their families. Social resources, in contrast, flow from ethnic solidarity, and they encompass such phenomena as social networks, ethnic ideologies and inclinations, and employer paternalism. The social resources embedded in the small-business owner's ethnic group may help the entrepreneur form and operate his or her business. An environment of strong ethnic solidarity may be conducive to increasing the scope of social resources accessible to the ethnic entrepreneur, or so the story goes.

Tastes and preferences peculiar to a particular ethnic group may be a type of social resource exploitable by an ethnic entrepreneur: serving those tastes can generate a loyal customer base. The desire of fellow ethnic-group members to conduct business in the language of their homeland may also generate a loyal clientele for the ethnic entrepreneur. In areas such as money lending, strong social trust among ethnic-group members may reduce transaction costs and default risks. Rotating credit associations (RCAs), informal financial systems that Asian immigrants to the United States have used to encourage thrift and to assemble business capital (Light, Kwuon, and Zhong 1990), for example, may facilitate access to the financial capital necessary to create or expand a small business.

Particularly among recent immigrants to the United States, a preference for familiarity, in conjunction with social distance from mainstream society, leads to a reliance on fellow ethnic-group members to find shelter and work. Newcomers seeking jobs frequently turn to firms owned by fellow ethnics. Paternalistic employment practices, such as helping out with housing, making a place in the business for newly arrived relatives, or extending a loan when unexpected financial obligations arise, may enhance loyalty among ethnic employees. If a common outcome of such practices is to secure a hard-working, loyal, low-cost workforce by employing fellow ethnics, then business viability is enhanced considerably. Of course, "'newcomers' dependence on their bosses/patrons makes them likely to accept conditions that may fall below standard" (Waldinger, Aldrich, and Ward 1990). And the impulse to find housing and work through fellow ethnics leads many to ethnic occupational and residential ghettos. But this process may build up the critical mass needed for formal ethnic institutions—churches, businesses, aid societies—that serve to reinforce ethnic identity in the new homeland. And transition to life in the United States may be eased by working and living in a familiar environment with those who speak the same language. At the same time, the presence of a generous pool of underemployed and disadvantaged ethnic workers enhances employers' prospects for securing a cheap and loyal workforce.

The greater success of Asian immigrants in small business relative to black Americans is widely asserted to be due to the latter's limited access to these social resources (Fratoe 1986; Waldinger, Aldrich, and Ward 1990; Light 1972). In their analysis of "the underdevelopment of black business," Waldinger, Aldrich, and Ward (1990, 62) point to "the lack of a large protected market and the fragmented social structure of black communities, which inhibits resource mobilization."

Blocked Opportunities

Possession of class resources and access to social resources are positive factors encouraging prospective entrepreneurs to take the plunge into self-employment. They are *pull factors*. Blocked opportunities to pursue wage and salary employment are *push factors*, dictating that self-employment be pursued, even though one may prefer to work as an employee in a managerial or professional occupation.

Bonacich and Light (1988) put forth a concrete measure of blocked opportunities for comprehending small-business creation decisions. Labor force disadvantage is expressed in terms of opportunity costs. Korean wage and salary earners in Los Angeles were earning, according to Bonacich and Light, only 70 percent of the return on human capital that non-Korean workers earned. Pursuing self-employment did not eliminate the Korean disadvantage, but it did narrow it. "Koreans' disadvantage was 22 percent greater in wage and salary employment than in self-employment. Arising from relative disadvantage, the obvious financial incentive explained the Koreans' overrepresentation in self-employment" (Light and Rosenstein 1995, 157).

Min expresses the push factors encouraging self-employment in terms of status incongruence. He measured status incongruence in terms of educational background and work status before and after migration (Min 1988). Examining Korean immigrant men in Atlanta, Georgia, Min found that over 90 percent had held white-collar jobs in Korea, but only 17 percent were white-collar employees in their first job in the United States. Similarly, 68 percent of self-employed Koreans in Atlanta had completed four or more years of college, but 83 percent of them were manual laborers when they were first employed in the United States.

Why are these Korean college graduates and other immigrants so often restricted to low-wage, blue-collar work? Kassoudji (1988) claims that Asian immigrants lacking English fluency face potentially diminished labor market prospects. ". . . Well educated, Korean immigrants probably have more language problems than other comparably educated immigrants" (Min 1993, 194). Professionals are often unable to pass applicable licensing exams, for example, because of limited English fluency. Kim, Hurh, and Fernandez (1989) argue that American employers often do not recognize the education and work experience that immigrants accumulated in their native countries. "Blocked mobility is a powerful spur to business activity" (Waldinger, Aldrich, and Ward 1990, 32).

The problem that sociologists frequently note about interpreting self-employment as a pragmatic response to labor market disadvantages is its seeming inapplicability to small-business ownership patterns among black Americans: "The logic of Asian-American business development raises questions about the absence of parallel developments among American blacks" (Light 1972, 6). Why have African Americans been less active than Asian Americans in responding to labor market discrimination by opting for self-employment? The consensus to date has been that internal deficiencies in the black community inhibit mobilization of social resources (Fratoe 1988; Waldinger, Aldrich, and Ward 1990). A secondary explanation is that public-sector employment opportunities have diverted blacks from entrepreneurship (Boyd 1991b). The black counterpart to the overeducated Japanese grocery-store owner in Los Angeles, for example, was a teacher in a segregated Alabama public school fifty years ago.

Findings of this study provide no support for either of these conclusions. Greater opportunity in government in urban areas throughout the United States coexists with greater business activity among black Americans (chapter 8). The evidence on social-resource mobilization provides little insight into differences in relative business performance between Asian immigrants and black Americans. Differing patterns of business formation and viability are powerfully shaped by differences in class resources. In comparison to blacks, greater human- and financial-capital endowments favor the self-employed Asian immigrant, while blocked opportunities disproportionately handicap them.

Government Policies Shaping Self-employment Patterns

A variety of government policies have shaped the opportunities minority entrepreneurs have faced in recent decades. The Reagan administration conceived of enterprise zones as inner-city areas in which a sharp reduction in government presence, along with tax relief, would create fertile ground for local entrepreneurial activity. This reduced public presence would be achieved largely by eliminating government regulation within the zone. As James Johnson notes, the federal government under Reagan made substantial progress toward the laissez-faire ideal when it "aggressively relaxed environmental regulations and reduced the budgets and slashed the staffs of government agencies that were charged with enforcing laws governing workplace health, safety, and compensation, as well as hiring, retention, and promotion practices" (1995, 152). Such policy changes sometimes predated the Reagan presidency as well. Decline in enforcement and subsequent rise in violations of minimum wage laws was a serious problem by the early 1970s (Levitan and Belous 1979).

Immigrant entrepreneurs were quick to realize that declining government enforcement of an array of health, safety, wage, and similar regulations to protect workers provided owners with a foot in the door, a comparative cost advantage in certain small-business sectors (Bonacich and Light 1988). Reaping cost savings from the "lax enforcement of wage and sanitary provisions of the labor code" (Light and Rosenstein 1995, 77), Korean-owned small businesses became prevalent in small-scale retailing in Los Angeles County in the 1970s and 1980s. Having a desperate, often destitute immigrant labor pool to draw upon (partially due to government tolerance of illegal immigration) further encouraged immigrant entrepreneurs to take advantage of the de facto demise of laws protecting workers. The personnel director of an Asian-owned fast-food chain in Los Angeles described the company's workforce in the following terms: "Most are tenuously here and here on fragile documents. I see them as very subservient" (Waldinger 1996, 282).

Government programs actively targeting minority-owned businesses have been in operation for over thirty years. After 1965, federal dollars were increasingly available to assist black enterprise. Destructive civil disorder during the second half of the 1960s in South Los Angeles, Detroit, Cleveland, and other cities drew national attention to the socioeconomic status of the black ghetto and thrust African American-owned businesses into the national spotlight. In 1968, presidential candidate Richard Nixon pledged to make government promotion of black capitalism the centerpiece of his civil rights platform; black capitalism was viewed as a potential cure for ghetto problems. But the typical firm in the black business community then was the barbershop, the beauty parlor, the mom-and-pop food store. The realities of black business ownership in the 1960s relative to the enormity of the economic and social problems of decaying urban areas made black capitalism an improbable vehicle for spurring economic development in the ghetto.

Efforts to promote Hispanic- and Asian-owned firms were added to the agenda in the 1970s. A wide array of support programs to promote minority-owned businesses were taken up in the 1980s by many state and local governments (Bates 1995d). The main group to benefit from federal loan assistance has shifted from blacks to Asian Americans. Institutional credit, notes Ivan Light, "is much easier for Koreans to obtain in Los Angeles than in Korea" (1980, 44). Koreans, according to Light, have been outstandingly successful in obtaining low-interest loans from the Small Business Administration (SBA). Furthermore, private loans have often secured government guarantees whereby 90 percent of the default risk for minority borrowers is assumed by public entities (Bates 1984).

Minority business investments forthcoming from the SBA's Minority Enterprise Small Business Investment Company (MESBIC) program were flowing predominantly to Asian-immigrant business owners by the late 1980s (Bates 1995a). These programs particularly facilitated increased access to small-business loans. The scope of minority business preferential procurement programs was substantial: over 10 percent of the minority-owned firms operating in 1987 reported that they had sold goods or services to government clients that year (Bates and Williams 1995). Greater access to loan funds and expanded access to public-sector clients have clearly typified America's minority business community. Minority business sales to government, however, appear to have stopped growing in the 1990s due to restrictive Supreme Court rulings regarding preferential procurement practices (Bates and Williams 1995).

RESEARCH PLAN

While class resources, social resources, and blocked opportunities are not the only factors believed to shape self-employment, other considerations—discriminatory access to bank loans, for example—will also be discussed throughout this book, these three factors are significant and so will be discussed in the next three chapters.

Chapter 2 examines the effects of class resources on self-employment entry and exit. First, I use the Census Bureau's Survey of Income and Program Participation (SIPP) database to follow the self-employment entry patterns of adults 21–60 years old. Using this nationwide survey of households, I track 24,428 adults to see whether they become self-employed over thirty-two months. The results show that those with a household net worth of over $100,000 and advanced educational credentials are the most likely to become self-employed. Second, I delineate firms going out of business from those remaining in operation based on a sample of firms drawn from the CBO database (described in table 1.1). The analysis shows that highly educated owners investing large sums of financial capital into their businesses at start-up are most likely to remain in operation.

In chapter 3 I extend my analysis of CBO data by narrowing the focus to a comparison of the social resources available to Asian American- and nonminority-owned firms. I then narrow the focus even further, analyzing the survival and profitability of Asian-immigrant-owned firms in terms of social resources to see if they add anything to findings derived solely from analyses of class resources. They do: my results show that weaker, more failure-prone Asian-immigrant-owned firms are more likely to rely on certain social resources.

In chapter 4 I delve into explanations of the behavior of firms owned by immigrants in terms of blocked mobility. My analysis shows that between 1987 and 1991 Asian immigrants who owned traditional small businesses, such as laundries, were more likely than members of the nonminority comparison group to leave self-employment, suggesting that self-employment is often a form of underemployment among Asian immigrants.

Chapter 5 sums up the roles played by class resources, social resources, and blocked mobility in explaining the self-employment behavior of Asian immigrants. I generalize my empirical findings into a theory of immigrant enterprise that explains the wide variations in self-employment rates among the major Asian subgroups pursuing self-employment in the United States: the combination of strong class resources and blocked mobility generates high rates of self-employment. I explore the further implications about this theory of immigrant enterprise by examining small-business profitability patterns as well as behavior variations over the life cycles of firm groups.

Chapter 6 examines how owners financed their entry into self-employment. Results emphasize the importance of the owner's class resources and indicate a direct correlation between firm weakness and reliance on social resources.

The analysis shifts in chapters 7 through 9 toward explanations of firm behavior in the African American business community. Chapter 7 describes the dual trends of growth and decline that typify black-owned firms. The traditional black business community, consisting largely of small-scale retail and personal service firms, is in a state of long-run decline. These firms cater to a minority clientele, and they are most commonly located in inner-city black communities. Emerging lines of black business, in contrast, most commonly serve racially diverse or largely nonminority clienteles, and their customers include other businesses as well as the government. Black-owned firms in emerging fields such as business services have been growing rapidly since the 1970s.

Chapter 8 explores trends in the primary markets served by traditional and emerging lines of black enterprise. Results show that cities headed by black mayors are particularly hospitable to new and growing African American-owned small businesses. Growth in government procurement opportunities accounts for some of this progress. The attraction of college-educated blacks into small businesses is perhaps the single most important element underlying rapid progress in penetrating nontraditional markets. Highly educated black Americans running small-scale, traditional firms, in contrast, have often found that self-employment is unremunerative. They often choose to leave their retail and personal service firms, since salaried employment is commonly more lucrative.

Chapter 9 explores how financial-capital constraints shape the black business community. Blacks typically lag far behind nonminorities and Asian Americans in small-business capitalization. This tends to minimize the black presence in larger, more capital-intensive fields, such as manufacturing and wholesaling. While influential scholars may assert that financial-capital constraints do not hinder small-business formation, the available evidence overwhelmingly points toward very real and enduring financial barriers to black business formation, growth, and survival.

Most of the small-business owners analyzed in this book—black, Asian, and white alike—are college educated. Chapter 10 focuses on small-business owners who have not attended college. Among firms owned by high-school dropouts, most generate sales revenues of under $20,000 annually, and profits are low. Small retail firms owned by blacks and Korean and Chinese immigrants who have not attended college generate sub–minimum wage returns given the hours their owners work. This translates into poverty-level incomes for many of the households reliant upon the profits generated by these small retail ventures.

Chapter 11 explores patterns of government assistance to small black- and Asian-immigrant-owned firms. Selling goods and services to government clients is particularly important: among young firms nationwide, 10.6 percent of black-owned businesses and 9.2 percent of Asian-immigrant operations sold to government customers. Detailed analysis of government procurement programs run by twenty-eight large cities revealed widely varying outcomes of these efforts: the policies of some cities promote minority front firms, while those of others effectively foster minority business development. The clear-cut finding is that the nature of the procurement program shapes whether or not minority vendors benefit from their sales to government.

Broadly, small-business ownership tends to work out best for those who are already successful. College-educated, experienced workers with significant financial resources are most likely to pursue self-employment, and they are also most likely to earn high financial returns from their small-business activities. Interesting variations on this broad theme typify both Asian-immigrant and black subgroups, and these variations are explored at length in this study. Some activities thought to benefit small firms—selling to government clients, borrowing from RCAs—turn out to be risky and potentially fatal to vulnerable firms. Small-business ownership, finally, is often a route to working poverty for those lacking the human and financial capital of successful entrepreneurs. The experiences of Asian-immigrant small-business owners in the United States do not disprove these conclusions; rather, they strongly confirm them.

CHAPTER TWO

Class Resources and Self-employment
Entry and Exit Patterns

S elf-employment rates vary widely across ethnic and racial groups in the United States. As discussed in chapter 1, Fratoe (1986) found that Korean adults who had recently immigrated to the United States were ten times more likely than Puerto Ricans to be self-employed. Defining self-employment broadly, Fairlie and Meyer (1996) found that 4.4 percent of employed African American men and 2.0 percent of employed African American women worked for themselves in 1990. Korean American men and women, in contrast, worked for themselves at rates of 27.9 percent and 18.9 percent respectively, according to 1990 U.S. Census data. Widely varying explanations for these substantial differences in rates of self-employment have been put forth. Some view self-employment as a strategy for avoiding labor-market discrimination. This explanation suggests that African Americans should be particularly active in pursuing self-employment (Moore 1983; Light 1972), but data consistently reveal that black self-employment rates are below national averages. Others contend that immigrant enclaves—Chinatown, Cuban Miami—create entrepreneurial opportunities for members of the predominant ethnic group to serve the unique tastes and preferences of their fellow ethnics (Aldrich et al. 1985; Borjas 1990). Still others (Fairlie and Meyer 1996) note that higher income, more advantaged racial or ethnic groups, not the more disadvantaged, are likeliest to become self-employed.

I will sort through the competing explanations of self-employment in chapters 2 through 5 of this volume. The self-employment incidence typifying a racially or ethnically defined group reflects both the rate of entry into and the rate of departure from self-employment. Stevens (1984) observed that entry was the key to understanding why the rate of Asian small-business ownership towered above the rate typifying African Americans. The annual rates at which Asians and blacks leave small business, according to Stevens (1984), were identical. Among self-employed persons, Fairlie (1994) found that black men were much more likely than white men to leave self-employment. Significantly, he also found that the higher black departure rate was heavily rooted in differences in educational level: the racial trait, per se, was less important than educational background, and the least educated were the most likely to quit self-employment.

As discussed in chapter 1, the conventional wisdom among sociologists is that differences in rates of self-employment reflect an interplay between group characteristics—class resources such as education and wealth, cultural norms, and social resources forthcoming from fellow ethnic-group members (Waldinger, Aldrich, and Ward 1990)—and opportunities, or the lack thereof, including constraints on employment, government policies, and various other factors. In contrast, this chapter will explain entry into self-employment for blacks, Asians, and non-Hispanic whites in terms of class resources and the owner's demographic traits; it will explain exit from self-employment for these groups in these terms as well, but it will also explain exit rates in terms of certain traits of the small business itself—whether the owner bought an existing firm or started one from scratch.

The class resources under consideration will be the owner's educational background, work experience, and household wealth, among others. Factors such as social resources, situational constraints, and government policies will be bracketed for the moment but will be taken up in later chapters. Delaying consideration of the sociological and political concerns shaping self-employment makes the analyses of this chapter consistent with the economist's simpler approaches to studying self-employment. The class and demographic variables being used here to explain self-employment behavior can be clearly defined and unambiguously measured, and the data needed can be drawn from Census Bureau databases that are large and national in scope. While some potential richness may be temporarily sacrificed, the uncluttered analysis of this chapter will provide a clear-cut analytical base upon which less tangible, more-difficult-to-measure variables can be added in later chapters.

ANALYSIS OF FINANCIAL AND HUMAN CAPITAL CONSTRAINTS

Reynolds and Miller suggest that roughly one in thirty of all adults active in the U.S. labor force "appear to be involved in a new firm startup at any point in time" (1992, 405). Many of these potential firms end up stillborn. Recent studies indicate that financial capital constraints act as effective barriers to self-employment entry (Acs and Audretsch 1989; Evans and Jovanovic 1989). People who would like to pursue self-employment find that their plans are frustrated simply because they lack the financial means to set themselves up in the small business of their choice. Greater personal wealth, of course, lessens the likelihood that one's self-employment plans will be undermined by capital constraints, and this is why people with a high net worth—across the board—are more likely to enter self-employment than others.

Would suddenly receiving a lump sum of cash increase the likelihood of self-employment? Holtz-Eakin, Joulfaian, and Rosen (1994) examined the 1981 labor force status of 3,023 people who were not self-employed in 1981 but who all received inheritances in 1982 or 1983; by 1985, nearly 20 percent of them were self-employed. Controlling for traits such as age and home ownership, the authors estimated the inheritors were quite sensitive to the size of their windfall: a $100,000 increase in the inheritance caused a 17 percent increase in the likelihood of becoming self-employed, other things being equal.

The role that financial capital plays in shaping self-employment is really quite straightforward: financial-capital requirements for setting up the desired small business are a barrier. Failure to overcome this barrier discourages entrepreneurs; a windfall such as an inheritance eliminates that barrier and makes the goal attainable.

Although most scholars concur on the role that financial capital plays in shaping self-employment, the role played by the owner's human capital has not been emphasized as essential to creating new firms: measures such as the educational background and work experience of owners have been seen as weak and erratic determinants of self-employment in empirical studies (Evans and Leighton 1989).

This chapter will demonstrate that the role of education and work experience in self-employment entry is, indeed, important, but it is often obscured in empirical studies by inappropriate aggregation across business types. The practice of placing entrepreneurs into overly broad groups, without regard to business-specific conditions, although quite common, "increases the imprecision of the research results and interpretations generated" (Carsrud, Olm, and Eddy 1986). Analysis in this chapter will be guided by the finding that paths to entrepreneurship differ depending on the owner's background and education, as well as the business sector in which the owner chooses to operate and other factors (Cooper and Dunkelberg 1982). Rather than examining general tendencies of entrepreneurship, this chapter will investigate diversity across major business groups. Statistics generally describing self-employment entrants mask wide differences in alternative paths to business ownership. Self-employment entrance varies significantly across business groups.

Entry into self-employment, then, will be viewed as a process shaped by the characteristics and resources of potential entrepreneurs as they interact with business-specific factors in the skill-intensive services, construction, and manufacturing and wholesaling. While barriers such as capital constraints clearly shape self-employment decisions, the nature of these barriers varies substantially across small-business sectors and affects not only the decision to enter but also the type of business entered. Characteristics associated with those starting a construction business, in particular, have little in common with the traits of people starting a skill-intensive service business. Further, when traits such as personal wealth and educational credentials are controlled for, African Americans and Latinos are less likely than nonminorities to become self-employed. They not only become self-employed less often than nonminorities, but their relative distribution across business groups also differs substantially.

Empirical studies of self-employment entry are rare. In their pioneering time series analysis of self-employment entry among nonminority men, Evans and Leighton (1989) found a strong, positive association between household wealth and self-employment entry. Further, they observed that the percentage of nonminority men who were self-employed increased with age until those men were in their early forties and then remained constant until they retired.

Qualitative studies by sociologists suggest that married people may be more likely to become self-employed because family members can serve as cheap labor if necessary (Waldinger 1986). Differences in self-employment rates among minority groups have been partially attributed to this factor. Higher self-employment rates among Asians, in particular, have been explained, in part, by their greater use of family help (Fratoe 1988).

While this study generally confirms the importance of personal wealth, age, and marital status as predictors of self-employment entry, it also attributes major importance to the human capital of potential business entrants. The barriers to self-employment entry in manufacturing and wholesaling are clearly financial, but human capital traits, particularly advanced educational credentials, are key to shaping entry into the large and rapidly growing skilled-services area, where self-employment growth among minorities is disproportionately concentrated. Evans and Leighton's finding (1989) that human-capital traits were poor predictors of self-employment entry reflects both their exclusive focus upon nonminority men and their implicit assumption that one model fits all, that the entry process is essentially the same across businesses—personal services, construction, professional services, and so forth. Disaggregation of dissimilar businesses was not considered by Evans and Leighton.

TRACKING ENTRY INTO SELF-EMPLOYMENT

The data source for the analyses in this chapter is the 1984 SIPP, a longitudinal survey of households carried out by the U.S. Bureau of the Census and one of the few household surveys that provides data on household net worth and detailed information on self-employment activity. For the 1984 SIPP, approximately 20,000 households were interviewed every four months between October 1983 and August 1986. The 1984 SIPP data analyzed in this chapter included 24,428 individuals aged 21 through 60 who did not own a business during the first interview period. Within this sample, business entry is considered to have taken place if the individual reported business ownership (as defined below) during any of the seven subsequent interview periods (twenty-eight months).

The SIPP data are particularly well suited for examining the impact of personal wealth on the likelihood of self-employment entry. A cross-sectional analysis of the factors underlying business ownership would not permit a clear interpretation of the wealth variable: because substantial wealth can be as much a result as a cause of business ownership, a positive relationship between business ownership and wealth could indicate either that high initial personal wealth facilitated new business entry or that business ownership, over time, generated wealth for the owner.

Researchers have rejected the notion that self-employment entry is an act that takes place all at once. A gestation or incubation period, which may or may not culminate in continued self-employment, may last months or even years (Reynolds and Miller 1992). Quitting one's regular job is commonly *not* the first step in this incubation process. People who do not define their primary labor force status as self-employed are particularly important (and numerous) among college-educated people dabbling in self-employment (Bates 1986).

This study is not attempting to identify a point of self-employment entry. Rather, it is attempting to identify traits of individuals in the gestation phase of self-employment and to compare these traits for selected business types. The criteria used to define (and identify) people in this stage of self-employment entry, furthermore, have a clear impact on the personal traits that emerge as important. This study will define *entry* in several ways in order to identify determinants that are sensitive to definitional changes in who is or is not self-employed. The primary measure of self-employment entry will include all firms that were incorporated or that were operating with annualized net profits or losses of at least $1,000 during an interview period. An alternative measure of business entry will include all firms in which the owner reported self-employment of at least ten hours per week during an interview period.

The variables used in the statistical exercises (tables 2.1 through 2.5) to determine the characteristics that distinguish business entrants from nonentrants are defined fully in the appendix, "Databases and Variable Definitions." The logistic regression exercise in table 2.1 delineates people pursuing self-employment from those not pursuing self-employment. Entrants are those generating annualized net profits or losses of $1,000 or more during any of the subsequent seven SIPP interview periods (28 months). Entry into self-employment (table 2.1) is strongly associated with a household net worth of $100,000 or more. Years of work experience, along with graduate education, are also clearly associated positively with self-employment entry. Age and marital status, further, show the expected relationship to self-employment entry. Controlling for these factors, as well as education, work experi-

Table 2.1

Logistic Regression: Delineating Self-employment Entrants
from Non-Entrants

	Logit coefficient	Standard error
Constant	−6.292[a]	.394
Education		
High school	−.129	.086
College, 1–3 years	.178[a]	.090
College graduate	.062	.108
Graduate school	.426[a]	.100
Work experience	.011[a]	.003
Wealth		
$10,000–$25,000	.252[a]	.096
$25,000–$50,000	.221[a]	.094
$50,000–$100,000	.157	.091
$100,000+	.911[a]	.084
Married	.223[a]	.068
Age	.144[a]	.021
Age²	−.002[a]	.0003
Gender	.823[a]	.062
Black	−.727[a]	.134
Hispanic	−.297[a]	.147
Asian	.020	.166

Source: Data from U.S. Bureau of the Census, Survey of Income and Program Participation (SIPP) database, 1988.

Notes: Variables are defined in the appendix, "Databases and Variable Definitions," pp. 268–9; $N = 24,428$ (1,520 entrants); chi-squared = 737.61; the hypothesis that the explanatory variables have no effect is rejected ($\alpha = 0.01$).

[a]Statistically significant at the 5-percent level.

ence, and wealth, women and minorities (particularly blacks) are much less likely to enter self-employment than nonminority men. Asians, however, display the same propensity to enter self-employment as their nonminority cohorts, and entry by Hispanics is higher than that by blacks.

The logistic regression equations summarized in tables 2.1, and 2.3 through 2.5 seek to identify personal traits that delineate people choosing to become self-employed from others. The characteristics used to predict self-employment entry—age, gender, race, work experience, educational background, and so forth—operate simultaneously and they are sometimes linked to one another. To disentangle these influences and measure the effect of each characteristic on the likelihood of becoming self-employed, logistic regression analysis is the appropriate statistical technique. Black Americans, for example, have lower levels of household wealth, on average, than whites, and they are less likely to be college graduates. If blacks are observed to enter self-employment less frequently than whites, this difference could be rooted in their lower wealth holdings, lower incidence of college education, or it could simply be a racial characteristic. Simple summary statistics looking at a single trait cannot unravel this issue. The regression technique permits black, white differences in self-employment entry to be investigated independent of differences in other factors such as educational background and wealth holdings. For example, if people are identical in terms of wealth, education, work experience, age, and other characteristics, but they differ in terms of race only, will their self-employment entry rates still differ? Relative to whites, table 2.1's logistic regression exercise indicates that the answer is "yes" for blacks and Hispanics, and "no" for Asians. Stating this conclusion in common statistical terms, blacks and Hispanics are significantly less likely than whites to enter self-employment, controlling for other factors. The other factors that are being controlled for (table 2.1) are educational background, household wealth, work experience, age, gender, and marital status.

Table 2.2 summarizes the mean values and frequencies of the variables in table 2.1, and it is disaggregated to highlight extreme differences in self-employment entry rates as well as wealth and educational backgrounds among the various racial and ethnic groups. The much lower self-employment entry rate among blacks (2.4 percent) relative to nonminorities (6.8 percent) clearly reflects their lower household wealth and weaker educational backgrounds. Among African Americans only 4.2 percent had a household net worth of $100,000 or more. The finding that high levels of wealth and education are strongly related to new business entry explains why Asians are overrepresented among self-employment entrants.

The coefficients on the two racial/ethnic group variables—"blacks" and "Hispanics"—do indicate significantly lower rates of new business formation, even after taking into consideration their lower levels of wealth and education and their demographic differences rela-

Table 2.2

Summary Statistics: Traits of Persons Analyzed in Table 2.1 Econometric Analysis, by Race

	Non-Hispanic whites	All minorities	Black	Asian
Percent entering self-employment	6.8%	3.5%	2.4%	7.1%
Education				
No high school	18.0%	33.5%	30.9%	21.5%
High school	37.4%	33.0%	36.3%	24.7%
College, 1–3 years	23.4%	20.7%	22.0%	19.8%
College graduate	10.7%	6.7%	5.9%	18.2%
Graduate school	10.4%	6.1%	4.9%	15.8%
Work experience (mean)	13.8	11.7	12.3	10.9
Wealth				
Under $10,000	30.2%	51.5%	56.6%	41.0%
$10,000–$25,000	13.3%	13.5%	14.0%	12.8%
$25,000–$50,000	15.6%	10.4%	14.5%	6.2%
$50,000–$100.000	20.3%	12.0%	10.6%	15.0%
$100,000+	20.6%	12.7%	4.2%	25.0%
Mean value of wealth	$68,768	$32,474	$22,232	$73,222
Percent married	67.8%	55.3%	45.0%	71.1%
Mean age (years)	37.7	36.7	37.0	36.6
Percent male	47.1%	43.7%	42.3%	46.9%
N	19,923	4,505	2,592	595

Source: U.S. Bureau of the Census, Survey of Income and Program Participation (SIPP), 1984, 1988.

Note: Variables are defined in the appendix, "Databases and Variable Definitions," pp. 268–9.

tive to nonminorities. This result can imply either that blacks and Hispanics face barriers to business entry that nonminorities do not face or that blacks and Hispanics have weaker preferences for business ownership than do nonminorities. At least for blacks, one can find clear-cut support for the interpretation of business barriers. The alternative possibility, that blacks have a weaker preference for business ownership, is inconsistent with a 1987 survey that found that blacks overall were more highly inclined toward business ownership than whites, Asians, or Hispanics (Development Associates, Inc. 1987).

Entry rates among African Americans are greatly sensitive to the definition of self-employment entry being used. When *entry* is defined as "pursuing self-employment at least ten hours per week during any interview period," entry among African Americans jumps by 52.4 percent above the self-employment entry rate reported in table 2.2.

When the logit exercise of table 2.1 is reestimated using the ten-plus-hours-per-week criterion for self-employment entry, the coefficient value for the variable "Wealth: $100,000" declines by nearly 10 percent, suggesting that high levels of household wealth are less of a prerequisite for entry into part-time self-employment. Wealth is clearly less likely to serve as a barrier to entry when the line of self-employment requires little financial capital. Generally, African American self-employment rates are highly sensitive to any sort of cutoff (such as net income or sales revenues) that excludes very tiny operations from the self-employment tally.

Tables 2.3 and 2.4 explore entry into two business groups: skilled services and construction. As in table 2.1, entrants are identified as those generating net profits or losses of $1,000 or more. In table 2.3, entrants solely include those starting a skilled-services business, while in table 2.4 entrants solely include those starting a construction business. The logistic regression equations explaining entry in tables 2.3 and 2.4 produced very different variable coefficients, suggesting that starting a construction business is a much different process from starting a skilled-services business, and both are quite different from the logit results summarized in table 2.1. The role of higher education in identifying self-employment entrants—highly positive for skilled services, highly negative for construction—is particularly revealing. The logit coefficients attached to the education variables in tables 2.3 and 2.4 are:

Education	Skilled services	Construction
High school	.703	−.246
College, 1–3 years	1.459	−.292
College graduate	1.827	−1.030
Graduate school	2.452	−1.138

Level of education is the most important factor in identifying those starting skilled-services businesses: probability of entry rises substan-

Table 2.3

Logistic Regression: Delineating Self-employment Entrants from Non-Entrants in Skilled Services

	Logit coefficient	Standard error
Constant	−9.690[a]	.917
Education		
High school	.703[a]	.302
College, 1–3 years	1.459[a]	.297
College graduate	1.827[a]	.310
Graduate school	2.452[a]	.294
Work experience	.017[a]	.008
Wealth		
$10,000–$25,000	.465[a]	.205
$25,000–$50,000	.299	.207
$50,000–$100,000	.284	.195
$100,000+	.552[a]	.186
Married	−.227	.134
Age	.194[a]	.047
Age^2	−.002[a]	.0006
Gender	.219	.125
Black	−.701[a]	.300
Hispanic	.196	.302
Asian	.192	.315

Source: U.S. Bureau of the Census, Survey of Income and Program Participation (SIPP) database, 1988.

Notes: N = 24,428 (309 entrants); chi-squared = 270.00; the hypothesis that the explanatory variables have no effect is rejected ($\propto$ = 0.01).

[a]Statistically significant at the 5-percent level.

tially at each of the higher levels of education, peaking among those who went to graduate school. In construction, the complete opposite situation prevails: people who never attended college are much more likely to start a construction business than college graduates. The vastly different role that education plays in explaining the entry process in construction as opposed to skilled services helps to explain the weak role played by education in explaining self-employment entry generally (table 2.1). Similarly, the weak and inconsistent explanatory

Table 2.4

Logistic Regression: Delineating Self-employment Entrants from
Non-Entrants in Construction

	Logit coefficient	Standard error
Constant	−9.250[a]	1.200
Education		
High school	−.246	.220
College, 1–3 years	−.292	.243
College graduate	−1.030[a]	.369
Graduate school	−1.138[a]	.372
Work experience	.0005	.012
Wealth		
$10,000–$25,000	.091	.252
$25,000–$50,000	−.426	.291
$50,000–$100,000	.232	.266
$100,000+	.486[a]	.244
Married	.393[a]	.207
Age	.167[a]	.063
Age^2	−.002[a]	.0008
Gender	2.154[a]	.261
Minority[b]	−.595[a]	.266

Source: U.S. Bureau of the Census, Survey of Income and Program Participation (SIPP) database, 1988.

Notes: Variables are defined in the appendix, "Databases and Variable Definitions," pp. 268–9.
$N = 24,428$ (153 entrants); chi-squared $= 156.21$; the hypothesis that the explanatory variables have no effect is rejected ($\propto = 0.01$).

[a]Statistically significant at the 5-percent level.

[b]Refers to all except non-Hispanic whites; small sample size necessitates use of *Minority*, defined as equal to 1 for blacks, Hispanics, Asians, and other minorities, 0 otherwise.

power of education in predicting self-employment entry observed by Evans and Leighton (1989) obviously reflects the fact that an advanced education is positively correlated to entry in some fields and negatively correlated in construction. Aggregation of these diverse business groups in studies seeking to identify the traits of likely self-employment entrants simply leads to a misrepresentation of human capital as it relates to self-employment entry in specific businesses.

The logit results in table 2.4 suggest that years of work experience have no relevance to construction self-employment entry. In fact, the human capital required to create a successful small construction business is apt to be very real and specific. Construction firms are often started by skilled craftsmen. The human capital of a journeyman plumber or an experienced sheet-metal worker, along with the experience most likely to translate into construction self-employment, is not commonly acquired in college, nor is it widely available to women or minorities (Waldinger and Bailey 1991; Bates and Grown 1992). The strong positive coefficient value for the variable "male" and the strong negative coefficient value for the variable "minority" suggest that the human capital that facilitates self-employment in construction is most accessible to white men.

Conversely, college education is the primary route to self-employment in skilled services. In the theoretical writings of Lucas (1978) as well as Evans and Jovanovic (1989), business entry is determined by the parameter "business acumen." At least in skilled services, the source of this acumen appears to be high levels of education. While years of work experience as well as household wealth of $100,000 or more are clearly associated positively with entry, college education is a much more important factor for identifying skilled-services entrants. Being male—the single most important factor in identifying construction self-employment entry—is a much weaker determinant in skilled services; 42.4 percent of the skilled-services entrants were women versus 12.4 percent in construction and 30.3 percent in all other fields. Similarly, for Hispanics, entry into skilled services is easier than it is in other lines of self-employment; the "Hispanic" variable coefficient in table 2.3 is positive but statistically insignificant. Only among African Americans is there a large, negative, highly significant variable coefficient, suggesting limited access to skilled-services self-employment, independent of education.

The largest scale, most capital-intensive lines of business, manufacturing and wholesaling, were entered by 87 of the 24,428 people described in table 2.2. Table 2.5 identifies the traits of these 87 entrants using the methods employed in tables 2.3 and 2.4. In sharp contrast to both construction and skilled services, educational background has no explanatory power whatsoever in identifying manufacturing and wholesaling entrants, and "years of work experience" emerges as an important explanatory variable in table 2.5 as it had not in earlier tables. People entering manufacturing and wholesaling have signifi-

Table 2.5
Logistic Regression: Delineating Self-employment Entrants from
Non-Entrants in Manufacturing and Wholesaling

	Logit coefficient	Standard error
Constant	−10.214[a]	1.655
Education		
High school	−.171	.352
College, 1–3 years	.285	.356
College graduate	−.039	.438
Graduate school	.242	.400
Work experience	.026[a]	.014
Wealth		
$10,000–$25,000	.263	.413
$25,000–$50,000	.137	.408
$50,000–$100,000	.100	.389
$100,000+	.1.091[a]	.339
Married	−.056	.270
Age	.178[a]	.085
Age^2	−.002[a]	.001
Gender	1.098[a]	.270
Minority[b]	−.813[a]	.433

Source: U.S. Bureau of the Census, Survey of Income and Program Participation (SIPP) database, 1988.

Notes: Variables are defined in the appendix, "Databases and Variable Definitions," pp. 268–9. $N = 24,428$ (87 entrants); chi-squared $= 76.03$; the hypothesis that the explanatory variables have no effect is rejected ($\propto = 0.01$).

[a]Statistically significant at the 5-percent level.

[b]Refers to all except non-Hispanic whites; small sample size necessitates use of *Minority*, defined as equal to 1 for blacks, Hispanics, Asians, and other minorities, 0 otherwise.

cantly more years of work experience (19.4 on average) than people starting small businesses in other fields. Manufacturing and wholesaling resemble construction in the sense that white men are much more likely to start such businesses than their similarly endowed female and minority counterparts. Manufacturing and wholesaling, finally, stand out as an area in which possession of $100,000 or more of personal wealth is very strongly associated with self-employment entry, as is consistent with the large-scale, more capital-intensive nature of these businesses.

A further logistic regression analysis exercise entailed redefining the dependent variable "self-employment entry," so that entrants included only those people reporting annualized net profits or losses of at least $5,000 during an interview period. Reestimating tables 2.3, 2.4, and 2.5 using this self-employment criterion, the significance of wealth as an entry determinant—the "wealth: $100,000" coefficient, most specifically—rose substantially, particularly in the table 2.5 analysis of entry into manufacturing and wholesaling. The coefficient "male" also increased substantially, but the racial grouping variable coefficients were not affected.

OVERVIEW: SELF-EMPLOYMENT ENTRY

The varying factors linked to self-employment entry in different business groups tend to obscure the role played by education and work experience in characterizing self-employment entrants. The likelihood of self-employment in skilled services increases with educational level, while the opposite situation prevails in construction. The likelihood of self-employment entry in manufacturing and wholesaling rises steadily as years of work experience accumulate; the same pattern, albeit weaker, prevails in skilled services. Several factors dominate the econometric models of self-employment entry for each type of business under consideration: the skilled-services entrant is highly educated and often in the $100,000-plus wealth category; the construction entrant is male and decidedly not highly educated in terms of formal schooling; the manufacturing and wholesaling entrant most commonly possesses household net worth exceeding $100,000 and is probably male.

The statistical findings also shed light on who may or may not emerge successful from the new-firm formation process, who may pursue self-employment long term versus who may abandon small-business ownership. Particularly for employees contemplating quitting their jobs to pursue self-employment full time, the ability to make a living will influence whether self-employment becomes one's primary labor force status. People commanding more household wealth are clearly more likely to report high self-employment earnings than those with less wealth, according to the findings of this chapter. Household wealth not only provides resources for business capitalization but is also positively associated with borrowing power (Bates 1990b). Thus, the person commanding significant household wealth is much more capable than the less wealthy of overcoming financial barriers to business entry. The less wealthy person, disadvantaged in the financially capital-intensive lines of self-employment—manufacturing and wholesaling—is less likely to make the transition from the formative stage to small-business maturity.

Several factors consistently identify self-employment entry across business types. The likelihood of entry increases with age, peaking as people approach forty and then leveling out. Blacks are less likely than others to pursue self-employment, other factors remaining constant. When the sample size is too small to identify blacks, Hispanics, and Asians separately, "minority" is substituted, and the "minority" category is dominated by blacks, followed by Hispanics. Being a member of a minority group is consistently a strong negative predictor of entry into construction and manufacturing or wholesaling self-employment. Barriers to self-employment entry are most binding to those who possess neither the human capital nor the financial capital associated with entry. Lack of wealth and advanced education are particularly pronounced barriers to black self-employment, at least outside of construction.

Part of the uniqueness of black entrepreneurship lies in the fact that the proportion of adult African Americans pursuing self-employment is quite low relative to whites as well as most other minority groups. An extensive body of literature, reviewed in Bates (1993b), cites discriminatory barriers to black Americans starting businesses. Specifically, limited access to debt capital and markets, entrenched old-boy networks in businesses such as construction, and a lack of training opportunities and on-the-job experience in skilled occupations are factors that discourage or prevent many black Americans from pursuing self-employment. In the absence of these constraints, what would the black business community look like? Applying the coefficients of a table 2.1 logit equation to the black population described in table 2.2 simulates what the black self-employment entry rate would be if blacks faced the same barriers as whites. Elimination of the negative influence of being black, while holding other factors constant, causes the estimated rate of self-employment entry to rise from 2.4 percent (table 2.2) to 3.0 percent, still less than half of the 6.8 percent and 7.1 percent typifying whites and Asians (table 2.2). The other factors, particularly a low incidence of high ($100,000 plus) wealth and graduate education, emerge from the analysis as more powerful determinants of black self-employment entry than race per se. For black Americans, therefore, large gains in self-employment await advances in human and financial capital.

The analyses of this chapter suggest that self-employment entry rates for Asian Americans are explained largely by patterns of household wealth and education, not by being Asian. Considerations of race, of course, may affect household wealth and education. The analyses of this chapter do not deny this obvious reality. But the distinction being made in this chapter among the effects of race, human capital, and financial capital is an important one for addressing the issues at hand. Asserting that Asian Americans have high self-employment rates because they are Asian implies that some sort of race-specific cultural uniqueness gives them an advantage over members of other races. The fact that advanced education and wealth provide entry into self-employment has an altogether different implication. Indeed, findings in later chapters show that Asian Americans lacking human and financial capital do poorly when they pursue self-employment. Variations in self-employment outcomes are consistently closely related to human and financial capital: people with an advanced education, work experience, and financial resources consistently do well in small business. Once these factors have been accounted for, incremental effects of race and ethnicity, while not trivial, are of less importance.

ANALYSIS OF SMALL-BUSINESS SURVIVAL PATTERNS

Black Americans become self-employed at lower rates than do whites and Asians, and those who start small businesses are somewhat more likely than whites and Asians to leave self-employment. Lower entry rates and higher exit rates combine to hold down the number of black-owned businesses operating nationwide. Asian Americans show the opposite pattern, becoming self-employed at a higher rate than blacks and whites, while leaving at a lower rate.

I will examine exit rates in this section by tracking the survival of 32,034 small businesses operating in 1987. These firms are weighted to be representative of all small businesses in the United States formed between 1979 and 1987 and still active in 1987. (These data are described in detail in the appendix, "Databases and Variable

Definitions.") The applicable small-business data—from the CBO database—were compiled by the U.S. Bureau of the Census in 1992. The 32,034 young firms active in 1987 were traced to late 1991 to delineate the firms that were still active. Firms that had changed hands were recorded as active if they were still in operation in 1991. The resultant data proved a very powerful tool for tracking firm longevity. Because minority-owned firms were heavily oversampled in the process of creating the CBO database, analysis of minority business by group was feasible, unlike in the SIPP database analyzed earlier in this chapter.

Analyses showed a strong consistency in the traits predicting business entry and longevity. Human and financial capital of owners broadly identified likely entrants as well as firms likely to remain in operation. Specifically, highly educated owners with a large financial investment in their small business start-ups were more likely to create lasting firms than poorly educated owners whose financial investments were less bountiful.

But the dynamics of small business survival depend heavily upon a variety of factors beyond those of the entrepreneurs' education and financial assets. Very young firms, for example, are much more volatile and failure-prone than older firms, which have built up customer goodwill and an established clientele. Boyan Jovanovic has pointed out that the instability of young firms is partially rooted in owners' uncertainty about their ability to operate their business successfully (1982). According to Jovanovic, people gradually learn about their managerial abilities as they run a business and observe how well they do. As they learn more about their entrepreneurial abilities, their behavior itself changes: those whose confidence grows expand their firms, while those whose confidence shrinks contract or dissolve their businesses. New owners may overestimate themselves and fail by overreaching or underestimate themselves and stagnate. It is therefore important to control for the age of the firm when analyzing firm survival. The firms of Asian immigrants, for example, are much younger, on average, than those owned by nonminorities, so failure to control for firm age can mistakenly make the businesses of Asian immigrants look to have poor survival prospects.[1]

Beyond the firm's age and the owner's education, a key determinant of whether or not a firm is likely to survive is the amount of time that its owner devotes to the small business. Owners of young firms are polarized: while most work long hours, a substantial group devotes less than twenty hours a week to their businesses. Many in this latter group are self-employed only part time because they still hold full-time jobs. Firms headed by part-timers are much less likely to remain in operation over the years than small businesses headed by owners whose main job is their small business. White and black self-employed people are much more likely than Asian immigrants to be self-employed part time. It follows that earnings from the small business are more likely to be the dominant source of household income among Asian immigrants than among blacks and whites.

The age of the owner is commonly a strong predictor of a small firm's survival prospects. Owners in their mid forties are the highest self-employment earners (Bates 1987), and their firms are most likely to remain in operation, other things being equal, than those owned by either younger or older cohorts (Bates 1990b). The owner's age, a broad proxy for work experience, boosts firm viability, but it is also correlated with lessening owner effort in old age.

All of these explanations of firm survival are really hypotheses used in this chapter (and later chapters) to investigate the traits of the firms (and their owners) that determine the likelihood of survival during the sorting process that characterizes the early years of small-business operation. Generally, the hypothesis here is that well-capitalized firms headed by college-educated owners who work full time in the small business are the most likely to remain active. Once these traits have been controlled for, the race or ethnicity of the owner is expected to have little impact on firm longevity.

In this section I have introduced appropriate racial identifiers of owners and other demographic variables into the analysis of firm survival. (Precise definitions of the applicable explanatory variables appear in the appendix, "Databases and Variable Definitions.") In the logistic regression exercise in table 2.6, I have delineated small businesses operating in 1987 and 1991 from firms operating in 1987 that had closed down by 1991. In the logit exercise in table 2.6, race/ethnicity variables exclude whites, the education variables exclude those not completing high school, and the year-of-firm-entry variables exclude 1979 to 1983 entrants.

Among the young firms formed from 1979 to 1987 that are analyzed in table 2.6, discontinuance rates in 1991 were 26.4 percent among black-owned firms, 23.1 percent among white-owned firms, 18.8 percent among Asian-immigrant-owned firms, and 19.5 percent among Asian American-owned firms.

Table 2.6

Logistic Regression Explaining Firm Survival, 1987–91 (Firms Formed 1979–87 Only)

	Regression coefficient	Standard error	Variable mean
Constant	−.450[a]	.181	—
Education			
High school	−.236[a]	.050	.281
College, 1–3 years	−.126[a]	.051	.233
College graduate	.202[a]	.054	.199
Graduate school	.414[a]	.058	.174
Married	.024	.035	.792
Age	.073[a]	.008	41.978
Age^2	−.0009[a]	.0001	1,896.4
Gender	.056	.032	.745
Black	−.011	.089	.024
Hispanic	.035	.080	.031
Asian immigrant	.179	.098	.025
Asian American	.246	.171	.008
Other minority	−.211	.373	.001
Owner-labor input	.023[a]	.001	19.568
Capital	.077[a]	.003	7.052
Leverage	.010[a]	.003	2.515
Entered			
1984–85	−.607[a]	.044	.220
1986	−.794[a]	.044	.211
1987	−1.463[a]	.041	.253

Source: U.S. Bureau of the Census, Characteristics of Business Owners (CBO) database, 1992.

Notes: Variables are defined in the appendix, "Databases and Variable Definitions," pp. 270–3.
$N = 32,034$; $−2 \text{ Log } L = 31,062.2$; chi-squared $= 3,613.3$.

[a]Statistically significant at the 5-percent level.

Table 2.6 shows that the firm most likely to remain in operation over 1987–91 was started with a substantial financial capital investment and operated by a full-time owner who had attended graduate school. Owners in their forties in 1987 were most likely to see their firms remain in operation, other factors remaining constant, while those over sixty were most likely to be connected to discontinued small businesses.[2] Except for age, demographic variables—including race/ethnicity—had little significance.

In the table 2.6 analysis, positive coefficient values are associated with firms in existence in 1987 and still operating in 1991. The explanatory variables that best delineate surviving firms were firm age and capitalization, and owner's age, labor input, and educational background. The variable "Entered: 1987" identifies the very youngest firms, and they were extremely prone to failure. This finding confirms not only Dr. Jovanovic's theories, but also the findings of previous analyses of small-business survival (Evans 1987; Bates 1994a; Bruderl, Preisendorfer, and Ziegler 1992). The longer the period since the owner entered the business, the more likely that the business will have remained in operation until 1991.

One seeming anomaly stands out in the pattern of findings in the survival analysis. While college graduates and graduate-school attendees were most likely to see their firms remain active, high-school graduates and owners with some college were less likely than high-school dropouts, the excluded group, to be connected with surviving firms. Low opportunity costs, rooted in a paucity of opportunities to work as paid employees, lure some people into self-employment. In inner-city minority communities, for example, beauty parlors run by African American women who dropped out of high school have very low failure rates (Bates 1989). Profitability of these beauty parlors is low, but the owners cling to self-employment because they typically face very bleak prospects in the broader job market. This is the crux of opportunity costs: if alternatives to self-employment are few and unattractive, then owners cling to small-business ownership. Alternatively, low-profitability firms tend to be abandoned by their owners if attractive alternatives for salaried employment become available. This exact phenomenon occurs with highly educated Asian immigrants who leave traditional small businesses (chapter 4). The findings in table 2.6 indicate that, on balance, the most educated people tend to stick to small-business ownership. Since this group has access to salaried employment, the findings suggest that they prefer self-employment.

The firms analyzed in table 2.6 have been weighted so that non-minority firms account for 91.1 percent of the young small businesses, while minorities, collectively, make up the other 8.9 percent, because the U.S. Bureau of the Census estimated that young, white-owned small businesses active in 1987 (i.e., generating gross sales of at least $5,000) accounted for exactly 91.1 percent of this business universe. Throughout this book, firms are weighted to reflect their frequency in the U.S. economy. Over 60 percent of the unweighted underlying sample described in table 2.6 was minority-owned, but weighting suppresses unique patterns of minority-business survival. Regression exercises in later chapters focus on minority subgroups specifically. The findings in table 2.6 are useful because they provide a context for comparing the dynamics of minority firms with those of the broader, nationwide (white-dominated) community of small businesses.

CONCLUSION

The norm in the small-business universe is for college graduates who own well-capitalized firms to show low business closure rates. Their firms are likely to remain in operation and are likely to be quite profitable. Significant deviations from this norm typify both Asian-immigrant and African American small-business owners. Unique patterns of firm viability among Asian immigrant subgroups will be investigated in the next two chapters.

APPENDIX: EXPLORING THE IMPLICATIONS
OF DIFFERENT ECONOMETRIC MODELS
OF FIRM SURVIVAL

Designing econometric models is something of an art, a subjective exercise in which various factors may be included or excluded at the whim of the investigator. This means that the econometric models used in social science research can readily be manipulated to strengthen or weaken observed relationships between independent variables, such as the education or financial assets of the business owner, and dependent variables, such as the firm's establishment or discontinuance. Since I believe that scholars using these techniques have a responsibility to report whether and how changes in the variables affect the results reported, this section will show how such variations alter the firm survival analyses reported in table 2.6.

Table A.1 reports variations of the logistic regression model analyzing firm survival patterns in table 2.6. The first model variation entails the addition of three new explanatory variables identifying the type of firm: "construction" identifying (you guessed it) construction firms; "skill-intensive" identifying firms operating in professional or business services, finance, insurance, or real estate; and "capital-intensive" identifying small businesses in manufacturing or wholesaling.

These three new business-identifier variables are related to certain other explanatory variables in the table A.1 logistic regression model, specifically, those picking out educational level: people with a college education are more likely to be in skill-intensive firms and less likely to be in construction firms than are other people who own small businesses. Comparing the logit coefficients attached to the education variables in table 2.6 with those in table A.1, model 1, is instructive:

Education	Table 2.6	Table A.1
High school	−.236	−.218
College, 1–3 years	−.126	−.067
College graduate	.202	.271
Graduate school	.414	.570

In table A.1, model 1, well-educated owners are shown to be even more likely than less well-educated owners to be connected to surviving businesses, other things being equal, because the added business-identifier variables pick out an important relationship between education and the nature of small-business operation in skilled services. The skill-intensive services are more volatile than the other firm types: they attract more college-educated people merely passing through self-employment. Highly educated and experienced managers who suddenly lose their jobs are likely to become independent consultants but likely also to go back to salaried employment as soon as a suitable job is forthcoming. Many skilled services are amenable to changes in the owner's status, from employee to self-employed and back again (lawyers, doctors, accountants, architects). Inclusion of a variable that identifies skilled-service firms, therefore, tends to result in a split—a strong positive relationship between college education and firm longevity as well as a strong negative relationship between skilled-services businesses and firm longevity.

Which is the correct approach to modeling small-business longevity—inclusion or exclusion of business-identifier variables? There is no correct response: designing models means making value

Table A-1

Varying the Specification of Logistic Regression Models Explaining Firm Survival, 1987–91 (Firms Formed 1979–87 Only)

| | Regression coefficient (std. error) | | |
	Model 1	Model 2	Model 3
Constant	−.411[a] (.183)	−.307 (.182)	−.450 (.190)
Education			
High school	−.218[a] (.050)	−.252[a] (.050)	−.187[a] (.052)
College, 1–3 years	−.067 (.052)	−.146[a] (.051)	−.060 (.055)
College graduate	.271[a] (.056)	.169[a] (.054)	.282[a] (.059)
Graduate school	.570[a] (.061)	.383[a] (.058)	.603[a] (.065)
Managerial experience	—	—	.015 (.035)
Bought ongoing firm	—	—	.406[a] (.050)
Married	.032 (.035)	.024 (.035)	−.002 (.038)
Age	.075[a] (.008)	.069[a] (.008)	.079[a] (.008)
Age^2	−.001[a] (.0001)	−.0008[a] (.0001)	−.0009[a] (.0001)
Gender	.012 (.033)	.041 (.032)	.038 (.034)
Black	−.012 (.089)	.007 (.089)	−.023 (.092)
Hispanic	.035 (.080)	.049 (.080)	.026 (.083)
Asian immigrant	.178 (.098)	.189 (.098)	.127 (.102)
Asian nonimmigrant	.261 (.171)	.258 (.171)	.226 (.177)
Other	−.243 (.373)	−.208 (.372)	−.262 (.391)
Owner-labor input	.023[a] (.001)	.021[a] (.001)	.021[a] (.001)
Capital	.073[a] (.004)	.071[a] (.004)	.052[a] (.004)
Leverage	.011[a] (.003)	.009[a] (.003)	.006[a] (.003)
Number of employees	—	.083[a] (.008)	.072[a] (.008)
Entered			
1984–85	−.612[a] (.044)	−.597[a] (.044)	−.561[a] (.045)
1986	−.797[a] (.044)	−.774[a] (.044)	−.822[a] (.045)
1987	−1.466[a] (.041)	−1.440[a] (.041)	−1.373[a] (.042)
Construction firm	.001 (.046)	—	−.052[a] (.048)
Skill-intensive firm	−.292[a] (.035)	—	−.244[a] (.036)
Capital-intensive firm	−.011 (.059)	—	−.070 (.060)
N	32,034	32,034	30,394
−2 Log L	30,985.8	30,882.2	29,189.5
Chi-squared	(3,689.8)	(3,793.3)	(3,163.7)

Source: U.S. Bureau of the Census, Characteristics of Business Owners (CBO) database, 1992.

Notes: Variables are defined in the appendix, "Databases and Variable Definitions," pp. 270–3.

[a]Statistically significant at the 5-percent level.

judgments. The ideal solution is to explore both approaches and to observe how the findings change.

Since large firms tend to stay in business longer than do small firms (Evans 1987; Bates and Nucci 1989), using number of employees as an explanatory variable is a popular way to measure the strength of the firm size–longevity relationship, so Model 2 in table A.1 drops the business-identifier variables and adds "number of employees" as an explanatory variable. In that portion of table A.1, coefficients attached to the "capital" and "owner-labor input" variables fall somewhat, but the coefficient for the number-of-employees variable, at .083, shows that this is, in fact, a powerful explanatory variable: more employees means enhanced survival prospects for the firm.

Yet adding this (or any other) measure of firm size to the analysis is controversial because of the very real interrelatedness of the factors that predict small-business survival: firms with full-time owners and large financial-capital investments are much more likely to hire paid employees than are poorly capitalized firms run by part-time owners. This interrelatedness can alter observed regression coefficients, standard errors, and reported statistical significance.

One of the virtues of the CBO data under consideration is that the key relationships between variables—such as that between owner-labor input, firm capitalization, and firm survival—are only altered slightly by inclusion of the "number-of-employees" variable. The findings of the logistic regression exercise are therefore robust, which is a cause for increased confidence in the reliability of the reported findings: we may change the econometric model, but the significant relationships between the firm's survival and its capitalization, its age, its owner's human capital, and the like remain strong.

Model 3 in table A.1 introduces a different sort of complication by adding two new explanatory variables—the owner's managerial experience and the owner's entry by buying an ongoing firm—to the logit analysis of firm survival. The new problem here involves item nonresponse. The question about the owner's managerial experience produced one of the lowest response rates on the CBO questionnaire: among black business owners responding to the survey, for example, only 91.1 percent answered that question. Nonresponse caused the sample size to drop by over 5 percent—from 32,034 to 30,394—when the "management-experience" and "bought-an-ongoing-firm" variables were added. Is the gain in explanatory power worth this loss in sample size? Do the variable coefficients change substantially when the number of firms analyzed drops by over 1,600 because of nonresponse to the relevant questions?

In fact, the dominant pattern of findings remains intact. Ongoing firms tend to be started with much larger financial-capital investments than do firms started from scratch; predictably, the coefficient for the capital variable drops in model 3 when the "bought-an-ongoing-firm" variable is introduced. In fact, model 3 shows that ongoing firms are much more likely than de novo firms to remain in business, other factors remaining constant, which is an interesting finding.

Overall, problems of the interrelatedness of explanatory variables pop up as alternative models are introduced in table A.1, but these variations also illuminate how, in fact, human-capital and financial-capital variables interact with the other factors that shape firm survival prospects. Ultimately, investigating alternative models and their ramifications enhances our understanding of the dynamics of firm longevity.

NOTES

1. Firm age in the CBO database is consistently measured by observing when the present owner entered the business. A firm in operation for twenty years thus becomes a start-up when a new owner takes over. Therefore, I delineated firms started de novo from those purchased from a previous owner in analyses of firm viability. I determined firm age in cases of multiple owners by the entry date of the dominant owner.

2. Summing the age and age^2 regression coefficients produces the following results: (1) owner = 30, coefficients = 1.38; (2) owner = 40, coefficients = 1.48; (3) owner = 50, coefficients = 1.40; (4) owner = 60, coefficients = 1.14. Thus, an owner who was sixty in 1987 had a smaller chance of being connected to a firm surviving in 1991 than a thirty-year-old owner; a forty-year-old owner, in contrast, was a better survival bet than a thirty-year-old owner. The owner age–firm survival relationship is decidedly nonlinear, with survival prospects dropping off most sharply among owners who were fifty-five or older in 1987.

CHAPTER THREE

Social Resources Generated by Group Support Networks: Do They Benefit Asian-Immigrant-Owned Small Businesses?

In the United States during the 1980s the number of small businesses owned by Asian Americans and Asian immigrants grew rapidly. Gross revenues of Asian-owned small businesses nearly tripled from 1982 to 1987, with the number of active firms growing from 187,691 to 355,331—an 89.3 percent increase (U.S. Bureau of the Census 1991). This rapid Asian business growth has been immigrant-driven: among firms operating nationwide in 1987 that were started since 1979, nearly 80 percent of the Asian small businesses were immigrant-owned. This chapter will examine the performance of recently formed Asian-immigrant-owned small businesses, tracing the survival of firms operating in 1987 through 1991.

Stressing the relevance of cultural factors, Waldinger, Light, Bonacich, and others have treated firm ownership and operation by immigrants as a group phenomenon, heavily dependent on social resources forthcoming from fellow ethnic-group members. The Asian-immigrant entrepreneur is seen as a member of supportive peer and community subgroups that assist in the creation of successful firms by providing customers, loyal employees, and financing.

This chapter will provide evidence that the success of Asian-immigrant-owned firms derives from the owner's heavy investment of financial capital and impressive educational credentials. It is the less profitable, more failure-prone small businesses owned by Asian immigrants that are likely to rely heavily on social-support networks. Successful firms often have little incentive to serve an ethnic community or enclave. They are more likely to serve nonminority clients, get credit from mainstream financial institutions, recruit nonminority employees, and generally conduct business outside the ethnic economy. Smaller, less viable immigrant-owned businesses, in contrast, are more likely to be connected to an ethnic economy composed of owners indebted to fellow ethnic-group members for start-up capital, loyal employees, and customers. For these businesses, reliance on the ethnic economy may be a precondition for success; the spatially clustered small firms that constitute the ethnic economy are disproportionately those that are too weak to exist elsewhere.

Researchers studying ethnic economies often define concepts inconsistently, leading to contradictory findings (Logan, Alba, and McNulty 1994). The analytical focus in this chapter will be on the businesses themselves rather than on geographically defined firm clusters or enclaves. Nonetheless, the overlap between concepts of an ethnic economy and immigrant business ownership are substantial, and two characteristics of ethnic economies are sometimes apparent in the business statistics summarized in chapters 3 through 5 of this volume:

1. *Sectoral concentration*   Urban immigrant communities that generate ethnic economies commonly produce minority-owned firms that are concentrated in several narrow business sectors. Logan, Alba, and McNulty (1994) note that the typical enclave is heavily based on the sale of ethnic foods and the manufacture of apparel. This specialization may reflect the segments of the economy that are open to immigrant firms, the outcome of informal networking, or the needs of the marketplace. Light (1980) describes Asian groups in Los Angeles selling liquor licenses within the group rather than to outsiders. Similar processes have been observed in hiring (Bailey and Waldinger 1991; Waldinger 1994).

2. *Geographic concentration*   The residential concentration of an immigrant ethnic community may correspond with the clustering of ethnic businesses. Lee (1992) has noted a strong correlation between the residential density of Koreans in Los Angeles and the incidence of Korean-owned firms. Kwong (1987) has documented an extensive relationship between residential concentration of immigrant

Chinese in New York City's Chinatown and the cluster of
ethnic businesses in that south Manhattan community.
Sassen-Koob (1989) suggests that this correspondence arises
to take advantage of the cheap, docile labor force that new
immigrants provide to the small businesses owned by fellow
ethnics.

Exactly what an ethnic economy is and is not, although widely discussed, has not been established to date, in part due to the paucity of
geographically specific data on small businesses. This chapter will consider manifestations of ethnic solidarity (perhaps rooted in ethnic
economies) that may affect small-business behavior.

Recent studies of minority entrepreneurship have often focused on
immigrants operating businesses in a specific location—Chinese in
New York, for example (Waldinger 1986). Within the same city, a large
immigrant ethnic community is a major factor shaping the behavior
of the immigrant small-business community under consideration.
Chinese garment manufacturers may retain a competitive edge,
according to Waldinger (1986), primarily because they use a loyal, low-
cost labor force made up of recent Chinese immigrants.

Yet discussions of business reliance on ethnic solidarity are often
blurred by the inclusion of family resources in the multifaceted concepts of social capital and the ethnic economy. Among recent Korean
immigrants, for example, Bonacich and Light (1988) note the effective
use of family resources, such as unpaid labor, to develop successful
small businesses. In this volume I strive to separate, whenever possible,
the effects of family resources on firm viability from those of social
resources forthcoming from the ethnic community.

Qualitative studies of immigrant entrepreneurs operating at one
geographic location do have certain advantages over the econometric
analyses of large national databases stressed throughout this book.
First, they delve into subjective determinants of business behavior that
are not easily subjected to statistical analysis, therefore capturing the
nuances of issues that might otherwise be overlooked. Second, the richer
detail captured by a well-written case study conveys more of the
human interest of the topic than statistical analysis and is therefore
more entertaining (see, for example, Waldinger [1986]). Third, sociological case studies are cheaper to carry out.

On the other hand, it is difficult for case studies alone to generate
reliable conclusions about small-business success and failure. Without

replicating case studies in a variety of locations, there is no way of establishing which features are peculiar to the situation and which are general (Reimers 1996). Case studies rarely sort out cause-and-effect relationships between the factors under consideration and small-business performance. A case study, at best, "can serve as a starting point by providing insights that suggest what information should be collected from a broader-based sample. The findings of a case study need to be placed into context before we can examine their meanings" (Reimers 1996, 198).

Data sources, such as the Census Bureau's CBO database, provide evidence that is not consistent with the social-resources explanations of minority business behavior forthcoming from qualitative studies, such as that of Bonacich and Light (1988). The alternative explanation of Asian-immigrant business patterns put forth in this chapter stresses education, skills, and financial capital. Immigrant entrepreneurs tend to be highly educated, have white-collar work experience, and possess substantial personal wealth. This study concludes that the very substantial investments of financial capital and the impressive educational credentials of business owners are what shape the success and survival of Asian-owned firms.

A COMPARISON OF ASIAN-IMMIGRANT AND NONMINORITY SELF-EMPLOYMENT PATTERNS

This chapter focuses on a nationwide sample of firms started by Asian immigrants between 1979 and 1987. Table 3.1 shows the distribution across business types of firms nationwide that are owned by Asian immigrants; the data are drawn from a representative sample of firms created since 1979 that filed small-business income-tax returns in 1987.[1] Small businesses owned by nonminorities are the norm in this country: such firms account for over 90 percent of the small businesses by number and 95 percent by total sales. A representative sample of nonminority-owned firms is presented in table 3.1 to highlight the traits unique to Asian-immigrant-owned small businesses.[2]

A consistent trait of the Asian-immigrant small-business community, noted by Bonacich and Light (1988), Logan, Alba, and McNulty (1994), and others is the extreme sectoral concentration, particularly in small-scale retailing. Table 3.1 indicates a heavy overrepresentation in three sectors—retailing, personal services, and professional services.

Table 3.1

Nationwide Distribution of Firms Operating in 1987 by Business Type
(Firms Formed since 1979 Only)

	Asian immigrant	Nonminority
Retail	31.8%	16.4%
Personal services	9.5%	6.8%
Business services	11.4%	12.0%
Professional services	14.8%	10.4%
Other services	9.0%	13.0%
Finance, insurance, and real estate	5.9%	9.1%
Construction	3.1%	12.8%
Manufacturing	2.7%	3.3%
Transportation	3.5%	4.6%
Wholesaling	3.1%	3.8%
Miscellaneous other	1.3%	3.0%
Unknown	4.0%	4.9%
	100.1%	100.1%
Key subsectors		
Food and beverage	10.7%	3.2%
Health services	12.5%	4.8%

Source: U.S. Bureau of the Census, Characteristics of Business Owners (CBO) database, 1992.

Relative to the mainstream, nonminority small-business community, Asian-immigrant-owned firms are heavily underrepresented only in construction and select services.

A significant industry broadening and diversification has taken place since 1960: laundries and restaurants accounted for less than 15 percent of the young firms owned by Asian-immigrant entrepreneurs nationwide in 1987. Firms in the high-yielding professional services, particularly health services, are now more numerous than the traditional businesses—the laundry and the restaurant. Professional-service firms have grown in number by extending beyond a traditional clientele of fellow ethnics; more than half of these firms nationwide rely on racially diverse or largely nonminority clienteles.

Broadening the industry base and expansion into more profitable self-employment niches typify the Asian-immigrant-owned small-business community in the United States today. But they are still heavily overrepresented in the two least profitable business groups—personal services (largely dry cleaning) and retailing: 41.3 percent of the

Asian-immigrant-owned firms described in table 3.1 are in retailing and personal services versus 23.2 percent of nonminority firms. A broader industry base notwithstanding, the Asian-immigrant community of small businesses still suffers from overconcentration in the lowest yielding business sectors.

Yet the public perception of Asian-immigrant small business is one of success, and table 1.1 briefly describes the factors behind that success.

1. Of the Asian-immigrant entrepreneurs operating young firms in 1987, 57.8 percent were college graduates versus 37.7 percent of the nonminority business owners. Professional services—the field in which both the owner's education and average self-employment remuneration are highest—accounted for 14.8 percent of the Asian business start-ups versus 10.4 percent of the nonminority start-ups.

2. Average initial financial-capital investment was $53,550 among the Asian immigrants versus $31,939 for non-minorities. The owner's equity investment—derived almost entirely from household wealth—averaged $26,838 among Asian-immigrant business entrants, 88 percent higher than the corresponding figure of $14,195 for nonminorities. Findings discussed in chapter 2 indicated that self-employment entry is very strongly and positively associated with the possession of household net worth exceeding $100,000; a higher proportion of Asian households nation-wide were in the $100,000-plus-household-net-worth category (25.0 percent) than nonminorities (22.1 percent). Highly educated entrepreneurs, large financial-capital investments in new firms, significant household wealth— these are important factors behind the growing diversity of small businesses owned nationwide by Asian immigrants.

SOCIAL CAPITAL AND PATTERNS OF BUSINESS BEHAVIOR

Theories of self-employment developed by sociologists often portray the entrepreneur as a member of a supportive network that assists firms by providing customers, loyal employees, and financing (Waldinger, Aldrich, and Ward 1990).

Protected Markets

What precise forms do these social resources take and how do they assist businesses? Social capital in the form of a captive, or protected, market, according to Ivan Light (1972), derives from the culturally based tastes of ethnic minorities that can only be served by ethnic businesses. Ethnic businesses offer fellow ethnics the comfort and security of conducting transactions in their own language. They also have an advantage in that ascertaining consumer preference costs the ethnic entrepreneur less than it would potential competitors from the "outside" (Evans 1989).

If highly visible minority population concentrations emerge, non-minority merchants may withdraw from the neighborhood, leaving the area open to minority businesses. This is how an ethnic enclave with a heavy concentration of small firms owned by ethnic entrepreneurs might emerge (Aldrich et al. 1985).

The protected-markets thesis presumes an ethnic neighborhood created more or less as described. As newly arrived immigrants cluster together for mutual support, they develop the critical mass of customers needed to support the businesses that cater to their distinctive ethnic tastes. Chinatown in Manhattan is such an ethnic neighborhood and offers such a protected market. In 1980 it was centered in four contiguous census tracts with populations more than half Chinese. This concentrated population "made Chinatown a hotbed of ethnic commerce, both large and small" (Waldinger, Aldrich, and Ward 1990, 108). When ethnic firms proliferate and the size and diversity of the ethnic marketplace attract customers from outside the neighborhood, agglomeration economies may develop, creating a regional ethnic shopping center.

Of the various forms of social capital associated with immigrant entrepreneurs, the protected-market concept has been the most controversial. The low incomes of most recent immigrants undermine the attractiveness of this market. The immigrant business that limits itself to the ethnic market sharply reduces its growth potential (Aldrich and Reiss 1976). Kwong described New York City's Chinatown in the 1980s as a saturated market undergoing suicidal competition because of "too many new businesses." "Many clothing stores, restaurants, and other businesses have hardly any business, yet they all continue to operate, forcing other firms to engage in suicidal competition and driving some out of business altogether" (1987, 47). Other studies, however, observe that Asian-immigrant-owned firms frequently operate outside of the ethnic marketplace. Fratoe, for example, reports that Asians are much less likely to sell to a minority clientele than are blacks or Latinos (1988). Reliance on ethnic markets may nonetheless be pragmatic during early stages of firm development because such markets provide an operational base from which later expansion can begin. The ethnic market may support immigrant entrepreneurs "in assembling a skilled labor force and gaining efficiency and expertise, qualities that . . . gradually allow . . . them to edge out into the broader market" (Waldinger 1986, 21).

Table 3.2 indicates that the two groups of Asian-immigrant entrepreneurs—those serving a clientele that is 50 percent or more minority versus those whose clientele is largely nonminority—differ systematically regarding sales, profitability, the owner's financial investment, and discontinuance rates. It is the very youngest among immigrant-owned businesses that appear to benefit most from serving clients in the broader, largely nonminority marketplace (table 3.2). Among those in business for no more than two years, the Asian firms catering to a predominantly minority clientele were much more likely to have closed up shop by 1991; although their profitability ($9,931 in 1987) was roughly comparable, they were smaller and their owners had less money to invest in them than owners of similar firms competing in the broader economy.

Among the firms analyzed in table 3.2 that were in operation for three to eight years, survival rates and mean sales were quite similar among businesses serving a minority clientele and those serving a broader market. Thus, it's not clear that immigrant firms benefit by avoiding the broader, largely nonminority marketplace at the outset. Note, however, that very young Asian-immigrant firms catering to a minority clientele are weaker in that they are run by owners who are, on average, less well educated and the amount of money invested in them is quite low ($35,581) relative to the amount invested in firms serving the broader economy ($62,066) (table 3.2).

Finally, I'd like to examine what constitutes a predominantly minority clientele by examining firms whose clientele was 75 percent or more minority; results of this exercise were highly consistent with the findings in table 3.2.[3] Do such firms benefit from a protected market?

One problem with using the data in table 3.2 as a test of the protected-markets thesis is the fact that the firms included in the "minority clientele" category need not be serving members of their own minor-

Table 3.2

Asian-Immigrant-Owned Firms by Clientele (Firms Formed 1979–87 Only)

| | Firm formed 1986 or 1987 | |
	Minority clientele*	Broader clientele
Firm's traits		
Gross sales, 1987 (mean)	$74,498	$95,715
Number of employees, 1987 (mean)	0.6	1.2
Net income, 1987 (mean)	$9,931	$9,371
Financial capital at start-up (mean)	$35,581	$62,066
Percent of firms still operating 1991	68.0%	79.2%
Owner's traits		
Percent with less than four years of high school	10.5%	9.4%
Percent with college degree	52.0%	59.6%
	Firm formed 1979–85	
	Minority clientele*	Broader clientele
Firm's traits		
Gross sales, 1987 (mean)	$172,495	$159,249
Number of employees, 1987 (mean)	1.4	1.8
Net income, 1987 (mean)	$19,143	$21,155
Financial capital at start-up (mean)	$47,643	$67,065
Percent of firms still operating 1991	91.2%	91.0%
Owner's traits		
Percent with less than four years of high school	13.1%	11.9%
Percent with college degree	58.4%	58.5%

Source: U.S. Bureau of the Census, Characteristics of Business Owners (CBO) database, 1992.

Note: Variables are defined in the appendix, "Databases and Variable Definitions," pp. 270–3.

*The clientele is defined as predominantly minority if 50 percent or more of the customers served were minority-group members.

ity group. Korean merchants often specialize in selling nonethnic products in minority markets—often in Latino or African American neighborhoods—whereas the concept of a protected market suggests that ethnic businesses are located in neighborhoods where members of the owner's ethnic group are concentrated. The Korean population of Atlanta, for example, is too small to support an ethnic Korean small-business enclave. Instead, Korean businesses serve the dominant minority group: almost 60 percent of Korean firms in 1982 were found in the inner city or in areas that were at least 50 percent black (Min 1988). According to Min (1984a), Korean business owners in Atlanta said that they would have much more difficulty competing in white areas than in black neighborhoods. The attraction of black communities was the reduced competition stemming from the paucity of mainstream business competitors. Yoon reports that Koreans often prefer to locate their businesses in black residential areas of Chicago because there is less discrimination and hostility from local residents than there would be in white neighborhoods. Store rentals in black communities are less costly than in white areas, and a limited knowledge of English is often sufficient. "Besides the light requirements for capital and managerial skills, the absence of competition from local black businesses lowers barriers to entry in black areas" (Yoon 1991b, 29).

In Los Angeles, half of the Korean businesses located outside of the Korean enclave were concentrated in the black and Latino areas of the county. Thus, catering to a minority clientele—while possibly beneficial for both Korean and Chinese businesses—entails serving fellow ethnics relatively more frequently for Chinese merchants than for Koreans. Yet recalculations of table 3.2—first, excluding Koreans and second, including Chinese only—do not alter the finding that very young Asian-immigrant firms (and firm subgroups) are smaller and more prone to failure when they serve a clientele that is predominantly minority.

Sources of Labor

Waldinger argues that loyal, low-cost employees drawn from the owner's own ethnic group may explain why self-employment is advantageous to Asian immigrants (1986). New arrivals often seek employment in an immigrant firm where they can work in a familiar environment with others who know their language. Bonacich and Light reported that Korean-owned businesses in Los Angeles—operating often in low-income, nonwhite neighborhoods—were very effective at generating jobs for fellow Koreans: "about 62 percent of Koreans found employment in the ethnic economy" (1988, 6). Ethnicity provides a common ground on which workplace rules are negotiated. "Authority can be secured on the basis of personal loyalties and ethnic allegiance . . ." (Waldinger, Aldrich, and Ward 1990, 38).

The view of paternalistic employment practices securing employee loyalty in the ethnic economy is challenged by descriptions of child labor abuses and unsafe, illegal working conditions. In his study of business practices in New York City's Chinatown, Peter Kwong claims that employers routinely violated fair labor practices. "The alliance between Chinese owners and workers is unfortunately a myth" (1987, 63). Employers, no doubt, pursue widely varying labor relations practices, covering the ground from paternalistic to exploitive. The conventional wisdom among sociologists, nonetheless, is that ethnic employers in immigrant enclaves are paternalistic on balance and that recent immigrants provide a productive and inexpensive workforce.

The relevance of this form of social capital may be constrained somewhat by Fratoe's findings that small businesses owned by Asians rely considerably less on minority employees than do blacks and Latinos (1988). Using CBO data, Bates and Dunham (1993) found that Asian-immigrant-owned firms predominantly hire minority group members, but less so than African American employers. The CBO database, however, cannot be used to test directly Waldinger's hypothesis of a loyal, low-cost, ethnic labor force, because, within its minority and nonminority employee groupings, minorities are not identified by ethnicity.

Family members may be another possible source of cheap, reliable labor for Asian-immigrant firms. Small-business owners face the possibility that their employees will shirk on the job. Married business owners can diminish this risk by hiring their spouses, since spouses presumably have the same incentive—maximization of family income. Borjas (1986) reports that married Asian immigrants are more likely to pursue self-employment than their unmarried Asian counterparts. Yet the evidence on this point is mixed. Boyd (1990a) used six different measures of family and extended family in logistic regressions to explain Asian involvement in self-employment: five of the six measures were insignificant statistically as predictors of self-employment among Asians in the United States. Chan and Cheung (1985) report that most Chinese-owned firms in Toronto had no family members as employees.

The impact of labor sources as well as a minority clientele, the owner's educational background and financial investment in the firm, and other factors of firm survival and discontinuance are investigated further below.

THE EFFECTS OF FINANCIAL CAPITAL, HUMAN CAPITAL, AND SOCIAL CAPITAL ON SMALL-BUSINESS LONGEVITY

Over the 1987–91 period, over 18 percent of the Asian-immigrant firms described in this chapter discontinued operations. Firms that were sold to a new owner, that merged with another firm, or that were otherwise altered are not counted as discontinued if they continue to operate. The logistic regression equations estimated in table 3.3 help explain small-business longevity. The independent variables I used to explain longevity among Asian-immigrant firms include measures of owner characteristics, firm traits, and social-capital proxies. While longevity is the primary measure of business viability under consideration, profitability will be analyzed later in this chapter to see just how robust the observed relationships between the explanatory variables and firm viability are.

Based on past econometric studies explaining small-business longevity, I expect that the greater the owner's investment of human and financial capital, the greater the chances that the Asian-immigrant-owned small business will survive (Bates 1994b).[4] The quality of the owner's human capital will be measured by the level of the owner's formal education and whether or not the owner had acquired managerial experience before starting the small business. Labor input will be measured by the number of hours the owner spent working in the business, as well as the owner's marital status and the number of paid employees the business had. I expect that married people living with their spouses will benefit from family labor, which potentially increases the amount of labor put into the business. Applicable demographic traits include the owner's age and gender. The owner's age is a broad proxy for work experience, so the greater the owner's age, the more I expect the firms to benefit until the diminishing effort associated with old age sets in.

To test the social-capital hypotheses examined earlier in this chapter, I have introduced the minority composition of the firm's clientele as a contributory factor, and I have investigated labor force composition as

Table 3.3

Logistic Regression Explaining Survival of Asian-Immigrant-Owned Firms, 1987–91 (Firms Formed since 1979 Only)

	Firms formed 1986 or 1987*		
	Regression coefficient	Standard error	Variable mean
Constant	1.487	.988	—
Education			
High school	.343	.264	.172
College, 1–3 years	1.082[a]	.280	.195
College graduate	.358	.246	.349
Graduate school	.594[a]	.275	.204
Management experience	.082	.159	.307
Bought ongoing firm	−.179	.171	.284
Married	.196	.201	.767
Age	−.063	.046	39.599
Age^2	.0005	.0005	1,660.6
Gender	−.267	.143	.668
Asian Indian	−.068	.223	.187
Chinese	.169	.205	.227
Korean	−.353	.195	.256
Vietnamese	−.132	.251	.115
Owner-labor input	.040[a]	.006	19.160
Number of employees	.144[a]	.053	1.015
Capital	.108[a]	.019	8.553
Leverage	.015	.014	2.279
Entered 1987	−.659[a]	.148	.571
Minority clientele	−.445[a]	.170	.540
Agglomeration	−.242	.135	.467

Continued on next page

[a]Statistically significant at the 5-percent level.

*$N = 1,615$; $-2 \log L = 1,540.9$; chi-squared = 299.5.

Table 3.3—*Continued*

	Employers only†		
	Regression coefficient	Standard error	Variable mean
Constant	−1.343	1.328	—
Education			
High school	.401	.281	.163
College, 1–3 years	.386	.312	.130
College graduate	.238	.253	.287
Graduate school	.496a	.261	.318
Managerial experience	.502a	.179	.395
Bought ongoing firm	−.350a	.171	.401
Married	−.384	.280	.873
Age	.179a	.058	42.695
Age²	−.002a	.0006	1,906.5
Gender	−.152	.187	.753
Asian Indian	−.302	.284	.218
Chinese	.232	.261	.308
Korean	.053	.263	.261
Vietnamese	.231	.361	.064
Owner-labor input	.031a	.007	26.124
Number of employees	.033a	.018	4.023
Capital	.099a	.036	10.413
Leverage	.040a	.019	2.689
Entered			
1984 or 1985	−1.128a	.237	.226
1986	−1.647a	.236	.213
1987	−.930a	.257	.208
Minority clientele	−.303	.184	.370
Minority labor force	.442	.259	.644
Agglomeration	−.102	.170	.360

aStatistically significant at the 5-percent level.

†$N = 2,623$; $-2 \log L = 1,323.5$; chi-squared $= 177.5$.

Table 3.3—*Continued*

	All Firms‡		
	Regression coefficient	Standard error	Variable mean
Constant	1.119	.717	—
Education			
High school	.255	.178	.162
College, 1–3 years	.987[a]	.200	.160
College graduate	.034	.162	.326
Graduate school	.408[a]	.179	.245
Managerial experience	.103	.110	.311
Bought ongoing firm	.159	.117	.278
Married	.075	.121	.819
Age	.043	.032	41.570
Age^2	−.0008[a]	.0004	1,817.9
Gender	−.152	.101	.689
Asian Indian	−.104	.158	.202
Chinese	.018	.144	.259
Korean	−.413[a]	.142	.239
Vietnamese	.061	.100	.095
Owner-labor input	.036[a]	.004	21.335
Number of employees	.080[a]	.026	1.411
Capital	.053[a]	.013	8.639
Leverage	.019	.010	2.116
Entered			
1984 or 1985	−.574[a]	.168	.226
1986	−1.251[a]	.161	.219
1987	−1.859[a]	.153	.292
Minority clientele	−.277[a]	.113	.501
Agglomeration	−.100	.095	.429

Source: U.S. Bureau of the Census, Characteristics of Business Owners (CBO) database, 1992.

Notes: Variables are defined in the appendix, "Databases and Variable Definitions," pp. 270–3.

[a]Statistically significant at the 5-percent level.

‡$N = 4,208$; $-2 \log L = 3,255.3$; chi-squared = 656.5.

a longevity determinant for firms with paid employees. I have introduced binary variables identifying major Asian ethnic groups into the analysis of firm longevity as control variables. An owner-ethnicity frequency distribution reveals that three groups dominate the Asian-immigrant entrepreneur sample described in table 3.1:

Chinese	26.7%
Korean	22.6%
Asian Indian	20.5%
All other	30.2%

Finally, I have introduced an agglomeration variable to test for possible effects on firm longevity of the intense clustering of Asian-immigrant businesses in several large metropolitan areas. Nearly 43 percent of the Asian-immigrant firms analyzed in this chapter operate in either the Los Angeles County–Orange County megalopolis, the New York City metropolitan area, or the San Francisco Bay region (including Oakland, San Jose, San Francisco, and surrounding suburbs). Large Asian populations live in each of these three areas. Yoon argues that the presence of complementary suppliers owned by fellow ethnic-group members facilitates successful business operation, because such suppliers provide "extended credit terms, lower prices, and easy access to information" (1991a, 198). A downside to concentration in geographic areas such as Los Angeles and New York is the prevalence of severe intraethnic competition (Kwong 1987). "Eighty percent of respondents (all Koreans) refer to Koreans as their primary business competitors" (Yoon 1991a, 199). (Exact definitions of the explanatory logistic regression variables are described in the appendix, "Databases and Variable Definitions.")

The dependent variable in each of the logistic regression exercises in table 3.3 is whether or not the business that was operating in 1987 was still functioning in late 1991. Logistic regression equations delineating active from discontinued businesses are reported in table 3.3, first, for Asian-immigrant firms that were started in 1986 and 1987 only. Table 3.2 highlighted the high discontinuance rates of these young firms, particularly among those serving minority clients. I examined the 1986 and 1987 entrant subsample to test the hypothesis that very young Asian-immigrant-owned firms benefited initially from operating in a minority market niche. Second, I analyzed the "employers only" firms in table 3.3 primarily to measure the impact of the minority composition of the labor force on firm survival and, secondarily, to assess the stability of the explanatory variable regression coefficients when only larger small businesses (the employer subset) are examined.[5] Finally, I analyzed all young Asian-immigrant firms in table 3.3 to provide a context for interpreting how very young firms and firms with paid employees differ from the broader group of Asian-immigrant businesses.

In the analyses in table 3.3 of firms that were operating in 1987, positive coefficient values are associated with firms still operating in 1991 and negative coefficients with those no longer operating. Five types of explanatory variables are particularly effective for explaining survival and discontinuance patterns for the Asian-immigrant firms started since 1979. The surviving firms that were active in 1991 are disproportionately those started with large financial-capital investments, the older firms, those serving a clientele that was not predominantly minority, and those headed by owners who had attended college. Firms with greater labor input—whether the labor was provided by the owner or by paid employees—were more likely to survive, particularly in comparison with firms with no employees and those headed by owners working in the business only part time. The very youngest firms—those started in 1986 and 1987—were most vulnerable to discontinuance, which is consistent with the findings of past studies (Jovanovic 1982; Evans 1987; Bates 1990b). The strong result that the firms better capitalized at start-up were more likely to stay active, other factors remaining constant, is also highly consistent with past findings (Evans and Jovanovic 1989; Bates 1990b). Thus, the same factors that explain firm longevity among small businesses generally are also important to explaining survival among firms owned by Asian immigrants.

Among the very youngest Asian-immigrant-owned firms, the negative impact of serving a minority clientele was most pronounced. While table 3.2 indicated that the young firms serving a predominantly minority clientele were generally those started with a lower financial investment and employing fewer people, table 3.3 indicates, other factors remaining constant, that firms owned by Asian immigrants oriented toward a minority clientele are much more likely to go out of business than similar firms operating in the broader marketplace. This finding is inconsistent with both Light and Waldinger's hypothesis regarding the benefits of serving fellow ethnic-group members as well as Min and Yoon's hypothesis that the neighborhoods of low-income minority clienteles generally offer attractive operating environments to Asian-immigrant firms due to the ease of entry and the lack of competition.

In the subset of firms with employees, those having a high percentage of minority employees were slightly more likely to remain active, but this relationship was not statistically significant at conventional significance levels. An explanatory variable identifying the percentage of employees drawn from the owner's ethnic group (rather than just "minority") might have produced a different result, one that would support the hypothesis concerning the beneficial effects of a workforce made up of fellow ethnic-group members. If this hypothesis were valid, minority employees of Asian-immigrant firms would be overwhelmingly drawn from the owner's ethnic group. Why would minorities from other ethnic groups be employed by Asian-immigrant firms in significant numbers if, indeed, workers drawn from the owner's ethnic group were cheaper and more loyal? On balance, the social-capital proxies analyzed in table 3.3 exhibit no strong, consistent relationship with the longevity of Asian-immigrant small businesses.

Among the immigrant entrepreneurs under consideration, the Asian-Indian subgroup relies least on minority employees and clients, while the Vietnamese subgroup relies most heavily on minority employees and is above average in orientation toward minority clients. The Asian Indian firms as a group have the lowest rates of discontinuance; the Vietnamese, in contrast, have the highest firm closure rates among the Asian subgroups (table 3.4). Thus, the use of social resources may be negatively associated with firm survival. A more likely explanation for differences in survival rates among Asian-immigrant ethnic groups is found in patterns of financial and human capital (table 3.4). Among the Asian Indian-owned firms, for example, mean financial capital at startup was $68,013 versus $25,626 among the Vietnamese. In the context of the logistic regressions explaining firm survival, ethnic group, by itself, generally had little explanatory power. While Koreans were somewhat more likely to see their firms fail, other factors remaining constant, this relationship did not characterize the larger firms, firms with employees. The agglomeration factor, finally, exhibited a consistently negative, although statistically insignificant, relationship to firm survival, suggesting that major concentrations of Asian-immigrant-owned firms in the New York, Los Angeles, and San Francisco areas may simply mirror broader patterns of residential concentration: agglomeration does not appear to boost the odds of firm survival.

Table 3.4

Traits of Asian-Immigrant-Owned Firms (Firms Formed since 1979 Only)

	Firm's traits (mean values)			
	Asian Indian	Chinese	Korean	Vietnamese
Gross sales, 1987	$161,675	$126,499	$128,022	$86,986
Total financial capital	$68,013	$61,521	$52,146	$25,626
Equity capital	$33,821	$33,231	$29,422	$12,186
Debt capital	$34,192	$28,290	$22,724	$13,440
Percent of firms still operating, 1991	84.3%	83.9%	78.4%	76.1%
	Owner's traits			
	Asian Indian	Chinese	Korean	Vietnamese
Percent with less than four years of high school	4.6%	20.0%	5.3%	16.7%
Percent college graduates	80.4%	53.9%	52.3%	26.4%
Owner-labor input (mean)	1,941	2,077	2,368	1,824
	Social capital proxies			
	Asian Indian	Chinese	Korean	Vietnamese
Percent serving predominantly minority clientele	42.3%	46.2%	68.3%	52.0%
Percent of minority employees (firms with employees only)				
0%	23.9%	16.8%	7.1%	8.5%
1–49%	18.0%	15.8%	9.1%	3.0%
50–74%	11.9%	9.9%	10.0%	12.7%
75%+	46.2%	57.5%	73.8%	75.8%
Percent in Los Angeles—Anaheim, New York City, or San Francisco—Oakland:	27.0%	56.8%	48.5%	47.1%

Source: U.S. Bureau of the Census, Characteristics of Business Owners (CBO) database, 1992.

Note: Variables are defined in the appendix, "Databases and Variable Definitions," pp. 270–3.

The logistic regression exercises in table 3.3 offer several other insights into survival and discontinuance among firms owned by Asian immigrants. Being married and living with one's spouse, both positively (for firms started in 1986 or 1987 and for all firms) and negatively (for firms with employees) related to firm survival, was statistically insignificant, suggesting that the access to family labor potentially available to married business owners is of minor importance.[6]

Entry into self-employment by buying an existing firm, much more common among Asian immigrants than among nonminority cohorts, other factors remaining constant, is negatively associated with firm survival; this relationship is statistically significant among the larger-scale firms, those with paid employees. Why? Buying an existing business is never easy: Owners may cook the books to make things look better than they are. Buyers are often naive, particularly if they have not owned a business before. People frequently end up buying a firm that is well on its way to failure.[7]

Asian-immigrant firms generally and the subset of such firms with paid employees specifically were broadly similar overall, regarding traits that predict longevity. The well-capitalized, well-established firms headed by college-educated owners were the businesses most likely to be active in 1991, particularly when their clientele was not predominantly minority. The larger scale firms (measured by number of employees) and those whose owners work full time in the business have the best survival prospects. These same traits accurately predict longevity among small businesses generally (chapter 2).

PROFITABILITY

Firm viability is a multidimensional phenomenon: small businesses that keep operating tend to be the larger, more profitable firms.[8] High profits not only serve to motivate the owner to remain self-employed, but they also make small businesses potentially salable to new owners when the present owner chooses to retire or move on to other pursuits.

The logistic regression equations in table 3.3 explaining firm discontinuance and survival serve as the basis for a complementary set of ordinary least squares (OLS) regression exercises analyzing the log of the dollar amount of before-tax profits (dependent variable). These OLS regressions use the same data and explanatory variables described in the logistic regression section of this chapter. I analyzed the Asian-immigrant groups of (1) all firms started between 1979 and 1987, and (2) firms with paid employees using the log of the dollar amount of 1987 before-tax profits as the dependent variable to test the robustness of the findings of the logistic regressions in table 3.3.[9] Results of the OLS regression explaining the dollar amount of firm profits for all young firms owned by Asian immigrants and Asian-immigrant-owned firms with paid employees only are reported below in table 3.5.

Inherent difficulties in the analysis of small-business profitability are rooted in the reality of widely varying accounting conventions regarding depreciation methods, inventory valuation, and so forth. Dollar measures of profitability, therefore, are apt to be much more random than the previously examined dependent variable—small-business longevity. In the CBO database, furthermore, nonresponse on the initial survey questionnaires was greater for the question regarding owner estimates of before-tax profits than for other questionnaire items. The OLS regression equations explaining profits for Asian-immigrant-owned firms, nonetheless, produced clear-cut results that are broadly consistent with those previously reported in the logistic regressions in table 3.3.

The portrait of Asian-immigrant businesses generating high profits is based on owners working full-time in their firms, being highly educated, and being in business for four or more years. Relative to the findings of the firm-longevity analysis discussed previously, the variables associated with the owner's human capital emerge as consistently positive, statistically significant determinants of firm profits.

The fact that human-capital measures, such as the owner's educational level and managerial experience, are consistent determinants of firm profitability and erratic determinants of longevity may be noteworthy. High rates of business ownership among Asian immigrants coexist with a narrow business base as well as annual sales and profits that are low, on average, relative to those reported by the dominant nonminority small-business sector. Waldinger (1986), for example, observes that Asian immigrants pursue self-employment less as a matter of preference and more as a matter of blocked mobility: impediments to more attractive alternatives include poor English-language facility and inappropriate skills. The lower rates of business discontinuance observed in table 1.1 among Asian immigrants may reflect their paucity of alternatives rather than their success in business. If this is true, then highly capable owners (profitability notwithstanding) may

Table 3.5

OLS Regression Explaining Profitability of Asian-Immigrant-Owned Firms, 1987 (Firms Formed since 1979 Only)

	All Young Firms*		
	Regression coefficient	Standard error	Variable mean
Constant	8.134[a]	.247	—
Education			
High school	.217[a]	.054	.167
College, 1–3 years	.265[a]	.052	.175
College graduate	.471[a]	.049	.294
Graduate school	.788[a]	.052	.244
Managerial experience	.117[a]	.032	.312
Bought ongoing firm	.046	.035	.246
Married	.103[a]	.041	.841
Age	.019[a]	.011	41.864
Age^2	−.0002[a]	.0001	1,841.9
Gender	.206[a]	.033	.746
Owner-labor input	.027[a]	.001	21.173
Number of employees	.010[a]	.003	1.350
Capital	.005	.004	8.169
Leverage	.007	.004	1.530
Entered			
1984 or 1985	−.266[a]	.039	.231
1986	−.372[a]	.041	.213
1987	−.356[a]	.041	.262
Minority clientele	−.087[a]	.031	.320
Agglomeration	.059	.030	.435
			Continued on next page

*$N = 3,647$; $R^2 = .275$; $F = 76.3$.

Table 3.5 — *Continued*

	Employers only[†]		
	Regression coefficient	Standard error	Variable mean
Constant	7.692[a]	.413	—
Education			
High school	.025	.081	.154
College, 1–3 years	.012	.083	.138
College graduate	.335[a]	.075	.287
Graduate school	.693[a]	.076	.298
Managerial experience	.188[a]	.046	.359
Bought ongoing firm	−.066	.044	.360
Married	.116	.069	.881
Age	.050[a]	.019	42.220
Age^2	−.0006[a]	.0002	1,858.6
Gender	.310[a]	.049	.790
Owner-labor input	.018[a]	.002	26.635
Number of employees	.008[a]	.002	3.900
Capital	.008	.011	10.215
Leverage	.015[a]	.004	2.711
Entered			
1984 or 1985	−.077	.053	.217
1986	−.368[a]	.057	.199
1987	−.273[a]	.062	.176
Minority clientele	−.055	.051	.202
Minority labor force	.042	.062	.620
Agglomeration	.169[a]	.044	.373

Source: U.S. Bureau of the Census, Characteristics of Business Owners (CBO) database, 1992.

Notes: Variables are defined in the appendix, "Databases and Variable Definitions," pp. 270–3.

[†]$N = 2,073$; $R^2 = .225$; $F = 24.8$.

[a]Statistically significant at the 5-percent level.

leave self-employment when better opportunities arise. This issue is explored in detail in chapter 4 of this volume.

Asian immigrants are very heavily crowded into several business groups—particularly retailing—and within a business group, they are often heavily overrepresented in the smaller scale lines of that business. Manufacturing, for example, is one of the larger scale industries where small businesses thrive. Yet Asian manufacturers are concentrated in several of the small-scale lines of nondurable goods manufacturing: garments, food processing, and printing. In retailing, Asian immigrants are overrepresented in restaurants and food stores, but they are underrepresented (relative to nonminorities) in larger scale retailing, such as building materials stores, new car dealerships, and appliance stores.

Based on CBO data, mean 1987 sales in major business groups are presented below for the Asian-immigrant and nonminority samples described in table 3.1.

	Asian Immigrant	Nonminority
Manufacturing	$173,240	$381,740
Wholesaling	$417,543	$520,223
Retailing	$167,583	$266,873
Services	$85,462	$91,930

Mean 1987 profits in two of these business groups were substantially lower for the Asian-immigrant firms than for nonminority-owned businesses.[10] Overall, the groups of Asian-immigrant and nonminority small businesses summarized in table 3.1 reported mean profits of $14,900 and $20,519 respectively. Operating marginally profitable small-scale firms may be a form of underemployment for many highly educated Asian-immigrant entrepreneurs. If applicable barriers to upward mobility can be overcome, many of these self-employed people could use their human capital more fully either by moving into managerial or professional salaried employment or by shifting into more skill-intensive, larger scale lines of small business.

CONCLUSIONS

The social-capital explanations put forth by Light (1972), Bonacich and Light (1988), Waldinger (1986), Waldinger, Aldrich, and Ward

(1990), and others to explain the success of Asian-immigrant-owned small businesses rest on an uncertain empirical foundation. The term *success* may be inappropriate: Asian immigrants, in spite of their much larger investments of human and financial capital, generate substantially lower sales and profits than similar nonminority-owned small businesses. Success may indeed typify the firms owned by immigrant Asian Indians; Fratoe and Meeks (1988) in their analysis of self-employment among individuals associated with the fifty largest ancestry groups in the United States found that Asian Indians ranked highest overall in mean self-employment income. Asian Indian small-business owners, however, are the Asian-immigrant subgroup that is least oriented to serving a minority clientele and least likely to employ a predominantly minority labor force, i.e., they are least likely to make use of the forms of social capital discussed above.[11] Vietnamese firms, in contrast, rely heavily on serving a minority clientele and on minority workers (table 3.4). Relative to their Asian cohorts, the Vietnamese run the smallest firms and suffer the highest firm discontinuance rates. Among Asian-Indian and Vietnamese firms active in 1987, 15.7 percent of the former and 23.9 percent of the latter had shut down their businesses by 1991.

In defense of the sociological approach, note that the quantitative analyses pursued in this chapter are too broad to reject the results of very specific studies of immigrant groups operating in individual businesses or cities. Waldinger (1986), for example, focused only on Chinese immigrants operating in the garment industry in New York. Waldinger's analysis may be on the mark for that group in that city. A legitimate concern, however, is the riskiness of generalizing about the behavior of Asian (or minority) business ownership nationally from such specific analyses.

The findings of this chapter call into question the validity of explaining success in self-employment in terms of protected markets and loyal employees drawn from the business owner's own ethnic group. Social-capital forms of start-up financing—rotating credit associations, for example—will be critically examined in chapter 6. Variations in the owner's human capital and ability to invest money in his or her firm, in contrast, do explain patterns of small-business viability. Many Asian immigrants have achieved success in self-employment in the United States; business owners who were highly educated and affluent before starting their businesses have been particularly successful.

NOTES

1. Detailed descriptions of the CBO database used throughout this chapter appear in the appendix, "Databases and Variable Definitions."

2. The Asian-immigrant and nonminority business samples described throughout this chapter are both drawn from the CBO database. To weed out the insubstantial businesses (largely employees who report small amounts of self-employment income) described in Bates (1990a), firms reporting gross annual sales in 1987 of under $5,000 were deleted. The statistics in table 3.1 are based on representative nationwide samples of 5,840 Asian-immigrant- and 12,490 nonminority-owned small businesses.

3. The minority composition of the clientele served by Asian-immigrant-owned firms tends to cluster at very high levels (75 percent or more minority) or very low levels (under 25 percent minority). The choice of the two cutoff points—50 percent and 75 percent—used to define "predominantly minority clientele" in this chapter was dictated by the nature of the questionnaire used to generate the CBO database.

4. The leverage variable cannot exceed 19; this constant is dictated by the nature of the questionnaire used to generate the CBO database. Leverage values above 10 are, in fact, quite rare in the CBO data.

5. The sample size for all Asian-immigrant firms formed between 1979 and 1987 that were still operating in 1987 was 4,208 in the table 3.3 logit analysis; the sample size dropped sharply to 2,623 after deleting the firms with no employees. Sample sizes underlying the various tables in this report vary due to item nonresponse on the relevant Census Bureau questionnaires. Firms providing information on any of the items covered in table 3.2 are included in that table; table 3.3, in contrast, includes only those firms providing information on all of the items covered in table 3.3. Imputed numbers are never used to fill in items left blank in the CBO questionnaires. A recalculation of business and owner traits among Asian immigrants in table 3.2 using the smaller sample of firms in table 3.3 produces no substantive changes in the relevant summary statistics.

6. The owner's gender and marital status interaction variables had no explanatory power when added to the logistic regressions in table 3.3 as explanatory variables.

7. This insight was provided by an anonymous referee.

8. Of the firms described in table 3.3, for example, mean sales in 1987 were $159,151 for the surviving firms and $51,479 for the firms that closed down.

9. In the regression analysis of log profits, firms reporting profits of less than $1 are excluded from the analysis.

10. Profit differences were large and statistically significant ($\alpha = .05$) in services and wholesaling; the lower mean profits reported by Asian immigrants operating in retail and manufacturing were not significantly different from the profits of similar nonminority firms. Firms' profit figures reported throughout this book are calcu-

lated to cope with outlyer problems that involve less than .01 of 1 percent of the CBO database firms: profits for an individual firm cannot exceed $100,000, nor can they be less than −$100,000. Outlyer values in the CBO database are not edited for reasonableness by the Census Bureau. Thus, a firm may report 1987 sales of $5,000 and profits of $3,000,000; indeed, some do. These data are constrained in the CBO data only to maximum/minimum values of +$3,000,000/−$3,000,000. Having an occasional −$3,000,000 profit figure can seriously skew calculated mean profits when a firm subset such as Asian-immigrant-owned manufacturing firms is involved. This makes the mean statistic a poor measure of central tendency. In Bates (1994b), unconstrained firm profit figures are reported for groups of firms summarized in this chapter. The impact of using unconstrained profits is always to depress Asian-immigrant business profitability relative to profit means typifying whites, blacks, and other comparison groups. By reporting constrained figures, the chapters in this book raise reported Asian-immigrant firm profitability and lower white, black, and Asian American firm profitability.

11. The findings discussed in chapter 6 indicate that the amount of financial capital available to Asian-immigrant firms from group support networks is similarly related to firm viability. Vietnamese firms rely most heavily on loans from group support networks, while Asian Indians are least reliant on loans from this source.

CHAPTER FOUR

Escaping from Self-Employment: An Analysis of Asian-Immigrant-Owned Small Businesses

The small-business creation process is shaped by a complex dynamic of push and pull factors. Many who pursue self-employment are pulled in by attractive opportunities and the prospect of rising earnings. Others are pushed into self-employment because their access to good jobs is blocked by barriers ranging from a lack of educational credentials to inappropriate work experience, limited facility in the English language, and so forth. Rapid growth in the number of small businesses owned by Asian immigrants living in the United States partially reflects the attractiveness of self-employment as a career choice. Often, however, self-employment offers meager returns but is taken up, nonetheless, because of a paucity of attractive alternatives.

This chapter will analyze self-employed Asian immigrants who have been pushed as well as pulled into the U.S. small-business sector. Being pushed into self-employment leads to sharply different behavior patterns from those of Asian immigrants who were pulled into self-employment. While the push dynamic creates business owners seeking to escape self-employment, pull factors produce owners whose firms are long lived. A poor use of the owner's human capital and low earnings often typify the firms of owners trapped in self-employment, whereas higher profits are more likely to accrue to businesses whose owners were pulled into self-employment. These effects are explored by comparing the performance of Asian-immigrant-owned small businesses to that of Asian American and nonminority cohorts.

EVIDENCE OF SELF-EMPLOYMENT SUCCESS
AMONG ASIAN IMMIGRANTS IS LACKING

Measures of success among self-employed Asian immigrants have been analyzed in several instances: Boyd (1991b) studied their earnings from self-employment, and Bates (1994b) investigated firm survival patterns from 1987 to 1991. Neither study supported the stereotype of business success. Empirical studies have most commonly sought simply to explain variations in the *rates* of self-employment among immigrant groups (Borjas 1986; Evans 1989; Kim, Hurh, and Fernandez 1989). Studies are often descriptive (Bonacich and Light 1988; Min 1986–87; Fratoe 1986), focusing on owners' traits as well as the operating environment of the immigrant firms.

The scarcity of empirical analysis has coexisted with the emergence of numerous suppositions to explain patterns of self-employment among Asian immigrants. Bonacich and Light (1988) imply that Korean immigrants have been successful in self-employment in Los Angeles, where their presence in small-scale retailing has increased rapidly since the 1970s. They assume that high self-employment rates and the rapid expansion of small-business ownership are evidence of success. Citing the growth of immigrant enclaves, Borjas (1990) argues that entrepreneurial opportunities for immigrants have increased in the past two or three decades. Evans (1989), Light (1972), and others claim that Asian-immigrant entrepreneurs have benefited from protected markets, particularly in the retail sector, where firms cater to fellow ethnic-group members. Self-employment, finally, is widely viewed as a strategy for escaping labor market discrimination (Moore 1983; Light 1972).

The conventional wisdom of Asian-immigrant success in self-employment rests, in fact, on a weak empirical foundation. One clear-cut fact discussed in earlier chapters is the rapid growth of self-employment among Asian immigrants. Using nationwide Census Bureau data, Borjas (1986) found that self-employed Asian immigrants reported higher mean annual incomes than any other racially defined group—immigrant or nonimmigrant, self-employed or salaried. Fratoe (1986) analyzed the earnings of the fifty largest groups reporting a single ancestry in the census of population: two immigrant-dominated groups—Asian Indians and Filipinos—ranked first and fourth in mean self-employment earnings.

Sociologists often infer Asian-immigrant success in the small-business realm from such statistics (Yoon 1991b), but economists have been more circumspect. Borjas (1990), after noting that self-employed immigrant men earn about 48 percent more than salaried immigrants, cautioned that this earnings pattern is not evidence of success in small business. Instead, Borjas found that the self-employed, whether native or immigrant, have somewhat lower incomes than demographically similar salaried workers. The mixed evidence to Portes and Zhou suggests a slight income advantage favoring the immigrant self-employed (1996).

Rapid self-employment growth is not necessarily motivated by the attractiveness of owning a small business. Increasing rates of self-employment clearly do suggest a shift in opportunities between employee and self-employed sectors. But the deterioration of the former (and not the attractiveness of the latter) can also encourage expanded small-business ownership. Borjas notes a "structural shift in the rate of wage convergence for Asian immigrants who migrated after 1970" (1994, 1682). Asian immigrants aged 35–44 who arrived in the United States between 1985 and 1989, for example, faced wages 30.6 percent lower than the wages earned by natives of the same ethnic background. This is over twice as large as the corresponding wage differential reported in the 1970 census by those arriving between 1965 and 1969 (Borjas 1994). Poor opportunities for salaried employment are clearly consistent with a growing propensity toward self-employment.

THE FIRM'S PROFITABILITY AND THE OWNER'S HUMAN AND FINANCIAL CAPITAL

This study analyzes small firms operating in 1987 that were created (or entered into) by their current owner since 1979. Over 70 percent of all Asian-owned small businesses active in 1987, as well as nearly 50 percent of nonminority firms, were started during this time span. The data source used in the following analysis is the CBO database described in the appendix, "Databases and Variable Definitions." The firms described below are representative of all small businesses active in the United States that generated gross revenues of at least $5,000 in 1987 and filed a small-business federal income-tax return (sole proprietorship, partnership, or corporate).

Asian-immigrant self-employment in the United States is dominated by five groups—Asian Indians, Filipinos, Koreans, Chinese, and Vietnamese—and mean self-employment earnings vary widely; Asian Indians possess the highest mean level of education among the self-employed and generate the highest earnings, while the Vietnamese are in last place in both categories. This chapter focuses heavily on the two highest earning Asian-immigrant business-owning subgroups—Asian Indians and Filipinos. Analysis of their self-employment income reveals that their returns trail those of nonminority and Asian American comparison groups. In fact, African Americans—characterized as earning very low self-employment returns by Fratoe (1986)—generate higher self-employment returns than do the firms of Asian immigrants started between 1979 and 1987.

Two important pieces of the context introduced in chapter 1 are illustrated in table 4.1. First, Asian immigrants entering self-employment, on average, have much greater human capital and invest much more financial capital into their ventures than do self-employed nonminorities. Second, self-employed groups of Asian immigrants differ widely in these areas, with Asian Indians (highest mean earnings) investing the largest amounts in their businesses and the Vietnamese (lowest mean earnings) investing the smallest amounts of financial capital, on average. Because the high-earning self-employed Asian-immigrant groups are more likely to be driving the stereotype of small-business success than low-income groups such as the Vietnamese, this analysis of self-employment will focus heavily on Asian-Indian and Filipino small-business owners.

The owner's rich human capital and substantial financial capital are advantages for new small businesses, but they are potentially counterbalanced by the limited English fluency that constrains occupational choice for many Asian immigrants. Levels of English fluency vary enormously: 79.9 percent of Asian Indian immigrants to the United States reported that they spoke English very well; only 20.8 percent of Vietnamese immigrants were similarly proficient in English. The majority of Filipino immigrants were also very proficient in English. These high levels of proficiency reflect the fact that English is commonly spoken in both countries, "particularly among the highly educated who have dominated recent immigration from India and the Philippines" (U.S. Commission on Civil Rights 1988, 57).

Table 4.1

Traits of Firms Nationwide Started 1979–1987, by Owner's
Race/Ethnic Group

	Nonminorities	All Asian Immigrants	Immigrants only		
			Asian Indians	Koreans	Vietnamese
Total financial capital at start-up (mean)	$31,939	$53,550	$68,013	$54,146	$25,626
Percent of owners who are college graduates	37.7%	57.8%	80.4%	52.3%	26.4%
Percent of owners with less than four years of high school	10.4%	11.4%	4.6%	5.3%	16.7%

Source: U.S. Bureau of the Census, Characteristics of Business Owners (CBO) database, 1992.

Note: Variables are defined in the appendix, "Databases and Variable Definitions," pp. 270–3.

Filipinos and Asian Indians are most fluent in English, have the largest endowments of financial and human capital invested in their small businesses, and earn the highest reported self-employment incomes among Asian-immigrant groups. The profitability analysis in table 4.2 is based on the same general sample as table 4.1: all firms filed a 1987 small-business federal income-tax return, and all generated gross revenues of at least $5,000. Asian Americans (excluded from table 4.1) are added as a comparison group.

Mean before-tax profits reported by immigrant Asian Indians and Filipinos, Asian Americans, and nonminorities in 1987 were $14,088, $17,835, and $15,838, respectively (table 4.2). Recall that all of these are young firms, and many of the owners were self-employed only part time. Most of the firms under consideration operated either in retailing or services. Retailing is noteworthy for its consistently low mean profits and the above-average input of labor and financial capital required of the owner. Reported profits are lower and the owner's hours of work in the firm are, in fact, higher in retailing than in any other major business group, and this pattern holds for Asian American- and Asian-immigrant-owned small businesses generally, as

Table 4.2

Traits of Asian and Nonminority Firms and Owners, 1987—Mean Values
(Firms Formed since 1979 Only)

	Immigrant Asian Indian/Filipino	Asian American	Nonminority
Before-tax profits			
All firms	$14,088	$17,835	$15,838
Firms whose owners worked at least 2,000 hours	$19,760	$23,260	$21,611
Full-time owners			
Annual owner-labor input in hours	2,958	2,900	2,832
Equity capital	$37,870	$28,860	$15,560
Profits divided by hours worked	$6.68	$8.02	$7.63
Profits less 10 percent equity return divided by hours worked	$5.39	$7.02	$7.08

Source: U.S. Bureau of the Census, Characteristics of Business Owners (CBO) database, 1992.

Note: Variables are defined in the appendix, "Databases and Variable Definitions," pp. 270–3.

well as for Asian Indian- and Filipino-owned firms specifically.
Services show the opposite pattern—higher profits and fewer hours
worked by owners—for all of the groups under consideration. A firm's
profit-per-hour-of-owner-labor calculation provides a crude mean
profitability measure illustrating the pronounced differences between
businesses:

	Retail	Service
Asian Indian and Filipino	$4.49 per hour	$8.97 per hour
Asian American	$6.60 per hour	$11.40 per hour
Nonminority	$5.66 per hour	$9.63 per hour

Owners of firms in service businesses are more often college educated than those in retailing, and opportunity costs alone suggest that
highly educated owners are likely to generate greater reported profits
than are the less well educated self-employed. The profitability figures
reported below set aside part-time self-employment by examining full-

time owners only (2,000 or more hours worked in the firm in 1987), and they are broken down by the owner's educational background. Attributing a 10 percent return to the owner's start-up investment of equity capital is one way to separate out returns to capital and labor. Resultant profits, minus a 10 percent return to equity capital investment, show the following average returns to the owners for their full-time work in their firms:

	College educated	No college
Asian Indian and Filipino	$5.63 per hour	$3.59 per hour
Asian American	$7.56 per hour	$5.71 per hour
Nonminority	$7.52 per hour	$6.39 per hour

Corresponding figures for various other groups identically sampled and analyzed are:

Korean and Chinese	$6.02 per hour	$3.40 per hour
African American	$6.41 per hour	$4.76 per hour

Studies of Asian-immigrant-owned small businesses frequently observe that unpaid family labor is used extensively, and this is cited as a cause of the greater viability of these firms, relative to small businesses generally and those of African Americans specifically (Fratoe 1988; Min 1986–87; Boyd 1991b). Use of family labor is not directly observable in CBO data, but a heavy reliance on family labor would widen the above profit-per-hour differences if family labor were factored in.

Another major strain of literature, besides the studies proclaiming the viability of Asian-immigrant small businesses, argues that blocked mobility often forces immigrants into self-employment. Waldinger, Aldrich, and Ward (1990) emphasize the interplay of situational constraints on job opportunities, access to small-business ownership, and group characteristics of Asian immigrants that encourage self-employment. Kim, Hurh, and Fernandez (1989) argue that American employers often do not recognize the education and work experience that immigrants have accumulated in their native countries. Min (1984a) claims that college-educated Koreans often confront serious language barriers that hamper their employment prospects, especially in jobs requiring contact with the public. Waldinger (1986) has observed that Asian immigrants pursue self-employment less as a matter of preference and more as a matter of blocked mobility: impediments to more attractive alternatives include poor English-language facility and foreign credentials that are viewed skeptically by potential employers. The self-employment behavior of Asian immigrants often reflects their lack of alternatives rather than their success in business. Professionals with specific skills—pharmacists, for example—are often unable to pass licensing exams because of their limited English fluency. In short, Asian immigrants may be unable to find jobs that use their training and professional skills, at least until they acquire a sufficient command of English to overcome this employment barrier. Thus blocked, the abundant human-capital and financial-resources of Asian immigrants come into play, making small-business ownership an appealing option for many.

The self-employed among Asian Indian and Filipino immigrants appear to be less constrained than other Asians in their choice of self-employment versus wage labor. Being highly educated as a group—over twice as likely as non-Hispanic, native-born whites to have college degrees—they are not limited to the same extent as the less well educated groups. Since the majority of Asian Indian and Filipino immigrants are fluent in English, they are again less constrained in their career choices than other Asian immigrants. Strong in class resources and English fluency, Asian Indians and Filipinos should be the Asian-immigrant groups most likely pulled (not pushed) into self-employment; blocked mobility should be weaker than it is among the less fluent groups of Asian immigrants. Yet the above evidence of low self-employment returns suggests that immigrant Asian Indians and Filipinos may yet be pushed into small-business ownership.

THE SELF-EMPLOYED ASIAN IMMIGRANT: DELINEATING PUSH FROM PULL

Absent blocked mobility, what sorts of businesses would most likely attract Asian Indian and Filipino immigrant entrepreneurs well endowed with financial and human-capital resources? Bates (1995c) has shown that individuals with a high net worth are disproportionately drawn to the most capital-intensive lines of small businesses—manufacturing and wholesaling. But the Asian Indian and Filipino firms described in table 4.2 are much less likely than comparison groups to operate in these capital-intensive fields: only 3.9 percent operate in manufacturing or wholesaling versus 7.1 percent and 7.5 percent for nonminorities and Asian Americans. College graduates (Bates 1995c) are disproportionately drawn to self-employment in skill-intensive services (business and professional services, finance, insurance, and real estate) other things being equal, and the most lucrative subfield in this group is professional services. Among new Asian Indian and Filipino firms operating in 1987, 46.2 percent were in the skill-intensive services versus 31.5 percent among firms owned by nonminorities and 36.4 percent among the Asian American self-employed. Finally, Asian Indian and Filipino immigrants are also heavily concentrated in the lowest-yielding self-employment fields—retailing and other services—where 38.0 percent of new firms were found versus 36.2 percent of firms owned by nonminorities and 39.8 percent of firms owned by Asian Americans. Among owners of the new firms under consideration (firms started between 1979 and 1987), the rough equality in proportions of each group self-employed in low-yielding retailing and other services must be seen in the context of the owner's human capital resources: 77.2 percent of the Asian Indian- and Filipino-immigrant owners were college graduates versus 37.7 percent of the nonminority and 46.4 percent of Asian American owners.

The strong educational backgrounds of Asian Indian and Filipino owners are consistent with their heavy overrepresentation in the single highest-yielding field of self-employment, professional services, where 27.4 percent of their firms (versus 10.4 percent among firms owned by nonminorities) operate. Highly educated people self-employed in high-yielding fields: this is the portrait of people *pulled* into self-employment by attractive opportunities. In contrast, the 38.0 percent of self-employed Asian Indian and Filipino owners in retailing and other services are the ones most apt to have been *pushed* into self-employment by considerations of blocked mobility. The two very lowest-yielding fields—retailing and personal services—are likely to harbor the highest frequency of owners experiencing blocked mobility.*

Studies of the work experiences of Asian immigrants indicate that their earnings rise with their years of residence in the United States

---

*"Other services" is a very heterogeneous field, including some areas, such as hotels and motels, that are financially capital-intensive. Personal services is the largest other-services subfield. Retailing is actually the lowest-yielding field among the Asian-immigrant self-employed; among nonminorities, personal services has the lowest average yields.

(U.S. Commission on Civil Rights 1988; Borjas 1994; Kassoudji 1988). Labor-market barriers, it seems, decline with the length of stay in the United States, reflecting the opening up of opportunities to Asian immigrants.

If Asian immigrants are held in self-employment by a paucity of opportunities and if opportunities expand over time, then the circumstances dictating self-employment should gradually alter. Since self-employment is often a low-yielding endeavor (table 4.2), then opportunity costs suggest that becoming someone else's employee would be the logical choice in an environment of expanding work opportunities. This hypothesis is tested in tables 4.3 and 4.4, which compare firm longevity and owner longevity in self-employment for Asian Indian and Filipino immigrants with those of a comparison group of self-employed nonminorities. A closely related hypothesis is that Asian Indian and Filipino immigrants in low-yielding fields are most likely to abandon self-employment and those in high-yielding fields are most likely to remain self-employed. That is, those pushed into self-employment are more likely to leave than those pulled into small-business ownership. Firm and owner characteristics are used in the logistic regression exercises in tables 4.3 and 4.4 to explain firm survival between 1987 and late 1991, and the owner's pursuit of self-employment continuously over the period. Over the period from 1987 to late 1991, 23.3 percent of new nonminority firms and 17.8 percent of Asian Indian- and Filipino-immigrant firms discontinued operations. In traditional retailing and personal services, firm discontinuance rates were 19.8 percent among nonminorities versus 26.0 percent among Asian Indians and Filipinos. The owner's continuity in the firm can diverge from the firm's continuity because enterprises continuing to operate over the 1987–91 period can be sold to new owners. Of the firms analyzed in tables 4.3 and 4.4, the phenomenon of firm survival *and* departure of the 1987 owner of record was much more common among Asian Indians and Filipinos than among nonminorities. What kinds of firms survived? What sorts of owners clung to self-employment? How were these patterns different for Asian Indians and Filipinos than they were for nonminorities? These are the issues addressed in tables 4.3 and 4.4.

Past econometric studies explaining small-business longevity identified the owner's investment of human and financial capital as the factor most strongly related positively to small-business survival (Holtz-Eakin, Joulfaian, and Rosen 1994; Bates 1990b). The well-capitalized

Table 4.3

Logistic Regression Explaining Firm Survival, 1987–91 (Firms Formed since 1979 Only)

	Regression coefficient (std. error)		Variable Mean	
	Asian Indian/Filipino	Nonminority	Asian Indian/Filipino	Nonminority
Constant	3.869[a] (.818)	.918[a] (.127)	—	—
Education				
High school	−.921 (.782)	−.157 (.086)	.079	.281
College, 1–3 years	−1.780[a] (.782)	−.001 (.091)	.116	.239
College graduate	−1.973[a] (.762)	.401[a] (.097)	.403	.203
Graduate school	−2.727[a] (.772)	.726[a] (.107)	.365	.178
Managerial experience	.537[a] (.165)	.062 (.057)	.398	.327
Bought ongoing firm	.134 (.190)	.512[a] (.083)	.258	.149
Married	−.774[a] (.219)	.075 (.060)	.858	.800
Gender	−.821[a] (.166)	.045 (.057)	.673	.747
Owner-labor input	.051[a] (.006)	.024[a] (.002)	19.03	19.69
Capital	.050[a] (.019)	.060[a] (.006)	8.14	7.17
Leverage	−.067[a] (.012)	.006 (.005)	2.67	2.59
Entered				
1984–85	−.063 (.247)	−.557[a] (.074)	.235	.224
1986	−1.177[a] (.232)	−.816[a] (.073)	.220	.210
1987	−1.302[a] (.225)	−1.370[a] (.068)	.282	.244
Traditional firm	−.965[a] (.202)	−.058 (.068)	.214	.236
Skill-intensive firm	.513[a] (.182)	−.223[a] (.062)	.452	.311
Capital-intensive firm	.873 (.526)	.001 (.099)	.036	.072
Minority clientele	−.268[a] (.148)	−.341[a] (.057)	.276	.195
N	1,937	11,248		
−2 Log L	1,383.2	10,738.7		
Chi-squared	(393.8)	(1,224.4)		

Source: U.S. Bureau of the Census, Characteristics of Business Owners (CBO) database, 1992.

Notes: Variables are defined in the appendix, "Databases and Variable Definitions," pp. 270–3.

[a]Statistically significant at the 5-percent level.

Table 4.4

Logistic Regression Explaining Owner Perseverance in
Self-Employment, 1987–91 (Firms Started since 1979 Only)

	Regression coefficient (std. error)		Variable Mean	
	Asian Indian/Filipino	Nonminority	Asian Indian/Filipino	Nonminority
Constant	3.208[a] (.641)	.910[a] (.118)	—	—
Education				
High school	−1.667[a] (.619)	.001 (.079)	.079	.281
College, 1–3 years	−2.595[a] (.605)	.189[a] (.083)	.116	.239
College graduate	−1.890[a] (.595)	.623[a] (.089)	.403	.203
Graduate school	−2.242[a] (.604)	.915[a] (.098)	.365	.178
Managerial experience	.501[a] (.136)	.079 (.053)[a]	.398	.327
Bought ongoing firm	−.526[a] (.150)	.012 (.069)	.258	.149
Married	−.234 (.165)	.002 (.056)	.858	.800
Gender	−.213 (.128)	−.034 (.054)	.673	.747
Owner-labor input	.025[a] (.005)	.020[a] (.002)	19.03	19.69
Capital	.123[a] (.016)	.033[a] (.006)	8.14	7.17
Leverage	−.074[a] (.010)	.012[a] (.004)	2.67	2.59
Entered				
1984–85	−.231 (.191)	−.517[a] (.063)	.235	.224
1986	−1.123[a] (.183)	−.771[a] (.066)	.220	.210
1987	−1.180[a] (.179)	−1.391[a] (.062)	.282	.244
Traditional firm	−.711[a] (.165)	−.129[a] (.062)	.214	.236
Skill-intensive firm	.148 (.153)	−.310[a] (.059)	.452	.311
Capital-intensive firm	.711 (.428)	−.049 (.093)	.036	.072
Minority clientele	−.550[a] (.127)	−.311[a] (.054)	.276	.195
N	1,937	11,248		
−2 Log L	1,854.0	11,990		
Chi-squared	(343.0)	(1,165.5)		

Source: U.S. Bureau of the Census, Characteristics of Business Owners (CBO) database, 1992.

Notes: Variables are defined in the appendix, "Databases and Variable Definitions," pp. 270–3.

[a]Statistically significant at the 5-percent level.

firm begun by a college graduate is much more likely to remain in operation than the poorly capitalized firm headed by a less well-educated owner. Among the firms founded by Asian Indians and Filipinos, mean start-up capital was $61,320, and 77.2 percent of the owners were college graduates; corresponding figures for the nonminority comparison sample were $31,939 and 37.7 percent respectively.

In the logistic regression exercises, owner involvement is also measured by the number of hours the owner spent working in the business, as well as that person's marital status. Married people living with their spouses are likely to benefit from family labor, which can increase the amount of labor put into the business. Financial capital is the sum of equity and debt capital invested in the firm at start-up. The owner's gender is a demographic trait to be considered. Three binary variables identify the type of small business: (1) traditional (a proxy for blocked mobility), (2) skill-intensive (a proxy for opportunity-motivated entry), and (3) capital-intensive. Owners entering self-employment by buying an ongoing business are delineated from firms started de novo in the logistic regression exercises. The youngest firms are identified to control for the effects of firm age on longevity. Finally, firms selling in the general market are delineated from those serving a minority clientele: Asian-immigrant firms that sell to nonminorities were shown in chapter 3 to be more viable than those serving a predominantly minority clientele. Exact definitions of the relevant explanatory variables are summarized in the appendix, "Databases and Variable Definitions."

The dependent variable in the logistic regression exercises of table 4.3 is whether or not the business operating in 1987 was still functioning in late 1991: the coefficient values are positive for firms still operating in 1991 and negative for those that had closed down. Regression results identify very distinctive survival patterns among firms owned by Asian Indian and Filipinos versus firms owned by nonminorities. Graduate education is the strongest single trait of the owner delineating surviving from discontinued firms: firms owned by the most highly educated Asian Indians and Filipinos are the ones *most* likely to close down. Exactly the opposite pattern typifies nonminorities: the more highly educated the owners, the less likely were their firms to close, other factors remaining constant. Among Asian Indians and Filipinos, traditional lines of business—a proxy for blocked mobility—were strongly associated with firm discontinuance, other things being equal, while this relationship was trivial among nonminorities.[1] The skill-intensive firms, in contrast, were more likely than others to remain in operation for Asian Indians and Filipinos but not for nonminorities. Consistent with the blocked mobility hypotheses in which impediments to mobility are presumed to decline over time, firms in the low-yielding, traditional fields were the ones most likely to close. Further, it has been presumed that the high-yielding, skill-intensive services would offer a fuller use of the owner's human capital and opportunities for increased earnings. In fact, firms in skill-intensive services were more likely to survive than those in less attractive industries. In light of the likely connection between skill-intensive firms and college education, the logistic regression in table 4.3 was reestimated solely for Asian Indian and Filipino firms in this area, yielding the result that there is a positive, statistically significant relationship between having a college degree and firm longevity.[2]

Many of the explanatory variables in the exercises in table 4.3 behaved similarly for Asian Indian and Filipino and nonminority firms. For both groups, the firms that remained active in 1991 were consistently and disproportionately those started with larger investments of financial capital, those that were older, those serving a clientele that was not predominantly minority, and those headed by owners working full-time in the business. Younger firms—those started since 1984—were the most vulnerable to discontinuance, consistent with the findings in chapters 2 and 3. Also consistent with earlier findings was the result that the firms better capitalized at start-up were much more likely to stay active, other factors remaining constant (Evans and Jovanovic 1989; Bates 1994b; Holtz-Eakin, Joulfaian, and Rosen 1994).

Abandonment of self-employment by the firm's owner does not always mean closure of the small business. Successful operations can often be sold to a new owner. Table 4.4 switches the focus from firm survival to continuity of the 1987 owner of record over the 1987–91 period. Continuing owners are those associated with the same firms in both 1987 and 1991; departing owners may be associated with either firms that were sold or firms that were closed. Positive coefficient values in the logistic regression analyses in table 4.4 are associated with surviving owners, negative coefficient values with departing owners. Using this dependent variable (surviving owner versus departing owner) creates problems of interpretation because the dependent variable ceases to be a measure of firm viability: a departing owner may be associated with either a closed (presumably unsuccessful) firm or an ongoing, sold (presumably viable) firm. Closed firms, as a group, are very small, poorly capitalized, and unprofitable (which supports the practice of associating closure with nonviability), whereas the sold firms that were still operating in 1991 were larger, better capitalized, and more profitable than cohort firms that were not sold.

The analysis of remaining, as opposed to departing, owners in table 4.4 reveals a pattern of leaving self-employment that was stronger for college-educated Asian Indian- and Filipino-immigrant owners than it was for nonminorities. In table 4.4, Asian Indian and Filipino high-school dropouts are shown to be much more likely to remain self-employed than better-educated owners, other factors remaining constant. The pattern is clearly one of better-educated Asian Indian and Filipino owners—across the board—moving away from self-employment over time, with abandonment most likely in traditional fields, especially retailing. No counterpart to this education–self-employment duration pattern is apparent in the nonminority comparison group: among the college-educated, higher levels of education are strongly associated with increased likelihood of remaining self-employed.

A THEORY OF SELF-EMPLOYMENT AMONG ASIAN IMMIGRANTS

High human and financial capital endowments enhance self-employment options but by themselves do not adequately explain the self-employment behavior of Asian immigrants to the United States. Particularly among college-educated immigrants in managerial and professional occupations, self-employment is motivated by barriers to salaried employment, such as employers' skepticism toward foreign credentials. Constrained alternatives for salaried employment lower the opportunity costs of self-employment, often pushing Asian immigrants with substantial financial and human capital toward self-employment, including small-business ownership in low-yielding traditional fields. Access to salaried employment tends to improve with length of residence, thus raising the opportunity costs of self-employment and encouraging business owners to rejoin the ranks.

The case of retailing is illustrative. Although 60.1 percent of all Asian Indian and Filipino owners of retail firms were college graduates, mean profits in 1987 for these firms were a mere $9,358. In contrast, the 1987 profits for the 27.4 percent of nonminority owners with college degrees in retailing averaged $12,278. In addition to their high human capital investments, the Asian Indian- and Filipino-immigrant owners invested substantially more financial capital—$61,453 at start-up, on average—than similar nonminority owners, whose mean financial capital outlay to enter retailing was only $51,828. Asian Indian and Filipino owners generated average 1987 revenues of $253,563 in their retail firms, while nonminority owners—with less human and financial capital—generated mean firm revenues of $274,214. Owners in both groups worked over 40 hours per week on average (over 2,080 hours in 1987) and firm profits, net a 10 percent return on the owner's investment of equity capital, averaged $3.15 per hour for Asian Indian and Filipino owners versus $4.67 for nonminority retail-firm owners. Recall that these are young firms (1979–87 start-ups) only. Thus, the nonminority owners generated income per hour that was nearly 50 percent higher than the hourly return reported by Asian Indian and Filipino immigrants. Bates (1994a) found that Korean-immigrant owners of retail firms produced similar results on average relative to nonminorities—higher investments in the firm of the owner's human and financial capital coexisted with lower levels of gross revenues and profits. Such low returns encourage owners to leave self-employment if they have access to salaried employment.

That Asian-immigrant owners of small businesses are indeed leaving low-yielding niches such as retailing is reflected in statistics describing the life cycle of the business community. Specifically, logistic regression findings from tables 4.3 and 4.4 show a pattern of owners leaving the lowest yielding lines of small business, while owners in the highest yielding skilled services remain. Thus, the older Asian-immigrant-owned firms should show a different industry distribution than the younger businesses, and they should be much more profitable.

Table 4.5 examines the life cycle of Asian-immigrant firm groups, highlighting trends in profitability and business distribution. All of the firms described in table 4.5 were operating in 1987, with old firms being those entered by the current owner before 1979. Comparison of business concentrations over the life of Asian-immigrant-owned firms shows a predictable movement away from traditional retail and personal-services fields into the skill-intensive services.[3] College-educated Korean and Chinese small-business owners show the largest shift away from traditional lines of self-employment. Fifty percent of well-educated Korean and Chinese owners running young firms were operating in traditional businesses (table 4.5); this concentration dropped precipitously to 26.6 percent among the older firms. Why are

Table 4.5

Young versus Old Firms Owned by Asian Immigrants (All Firms Operating in 1987)

	Asian Indian, Filipino		Korean, Chinese	
	Young Firms	Old Firms	Young Firms	Old Firms
All firms				
Industry distribution				
Skill-intensive services	46.2%	59.2%	24.7%	33.9%
Traditional firms[a]	20.6%	14.5%	52.8%	40.4%
Before-tax profits, 1987 (mean)				
All firms	$14,088	$36,573	$15,740	$27,613
Firms with full-time owners	$19,760	$45,703	$18,308	$29,572
Firms with College-Educated Owners				
Industry distribution				
Skill-intensive services	50.7%	60.2%	31.4%	42.5%
Traditional firms[a]	17.8%	11.6%	50.0%	26.6%
Before-tax profits, 1987 (mean)				
All firms	$15,367	$38,851	$17,436	$30,692
Firms with full-time owners	$20,351	$48,690	$22,422	$34,350

Source: U.S. Bureau of the Census, Characteristics of Business Owners (CBO) database, 1992.

Notes: Variables are defined in the appendix, "Databases and Variable Definitions," pp. 270–3.

[a]Retail and personal services.

there so few old Korean and Chinese firms in retailing and personal services? As owners became acclimated to U.S. society and became fluent in English, most simply moved on, thus dropping out of the small-business sector. Many sold their firms to newly arrived immigrants, but these firms are counted as young in the CBO database, because firms are dated from the owner's point of entry. Thus, some of the firms remain in operation at the same location, forever classified as young, as owners enter and then leave these businesses by selling them to new owners.[4]

Older groups contain fewer personal-service and retail firms, and more skill-intensive firms. Differences in income generated by firms owned by Asian Indians and Filipinos and those owned by Koreans and Chinese actually widened as the firms grew older. High self-employment returns are necessary to retain well-educated members of the former group in self-employment over the long run. Highly educated members of the latter group who remain self-employed often shift out of personal service and retail and into higher-yielding businesses during their careers, giving Korean and Chinese owners less time to accumulate goodwill and work experience in lucrative industries relative to cohorts who, already fluent in English, started out in the more attractive lines of self-employment.

Owners who stick with firms for ten or more years commonly do so because the underlying business is successful. Considerations of blocked mobility fade in significance as the years go by, which means that Korean and Chinese owners of old firms, just like their Asian Indian and Filipino counterparts, often remain self-employed because they prefer this status to wage labor: they are pulled more than pushed into self-employment. This self-selected group of owners operating old, established firms earns much higher returns than similar owners of young firms. Among the Koreans and Chinese self-employed full time, 1987 profits averaged $18,309 among the young firms, $29,572 among the old. As befits a highly educated entrepreneur group, old firms owned by Koreans and Chinese were more profitable than non-minority old firms (they averaged $27,088 in 1987) but still less profitable than the firms of Asian Americans ($32,732).

Old firms operated by Asian Indian and Filipino immigrants, not surprisingly, were much more profitable than firms run by any other subgroup defined by race or ethnicity. This group of firms is operated by a highly educated group of owners who have concentrated much more heavily in the skill-intensive services than anyone else. Looking solely at old firms, nearly 60 percent of the Asian Indian and Filipino small businesses in operation in 1987 were in the skill-intensive services far above the corresponding 33.9 percent of Korean and Chinese firms, only 14.5 percent were in retailing or personal services, whereas 40.4 percent of the Korean and Chinese firms were in these areas. Among college-educated owners who pursued self-employment full-time, in the Asian Indian and Filipino group of old firms, mean 1987 earnings were $48,690 (table 4.5).

CONCLUSIONS

Self-employment patterns among Asian immigrants have been analyzed in this chapter without direct reference to factors such as the ethnic-solidarity and social-capital considerations that dominate the social science literature on immigrant entrepreneurship. These factors were explored in chapter 3, but their explanatory power was not apparent.

Crowding Asian immigrants into traditional fields, such as small-scale retailing, has often been interpreted as evidence of success or expanding opportunities (Bonacich and Light 1988; Borjas 1986). In light of the very low returns earned by Asian immigrants in traditional lines of business and the departure from these fields over time, such crowding appears to be rooted in blocked mobility. To the extent that Asian immigrants increasingly enter these fields, such behavior reflects declining opportunities for salaried employment (Borjas 1994) rather than attractive self-employment options.

The finding that college-educated Asian immigrants often earn low returns in traditional lines of self-employment has ramifications for comparisons of small-business ownership patterns among minority groups. The assumption that a proliferation of Asian-immigrant–owned small businesses signals opportunities has caused scholars to speculate about why African Americans have shown less inclination toward self-employment than immigrant groups such as the Koreans (Bonacich and Light 1988; Waldinger, Aldrich, and Ward 1990). The recognition of higher self-employment returns among African Americans—after controlling for human and financial capital investments—puts comparisons of black and Asian-immigrant business viability in a different light. An alternative to the literature's assertions of relative weakness in the black business community is the hypothesis that college-educated African Americans rationally choose to forgo self-employment in traditional businesses because opportunity costs are high.

NOTES

1. Among Korean- and Chinese-owned firms operating in traditional businesses, having a college degree was negatively related to firm survival, but the relationship was not statistically significant.

2. Numerous interesting variations of these regression exercises are possible. When exercises from tables 4.3 and 4.4 are replicated for self-employed Asian Americans, results closely approximate those for self-employed nonminorities.

3. Self-employed Vietnamese are excluded from table 4.5. The four dominant groups in the Asian-immigrant small-business community—Asian Indians, Filipinos, Koreans, and Chinese—are all quite similar in the sense that the average business owner at start-up is more highly educated (more likely to be a college graduate) than nonminority counterparts, and their firms begin operation with significantly greater financial capital. Vietnamese firms, in contrast, do not fit the high human capital–high financial capital profile of the Asian-immigrant small-business community.

4. The CBO database does not record the age of the firm, as such, in its data files: firms are dated by years of the current owner's involvement only.

CHAPTER FIVE

Explaining the Self-employment Patterns of Asian Immigrants in the United States

P articularly successful entrepreneurs tend to be highly educated and their firms, well capitalized; they are also overrepresented in the growth sectors of the small-business world, the skill-intensive services, for example. The Asian-immigrant business community in the United States is unique in that many among the highly educated start very small-scale, low-yielding retail and personal-service businesses. Self-employment most often degenerates into underemployment in these traditional lines. As recently as 1960, most self-employed Asians in the United States worked in three traditional businesses—restaurants, grocery stores, and laundries (Bates 1987). While Asian American entrepreneurs have moved away from these lines of business en mass, they are still major areas of concentration in the Asian-immigrant community of small firms. No counterpart to this phenomenon exists in the nonminority small-business realm, nor do highly educated African Americans concentrate in these least prof-itable lines of self-employment. Self-employment has often produced working poverty for Asian immigrants operating traditional businesses.

In the Asian-immigrant business community in 1987, 19.7 percent of businesses were owned by Asian Indians, 27.7 percent by Chinese, 21.7 percent by Koreans, and 10.1 percent by Filipinos.[1] Fratoe (1986), using data from the Bureau of the Census, calculated the following

nationwide self-employment rates for people reporting a single ancestry group:

Koreans	6.9%
Chinese	6.0%
Asian Indians	4.7%
Filipinos	2.2%

(The national average for self-employment was 4.9 percent.) Among all
ancestry groups, Fratoe observed that high rates of self-employment
were closely associated with high mean income among the self-
employed and low rates with low mean income, but this pattern did not
typify major self-employed Asian subgroups, whose mean incomes were:

Asian Indian	$29,800
Filipino	$27,800
Chinese	$18,980
Korean	$18,500

(The national average for self-employment income is $18,630.)

Why would people of Korean ancestry have the highest self-
employment rates and the lowest average earnings, while Asian Indians
show the opposite pattern? More broadly, why do some ethnic and
immigrant groups pursue self-employment at much higher rates than
others, and why are some groups so much more successful than others?

Rapid growth of small-business ownership is clearly immigrant-driven among Koreans. Census data show that among newcomers arriving
in the United States between 1970 and 1980, Koreans ranked higher in
self-employment—at 11.5 percent—than any other group (Waldinger,
Aldrich, and Ward 1990, 40). The seeming paradox of high self-employment rates coexisting with low earnings heightened during the 1980s as
the incidence of self-employment among Koreans expanded more
rapidly than any other immigrant group. Fairlie (1994), examining
employed men only (a much narrower reference group than Fratoe
examined in his 1986 study of self-employment by ancestry group),
reported the following nationwide self-employment incidences for 1990:

Koreans	27.9%
Chinese	13.5%
Asian Indians	11.7%
National average	10.8%
Filipinos	5.1%

Chapter 2 showed that substantial household wealth and advanced education were commonly associated with high rates of self-employment entry. The college graduate who is doing poorly as an employee is the likely self-employment candidate; the high-school dropout mired in working poverty is not likely to pursue self-employment. Chapter 4 introduced another factor that promotes self-employment: blocked mobility. Blocked mobility promotes high rates of self-employment when the constrained group—Korean immigrants, for example—possesses strong class resources. "Lacking the same alternatives for stable career employment as natives, immigrants are more likely to strike out on their own" (Waldinger, Aldrich, and Ward 1990, 32).

This chapter will draw together and extend the findings from chapters 2 through 4 regarding self-employment entry and exit, and small-business profitability. Here, the empirical findings discussed in those chapters will be generalized into a theory of immigrant enterprise, and that theory will be used to explain the wide variations in the rates at which Asian-immigrant subgroups pursue self-employment in the United States. Implications of this theory of immigrant enterprise will be drawn out further by examining small-business profitability patterns.

HUMAN CAPITAL AND FINANCIAL CAPITAL

Consider the hypothesis that highly educated people are much more likely to become self-employed than others. Tabulations from the census data show the following years of school completed among all men 25–64 years old in 1980:

	Years of school (mean)	Percent with 16 or more years of school
Foreign Born		
Asian Indian	16.7	73.1%
Korean	14.9	55.6%
Vietnamese	12.1	17.5%
Chinese	13.6	46.5%
Filipino	14.0	42.6%
Non-Hispanic White	12.8	28.4%
Native Born		
Non-Hispanic White	12.9	24.5%

Educational patterns alone suggest that Asian immigrants should be self-employed at higher rates than nonminorities, who are much less well educated than all major Asian-immigrant groups except the Vietnamese. The Vietnamese are introduced into the analysis precisely because of their below-average rates of self-employment (Fairlie 1994; Fratoe 1986) and their low incidence of college education.

If advanced educational credentials, by themselves, accurately predicted self-employment, then self-employment rates for Asian immigrants would be highest among Asian Indians and lowest among the Vietnamese. Koreans would be in second place, while the Chinese and Filipinos would rank third and fourth; all of these groups (except for the Vietnamese) would be far ahead of non-Hispanic whites. Clearly, education by itself cannot explain the range of self-employment rates that typifies Asian-immigrant groups. Asian Indians and Filipinos in particular are much less likely to pursue self-employment than the simplistic model—self-employment propensity is solely a function of educational attainment—suggests.

A second possible determinant of self-employment propensity is household net worth: high personal wealth is strongly associated with high self-employment activity. No direct measure of household wealth is available for specific Asian-immigrant subgroups, but fragmentary evidence does indicate a high incidence of substantial personal wealth. Median wealth, as indicated in chapter 2, is higher among Asian households nationwide than it is among nonminorities. The proportion of Asian households with marketable net wealth exceeding $100,000—25 percent—is similarly higher than the corresponding figure for nonminorities—20.6 percent. The mean equity investment by owners to finance new businesses was much higher among Asian immigrants ($26,838) than among nonminorities ($14,195) during the 1979–87 period (chapter 1). High wealth, high firm capitalization, and high educational attainment go hand in hand. All of this suggests that Asian immigrants (with the exception of the Vietnamese) should be more likely than members of other groups to enter self-employment.

The data presented below from chapters 1 and 3 describe nationwide samples of firms that were started between 1979 and 1987; the selected groups are distinctly different regarding firm capitalization, with Asian immigrants exhibiting the expected advantages over nonminorities.

	Nonminorities	All Asian Immigrants	Immigrants only		
			Asian Indians	Koreans	Vietnamese
Mean total firm capitalization at start-up (equity and debt)	$31,939	$53,550	$68,013	$52,146	$25,626
Percent of owners who are college graduates	37.7%	57.8%	80.4%	52.3%	26.4%
Percent of owners with less than four years of high school	10.4%	11.4%	4.6%	5.3%	16.7%

Available evidence indicates that the high incidence of self-employment among Asian immigrants is consistent with their education and their substantial personal wealth. The traits of actual firms created between 1979 and 1987 reflect these profiles of human capital and household wealth. Consistent with the class resources explanation, the Vietnamese—lagging behind cohort Asian immigrants—showed the lowest incidence of self-employment and created firms possessing the smallest investments in terms of money and the owner's human capital.

A deficiency of the human capital–financial capital model is its inability to explain why better-endowed groups, such as Asian Indians, have lower rates of self-employment than do less well-endowed groups, like the Koreans. The Chinese, similarly, are over twice as likely to pursue self-employment as Filipinos even though education among these two groups is broadly similar and their businesses are nearly identical in terms of the owner's investments of human and financial capital. Clearly, human and financial capital, by themselves, provide an incomplete explanation of self-employment behavior among Asian immigrants.

BLOCKED MOBILITY

Chapter four's findings emphasized that Asian immigrants pursue self-employment less as a matter of preference than as a matter of blocked mobility: impediments to more attractive alternatives include poor English-language facility, inappropriate skills, and foreign credentials that are viewed skeptically by potential employers. As observed elsewhere, the high rates of self-employment among Asian immigrants may reflect their paucity of alternatives rather than their success in business. The various studies suggesting possible links between blocked opportunities for salaried employment and inclinations toward self-employment among Asian immigrants are summarized in chapter 4 of this volume.

It is essential to understand that different immigrants face differing degrees of blocked mobility, and herein lies a key cause of the dissimilar self-employment rates characterizing Asian Indians and Koreans, Filipinos, and Chinese. Many immigrants arrive in the United States already speaking English fluently, and these newcomers face a much broader range of employment opportunities than newcomers whose English is barely serviceable. To the extent that blocked mobility pushes immigrants toward self-employment, those facile in English are less likely to start small businesses than are non–English speakers.

Among Asian groups, levels of English fluency vary enormously: 79.9 percent of Asian Indian immigrants to the United States reported that they spoke only English or that they spoke English very well; only 20.8 percent of Vietnamese immigrants were similarly proficient in English (table 5.1). Nearly 65 percent of Filipino immigrants were very proficient in English, as opposed to 38.2 percent of Chinese and 29.5 percent of Koreans.

Many Koreans are very recent immigrants: among those who have lived in the United States for five years or less, only 15.4 percent were very proficient in English (table 5.1). A 1986 predeparture survey conducted in Seoul revealed that 90.8 percent of departing Koreans used an interpreter for their visa interviews, which are conducted in English (Park 1990). In sharp contrast, over 50 percent of recent Filipino immigrants were highly fluent in English, as were 70 percent of Asian Indians (table 5.1).

The blocked-mobility explanation of self-employment suggests that the less fluent immigrant groups are more inclined to start small businesses, since the employment alternatives they face are narrower than those faced by Asian Indians and Filipinos. Three important groups— the Chinese, the Koreans, and the Vietnamese—will thus be labeled "less proficient" for purposes of analysis: members of these groups

Table 5.1

English Proficiency among Male Asian Immigrants (25–64 Years Old)

	Very proficient	Less proficient
All foreign born		
Asian Indian	79.9%	20.1%
Chinese	38.2%	61.8%
Filipino	64.1%	35.9%
Korean	29.5%	70.5%
Vietnamese	20.8%	79.2%
	1–5 years since migration	6–15 years since migration
Foreign-Born who immigrated within 15 years—percent "very proficient"		
Asian Indian	70.0%	85.2%
Chinese	23.6%	40.3%
Filipino	51.0%	67.3%
Korean	15.4%	35.4%
Vietnamese	18.7%	59.4%

Source: U.S. Commission on Civil Rights, *The Economic Status of Americans of Asian Descent.* (Clearinghouse Publication, October 1988) tables 5.6 and 5.7. These tables are derived from the 1980 U.S. Census, public use microdata, sample A.

accounted for 56.9 percent of all Asian-immigrant owners of firms operating in the United States in 1987.

EXPLAINING DIFFERENCES IN SELF-EMPLOYMENT
RATES: INTERACTIONS AMONG CLASS
RESOURCES, BLOCKED MOBILITY, AND
LABOR MARKET OPPORTUNITIES

Blocked mobility, by itself, inadequately explains the different rates of self-employment among Asian-immigrant groups. The Vietnamese and Koreans, for example, are both typically less fluent in English than other immigrant groups, but the Vietnamese rank close to the bottom in self-employment (forty-sixth) among the fifty largest ancestry groups), while Koreans rank close to the top (Fratoe 1986). Mexicans,

Native Americans, and other minority groups that rank far below national self-employment averages report rates above those typifying the Vietnamese.

Self-employment rates for various subgroups defined by race or ethnicity are a reflection of a complex social processes. An accurate first approximation for understanding the diverse self-employment rates typifying Asian-immigrant groups is sketched below, and it entails seeing self-employment as a two-step process.

Step One: Class Resources—Human and Financial Capital

The bedrock of small-firm creation is most commonly found in the owner's human capital, that is, the founder's education, training, work experience, and skills. In the rapidly growing skill-intensive services, most firms are created by highly educated individuals, particularly those with graduate training. The self-employment growth areas peopled by such owners include health care, computer software, engineering services, and so forth (chapter 2). Those lacking the human capital needed to create successful small businesses have low self-employment rates, and they concentrate in several low-yielding fields—small-scale retailing, for example—when they do start their own firms.

In many lines of business, appropriate human capital must be matched by substantial financial capital if the planned firm is to see the light of day. Manufacturing is the most financially capital-intensive major small-business field, followed by wholesaling. The trait that most accurately predicts self-employment in financially capital-intensive fields is the owner's possession of household net worth exceeding $100,000 (chapter 2). Of course, some individuals who lack the requisite financial capital nonetheless enter self-employment, even in manufacturing, but they are usually relegated to several small-scale niches.

Human-capital and financial-capital requirements are properly thought of as prerequisites for success in most lines of self-employment. For people lacking the necessary skills and capital, self-employment entry rates are low. For those lacking appropriate human and financial capital who nonetheless become self-employed, business failure and self-employment exit rates are high (chapter 2). Thus, the limited ability to compete that typifies the weaker small businesses combines with entry barriers to keep many potential entrepreneurs on the sidelines: low human-capital and financial-capital endowments translate into low self-employment rates. These factors explain the very low self-employment rates typifying Vietnamese immigrants.

Step Two: Employment Alternatives, Opportunity Costs

Assume, for purposes of illustration, that everyone lacking the human- and financial-capital traits typifying successful small-business owners has dropped by the wayside, screened out at step one of the two-step self-employment entry process. The residual group under consideration would contain a high proportion of Asian immigrants simply because so many of them are highly educated and affluent, with substantial managerial and professional experience (Waldinger 1986; Min 1984a; Bates 1994b; Lee 1992; Kim 1981). Yet most often people for whom self-employment is realistic become employees; only a small fraction of them become self-employed.

Particularly among college graduates, choosing self-employment often means giving up high-yielding employee positions in managerial and professional occupations, so self-employment is often pursued part time by college-educated, full-time employees. Yet self-employment invariably competes with wage employment, and there are opportunity costs to be incurred (lost wages, reduced chances of promotion) if time is spent in self-employment that would have been devoted to one's regular job. If one's salary is high, then the opportunity costs of starting a business on the side are high; the higher the opportunity costs of self-employment, other things being equal, the more attractive self-employment must be to lure the potential entrepreneur down that avenue. This explains why college graduates with high salaries rarely establish barbershops or mom-and-pop food stores. The opportunity costs of choosing self-employment usually rule out such low-yielding lines of small-business ownership.

Immigrants who speak no English, however, may face completely different self-employment opportunity costs than native-born college graduates. If managerial and professional jobs are inaccessible to highly educated Asian immigrants, then self-employment becomes attractive because the alternatives are low-wage service and blue-collar jobs. Because of the inaccessibility of jobs in keeping with their backgrounds, "a large majority of college-educated Korean immigrants have to accept blue collar jobs" (Min 1993, 194). The opportunity costs of self-employment are low when employment alternatives are unattractive. This explains the importance of blocked mobility for comprehending self-employment patterns among Asian-immigrant groups, such as Koreans.

In summary, the immigrant trait, by itself, should not be uncritically associated with high rates of self-employment. In Fratoe's study of the fifty largest ancestry groups in the United States (1986), the five groups with the lowest self-employment rates (the bottom tenth) were the Vietnamese, the Haitians, the Dominicans, the sub-Saharan Africans, and the Puerto Ricans, i.e., three of the lowest five groups were made up predominantly of immigrants. Immigrants turn to self-employment most frequently when:

1. they are well-educated, affluent people who worked as professionals and managers prior to migration;
2. upon arrival, they are blocked from working in the kinds of managerial and professional jobs they held at home.

DEGREES OF BLOCKED MOBILITY FOR IMMIGRANTS: ASIAN INDIANS AND FILIPINOS VERSUS KOREANS AND CHINESE

Waldinger, Aldrich, and Ward (1990, 45) observe that "immigrants who arrive in the United States with English-language facility have a broader range of employment opportunities than do those newcomers whose English is virtually nonexistent or barely serviceable." In this section I will compare the self-employment experiences of two immigrant groups with high proficiency in English—Asian Indians and Filipinos—to two groups in which most immigrants are not highly fluent—Koreans and Chinese. I will not consider the Vietnamese here because their endowment of class resources is so much lower than that of the other four groups. The four Asian-immigrant groups analyzed in this section possess higher average years of education than the U.S. nonminority population.

I am focusing on immigrant groups with substantial class resources in order to isolate the impact of English fluency on self-employment. My guiding hypothesis is that the opportunity costs of self-employment are much higher for the Asian Indians and Filipinos than for the Koreans and Chinese. Thus, the high-fluency groups must be pulled into self-employment by attractive opportunities and high earnings, while the low-fluency groups are often pushed into self-employment by the lack of job opportunities in managerial and professional occupations. I expect the very different self-employment dynamic at work here to result in higher household earnings and higher self-employment earnings for Asian Indians and Filipinos than for Koreans and the Chinese. Further, I expect the high-fluency group to avoid low-yielding, traditional lines of business (chapter 4) while the low-fluency group, facing low self-employment opportunity costs, enters these fields actively. Furthermore, I expect highly educated Asian Indians and Filipinos to concentrate in skill-intensive fields, such as professional services, because these lines of business use their human capital most fully. In contrast, I expect Korean and Chinese college graduates often to be blocked from these attractive fields, forcing them into low-skill businesses that do not make full use of their talents.

Table 5.2 compares traits of businesses and owners for four groups: the Asian immigrants with high and low English fluency, and two comparison groups, Asian Americans and nonminorities. All of the firms described in table 5.2 were active in 1987, and all were traced to late 1991 to see whether they were still in business. In terms of class resources, it is noteworthy that all of the Asian self-employed groups entered self-employment by investing substantially more financial capital into their firms than the nonminorities. The dollar amount of start-up capital is strongly and positively associated with subsequent firm size and survival (Bates 1993b; chapters 3 and 4). The proportion of firm owners who are college graduates is similarly higher for self-employed Asians than it is for nonminorities. Further, the immigrant groups—Asian Indians and Filipinos and Koreans and Chinese—were far ahead of Asian Americans in terms of both mean financial-capital investment and owner's educational background. Yet the firms owned by Asian Americans reported higher average profitability than did the businesses owned by either the high English-fluency group (Asian Indians and Filipinos) or the low English-fluency group (Koreans and Chinese). Similarly, the businesses owned by nonminorities generated greater profits with much lower investments of financial and human capital by owners than did either of the Asian-immigrant groups. The greatest surprise in table 5.2 was the finding that Korean and Chinese firms earned higher average profits ($17,397) than did the firms of Asian Indians and Filipinos ($16,443).

Table 5.2

Traits of Asian- and Nonminority-Owned Firms, 1987

	Immigrants		Nonimmigrants	
	High fluency (Asian Indian and Filipino)	Low fluency (Korean and Chinese)	Asian American	Nonminority
All Firms (young and old)				
Firm's traits				
Gross sales, 1987 (mean)	$138,158	$145,948	$126,401	$208,563
Total financial capital at start-up (mean)	$58,363	$55,315	$36,679	$30,518
Number of employees (mean)	1.2	1.7	1.2	2.2
Percent of firms still operating, 1991	82.2%	82.6%	81.9%	80.4%
Owner's traits				
Percent with less than four years of high school	4.1%	13.0%	12.1%	12.3%
Percent college graduates	77.8%	54.1%	44.8%	36.4%
Annual owner-labor input in hours (mean)	1,917	2,236	1,930	2,020
Before-tax profits, 1987				
All firms (mean)	$16,443	$17,397	$20,367	$17,898
Firms with full-time owners (mean)	$23,471	$20,899	$25,935	$23,614
Young firms				
(firms formed since 1979)				
Firm's traits				
Gross sales, 1987 (mean)	$130,556	$127,188	$119,678	$154,274
Total financial capital at start-up (mean)	$61,320	$57,191	$43,186	$31,939
Number of employees, (mean)	1.2	1.5	1.2	1.5
Percent of firms still operating, 1991	81.4%	81.9%	80.5%	76.9%

Continued on next page

Table 5.2—*Continued*

	Immigrants		Nonimmigrants	
	High fluency (Asian Indian and Filipino)	Low fluency (Korean and Chinese)	Asian American	Nonminority
Owner's traits				
Percent with less than four years of high school	4.1%	13.2%	10.0%	10.4%
Percent college graduates	77.2%	53.2%	46.4%	37.7%
Annual owner-labor input in hours (mean)	1,874	2,210	1,906	1,960
Before-tax profits, 1987 (mean)				
All firms	$14,088	$15,740	$17,835	$15,838
Firms with full-time owners	$19,760	$18,308	$23,260	$21,611

Source: U.S. Bureau of the Census, Characteristics of Business Owners (CBO) database, 1992.

Note: Variables are defined in the database, "Databases and Variable Definitions," pp. 270–3.

This advantage is rooted in the tendency of the low English-fluency groups to devote themselves full time to self-employment, while the high-fluency Asian Indians and Filipinos are more likely to pursue self-employment part time.

Because self-employed Asian immigrants are more likely than others to be newcomers to small-business ownership, a comparison of firms of all ages incurs the danger of attributing the traits of young firms (lower profitability and sales) to those of ethnic groups. To avoid this bias, figures on the traits of firms and owners in the second half of table 5.2 report solely on young firms (those started between 1979 and 1987). All of the patterns identified above—higher financial- and human-capital investments coexisting with lower profits—continue to typify young firms started by Asian Indians, Filipinos, Koreans, and the Chinese in comparison with young small businesses started by nonminorities and Asian Americans.

Korean and Chinese owners of young firms worked an average of 2,210 hours in their firms in 1987, well above corresponding figures for Asian Indians and Filipinos (1,874 hours) and the comparison groups. This difference is partially rooted in the very different kinds of businesses in which Korean and Chinese owners concentrate. Restaurants, grocery stores, dry-cleaning establishments, and the like operate on fixed schedules, commonly requiring owners to work long hours and to be more dependent on paid employees than firms in skilled services. Skill-intensive services—particularly professional services but also finance, insurance, real estate, and business services—are the stronghold of highly educated self-employed persons. These skill-intensive fields lend themselves to part-time self-employment, which is a major reason why college graduates often pursue self-employment part time while maintaining full-time jobs. Typical weekend niches in the self-employment world for full-time employees are consulting, research, and selling real estate. Professionals contemplating self-employment as a full-time endeavor often try it out first part time, while they continue to work as employees (Bates 1986). If the part-time activities are sufficiently successful, then self-employment is likely to become full time.

Korean and Chinese business owners, the majority of whom are college graduates, stand out from other groups quite sharply in their industry concentrations (table 5.3): among immigrant Asian Indians and Filipinos who established firms between 1979 and 1987, 27.4 percent were in professional services (the highest earnings field) and 2.7 percent were in personal services (the lowest earnings field in the small-business community nationwide), which is consistent with the self-employment patterns typifying highly educated owners generally (Bates 1987). Korean and Chinese owners, in contrast, were more likely to work in personal services (12.4%) than professional services (8.8%). Their major concentration, however, was in the second lowest-yielding small-business field—retailing—where 40.5 percent of their firms were operating.[2] The most common self-employment field for Asian Indians and Filipinos was health services (24.5%) and for Koreans and Chinese—eating and drinking establishments (16.2%).

Narrowing the focus to firms started by college-educated owners does not markedly alter the business distributions reported by the Asian-immigrant groups under consideration. Young firms started by college-educated Koreans and Chinese are most likely to be in retail-

Table 5.3
Nationwide Industry Distribution of Firms Operating in 1987 That Had
Been Formed since 1979

	Immigrants only		Nonimmigrants	
	Asian Indian and Filipino	Korean and Chinese	Asian American	Nonminority
Young Firms				
Business type				
Retail	17.8%	40.5%	20.9%	16.4%
Personal services	2.7%	12.4%	9.6%	6.8%
Business services	13.2%	9.0%	11.5%	12.0%
Professional services	27.4%	8.8%	18.1%	10.4%
Other services	17.5%	4.5%	9.3%	13.0%
Finance, insurance, and real estate	5.6%	6.9%	6.8%	9.1%
Construction	2.4%	3.5%	6.4%	12.8%
Manufacturing	1.6%	2.7%	3.6%	3.3%
Transportation	4.4%	2.6%	3.2%	4.6%
Wholesaling	2.3%	3.8%	3.9%	3.8%
Miscellaneous	0.8%	0.4%	3.2%	3.0%
Unknown	4.4%	4.9%	3.4%	4.9%
	100.1%	100.1%	99.9%	100.1%
Key subsectors				
Food and beverage	3.0%	16.2%	7.1%	3.2%
Health services	24.5%	6.4%	13.6%	4.8%
Young Firms Started by College-Educated Owners Only				
Industry				
Retail	15.6%	37.5%	17.0%	14.9%
Personal services	2.2%	12.5%	10.2%	5.2%
Business services	14.8%	9.7%	12.6%	15.0%
Professional services	29.7%	12.5%	22.3%	15.2%
Other services	17.3%	4.0%	10.6%	12.8%
Finance, insurance, and real estate	6.2%	9.2%	8.8%	11.8%
Construction	1.8%	2.0%	3.6%	7.9%
Manufacturing	1.6%	1.9%	2.9%	3.0%
Transportation, communication	3.6%	2.0%	2.2%	2.2%
Wholesaling	2.5%	4.4%	4.2%	4.1%

Continued on next page

Table 5.3—*Continued*

	Immigrants only		Nonimmigrants	
	Asian Indian and Filipino	Korean and Chinese	Asian American	Nonminority
Young Firms Started by College-Educated Owners Only (Continued)				
Miscellaneous	0.8%	0.3%	2.4%	2.8%
Unknown	3.9%	4.0%	3.2%	5.1%
Key subsectors				
Eating, drinking establishments	2.6%	13.0%	5.6%	2.7%
Health services	26.6%	9.2%	16.3%	7.6%

Source: U.S. Bureau of the Census, Characteristics of Business Owners (CBO) database, 1992.

ing (37.5%); corresponding retailing concentrations for Asian Indians and Filipinos, Asian Americans, and nonminorities were 15.6 percent, 17.0 percent, and 14.9 percent respectively. Concentration in personal services was similarly higher among college-educated Korean and Chinese owners than for any other group.

The business pattern typifying immigrant Korean and Chinese owners—heavy concentration in retailing and personal services, severe underrepresentation in professional services—is consistent with blocked mobility. Waldinger, Aldrich, and Ward (1990) stress that Asian-immigrant entrepreneurs find opportunities in underserved markets, those in which long hours, low returns, and a lack of prestige discourage natives from establishing firms. Older immigrant groups often move out of self-employment in these underserved markets, creating opportunities for Asian immigrants. In New York City, for example, Waldinger argues that the sons and daughters of Jewish and Italian small-business owners often do not want to take over family firms when their parents retire. This intergenerational abandonment of small family businesses is most pronounced in less attractive industries, such as food retailing and garment manufacturing (Waldinger 1986). Thus, family firms are often sold off to Asian immigrants. In fact, the Korean and Chinese owners described in table 5.2 were much more likely than other groups to become self-employed by buying an existing firm; most such buyouts were in retailing.

Yet the practice of entering self-employment by moving into under-served markets, buying small retail businesses, and the like does not typify Asian-immigrant entrepreneurs generally: the low English-fluency Korean and Chinese group fits this stereotype, but the high English-fluency Asian Indian and Filipino group does not. While many Korean and Chinese immigrants may indeed be pushed into self-employment by blocked mobility, the Asian Indian and Filipino self-employed appear more likely to be pulled into small business by attractive opportunities. The "lure of opportunity" hypothesis is consistent with a very high Asian Indian and Filipino concentration in professional services and low involvement in retailing and personal services. Blocked mobility explanations of Asian-immigrant self-employment are clearly most applicable to those with low English-language fluency.

FUNDAMENTAL DIFFERENCES IN THE SELF-EMPLOYMENT EXPERIENCES OF HIGH- AND LOW-FLUENCY ASIAN-IMMIGRANT GROUPS

I proposed a model of self-employment entry earlier that was partially tested in the last section by comparing the self-employment experiences of Asian Indians and Filipinos with those of the Chinese and Koreans. In brief, the model considers, first, the class resources of various immigrant groups and, second, the employment barriers facing group members seeking work in the broader economy. An application of the self-employment model is sketched below:

Step One: Class Resources—Human and Financial Capital

Low human- and financial-capital endowments severely constrain self-employment options. For this reason, Vietnamese immigrants show below-average self-employment rates, and the firms they create have low human- and financial-capital investments by owners.

High human- and financial-capital endowments enhance self-employment options but these endowments, by themselves, inadequately explain differences in self-employment rates among Asian-immigrant groups. Firms created by high-endowment groups show high investments of human- and financial-capital by owners on average. Firms owned by Asian Indians, Filipinos, Koreans, and the Chinese fit this pattern.

Step Two: Blocked Mobility, Limited Employment Options

Barriers such as limited English fluency restrict access to employment, particularly among college-educated Asian immigrants seeking jobs in managerial and professional occupations. Such barriers vary greatly among Asian-immigrant groups.

If employment alternatives are unattractive, then the opportunity costs of self-employment are low. A lack of alternatives pushes those with substantial class resources toward self-employment, including small-business ownership in low-yielding traditional fields. The group self-employment rates that result are inversely related to the opportunity costs of self-employment.

If employment alternatives are attractive, then the opportunity costs of self-employment are high, which reduces self-employment rates. Potential entrepreneurs must be pulled toward self-employment, which leads to concentrations in high-yielding areas, such as professional services, among those having the requisite human capital to enter these fields. Personal services and retailing tend to be avoided because they are commonly less attractive than the alternative of working as an employee in a white-collar job. Self-employment patterns among Asian Indians and Filipinos are heavily skewed by opportunity costs that encourage the highly educated to remain employees.

Focusing more narrowly on those who actually become self-employed, the above considerations should cause the Asian-Indian and Filipino small-business community to be profoundly unlike its Korean and Chinese counterpart: Asian Indians and Filipinos should be more likely than Koreans and the Chinese to become self-employed part time. Like highly educated entrepreneurs who work in skill-intensive services generally, Asian Indians and Filipinos should have the flexibility of mixing salaried labor with self-employment. So differences in total income between the Asian Indian and Filipino and Korean and Chinese immigrant groups should be greater than differences in self-employment income, since members of the latter group must rely much more heavily on self-employment for their livelihood.

The above statements about the expected behavior of Asian-Indian and Filipino versus Korean and Chinese small-business groups are tested by the evidence in table 5.4. Recall from table 5.2 that average 1987 profits among the Korean and Chinese firms were $17,397, nearly $1,000 above the corresponding figure ($16,443) for Asian Indians and Filipinos, and not much below the $17,898 profitability

Table 5.4
Traits of Owners Whose Firms Were Operating in 1987

	Immigrants		Nonimmigrants	
	High fluency (Asian Indian and Filipino)	Low fluency (Chinese and Korean)	Asian American	Nonminority
All Young Firms (Started 1979–87)				
Percent with total household income under $15,000 (1987)	14.7%	26.4%	16.0%	20.8%
Percent with total household income of $75,000+ (1987)	22.7%	8.5%	13.9%	12.4%
Household income from self-employment under 10 percent	34.3%	20.5%	22.3%	29.3%
Household income from self-employment 75 percent or more	35.4%	46.5%	32.9%	35.2%
Percent employed in traditional retail, personal services	20.6%	52.9%	30.4%	23.2%
Percent employed in skill-intensive services[a]	46.2%	24.7%	36.4%	31.5%
Young Firms: College-Educated Owners Only				
Percent with total household income under $15,000 (1987)	11.9%	21.5%	12.7%	12.3%
Percent with total household income of $75,000 (1987)	25.5%	11.5%	15.9%	17.9%
Household income from self-employment under 10 percent	34.2%	21.3%	23.0%	27.4%
Household income from self-employment 75 percent or more	35.6%	46.2%	32.4%	36.7%

Continued on next page

[a]Including professional and business services, finance, insurance, and real estate.

Table 5.4—*Continued*

	Immigrants		Nonimmigrants	
	High fluency (Asian Indian and Filipino)	Low fluency (Chinese and Korean)	Asian American	Nonminority
Percent employed in traditional retail, personal services	17.8%	50.0%	27.1%	20.1%
Percent employed in skill-intensive services[a]	50.7%	31.4%	43.7%	42.0%

Source: U.S. Bureau of the Census, Characteristics of Business Owners (CBO) database, 1992.

[a]Including professional and business services, finance, insurance, and real estate.

mean for all nonminority firms. Is this such a bad showing for a business community heavily mired in the low-yielding retail and personal services? Evidence from table 5.4 helps put these relative profitability figures into perspective.

Table 5.4 describes young firms (those formed between 1979 and 1987) that were still operating in 1987. Recall that anyone who generated gross sales of $5,000 or more and filed a 1987 federal small-business income-tax return was counted as a firm in this analysis, and that definition captured many for whom self-employment was a secondary source of income. Particularly among young firms, lots of part-time self-employment was picked up, but Korean and Chinese immigrant small-business owners are much less likely to pursue self-employment part time than other groups.

Among the Asian Indian and Filipino owners of young firms, nearly 35 percent relied on self-employment for under 10 percent of their total household income; only 20.5 percent of the Koreans and Chinese similarly did not rely on self-employment income (table 5.4). The Korean and Chinese owners were likely to rely on self-employment for most of their household income, much more so than Asian Indians and Filipinos or the comparison groups of Asian Americans and nonminority business owners (table 5.4).

Heavy reliance on the earnings generated by young firms translated into a high incidence of very low household incomes among Korean and Chinese owners; percentages of households earning under $15,000 from all sources (table 5.4) highlight this pattern.

Total income under $15,000 from all sources

Korean and Chinese	26.4%
Asian Indian and Filipino	14.7%

Less reliance on the incomes of young firms similarly means that Asian Indian and Filipino owners were much more likely to be in high income brackets than were Korean and Chinese owners. Percentages of households earnings $75,000 or more from all sources are listed below.

Total income over $75,000 from all sources

Korean and Chinese	8.5%
Asian Indian and Filipino	22.7%

Recall that Korean and Chinese owners worked much longer hours in their firms than Asian Indian and Filipino owners did. The nature of the firms most commonly owned by Koreans and Chinese—particularly retail firms—often requires additional labor from family members, further reducing opportunities to earn money from sources other than self-employment. Bates (1994a) found that unmarried Korean business owners were significantly less likely to survive in self-employment than married small-firm owners; similar patterns do not exist among married and unmarried nonminority business owners. Areas of Asian Indian and Filipino self-employment, in contrast, more often coexist with wage and salary work. Thus, the slightly lower average earnings from self-employment of Asian Indians and Filipinos, in comparison with those of Koreans and the Chinese, are typically combined with a salary, resulting in much higher total household incomes.

The greater incidence of working poverty among Chinese and Korean owners of young firms comes into sharper focus when household incomes among the college educated are examined. The incidence of those earning less than $15,000 from all sources is:

Korean and Chinese	21.5%
Asian Indian and Filipino	11.9%
American Asian	12.7%
Nonminority	12.3%

At the other end of the earnings spectrum, college-educated Asian Indian and Filipino owners of young firms are more than twice as likely as Korean and Chinese owners to have household incomes over $75,000 (25.5 percent versus 11.5 percent).

IS SOCIAL CAPITAL IRRELEVANT?

Self-employment patterns have been analyzed in this chapter without direct reference to considerations of ethnic solidarity and social capital. In the sociology literature analyzing the self-employment experiences of Asian immigrants to the United States, theories stressing interactions among multiple causes are fashionable. Waldinger, Aldrich, and Ward (1990), for example, emphasize the interplay between characteristics of immigrant groups and opportunity structures in the new homeland. The applicable opportunity structures include situational constraints on job opportunities, along with access to small-business ownership and related factors such as government policies. The relevant group characteristics encompass class resources, such as education and wealth, cultural norms, and various social resources forthcoming from the broader community of fellow ethnic-group members. Kim, Hurh, and Fernandez (1989) explain patterns of Asian immigrant entrepreneurship as a function of interacting factors, including the owner's class resources and blocked mobility in the labor market, as well as the social capital forthcoming from fellow ethnic-group members. The theory of Asian-immigrant self-employment patterns offered in this chapter is intended to revise this conventional wisdom.

The empirical research summarized in chapters 2 through 5 indicates that substantial class resources and blocked labor-market opportunities often inclined Asian immigrants toward self-employment. The human- and financial-capital resources they invested in their small businesses enhanced firm viability. Highly educated owners, however, left self-employment in the low-yielding retail and personal service fields, which suggests that they overcame the blocked-mobility constraints that initially pushed them toward self-employment. The data reviewed thus far do not support the hypothesis that social capital from fellow ethnic-group members promotes firm viability. Consistent with Boyd's results (1991b), a concentrated ethnic population and agglomeration effects were found to be of no apparent benefit to Asian-immigrant entrepreneurs (chapter 3). Rather, selling to a predominantly nonminority clientele was associated with increased firm longevity and profitability among Asian-immigrant-owned firms (chapter 3), particularly for very young firms. Greater reliance on non-minority employees, finally, is generally found among the larger, more successful Asian-immigrant-owned firms. The Vietnamese are most heavily reliant on fellow ethnics for financial capital, customers, and employees, while Asian Indians are most likely to sell to nonminorities, employ nonminorities, and borrow from commercial banks.

Reliance on social capital appears to be strongly correlated with smaller, less successful firms, both within and across Asian-immigrant groups, but the evidence is not adequate to support the conclusion that making use of social capital is harmful to Asian-immigrant-owned firms. Still, it is important to note that empirical studies of self-employed Asian immigrants in the United States have not established causal links between the use of social capital and improved firm via-bility (or increased likelihood of self-employment). These matters will be pursued further in chapters 6 and 11 of this study. Chapter 6 demonstrates that the use of social resources is not of major impor-tance for financing small-business entry. Personal wealth and main-stream financial institutions are the primary capital sources used by Asian immigrants to finance small businesses. Yoon's study of Korean-owned firms operating in Chicago revealed that borrowing from fellow ethnics typified weaker firms and resulted in reduced loan sizes (1991a). Analyses in chapter 6 confirm that Yoon's results accurately describe the experiences of Asian-immigrant-owned firms nationwide. The evidence considered collectively suggests (but does not prove) that relying on the social resources of fellow ethnic-group members allows some marginal firms owned by Asian immigrants to come into existence. Absent social resources, they would have been too weak to start on their own. Because these very weak firms are typically tiny and failure prone, statistical analysis tends to equate their use of social resources with failure. Chapter 10 examines retail firms owned by those who are not college educated. Such firms, when owned by Asian immigrants, rely heavily on fellow ethnics for start-up capital; they avoid competing in the mainstream economy for nonminority cus-tomers; they rarely hire nonminority employees. The profitability of such firms is typically very low, generating an existence of working poverty for their owners. Availability of resources from fellow ethnics may indeed increase somewhat the number of these marginal firms that come into existence.

CONCLUSIONS

In this chapter I constructed a theory of Asian-immigrant self-employment based on three interrelated concepts—class resources, blocked mobility, and opportunity costs. Diverse aspects of that behavior were shown to be consistent with the theory. The self-employment behavior of Asian-immigrant subgroups is broadly explainable without reliance on ethnic solidarity or social capital. Such concepts may nonetheless be relevant to describing some of the behavior of firms owned by immigrants at the fringes of the ethnic economy.

NOTES

1. Figures reported in chapter 3 indicated that incidences of business owners in 1987 were somewhat different, but the chapter 3 figures referred solely to Asian-immigrant-owned firms started since 1979. Chapter 5's figures include older firms.

2. Solely among firms owned by Asian immigrants, retailing is actually the least profitable business group, while personal services ranks second from the bottom. Among white- and black-owned firms, personal services ranks last in profitability.

CHAPTER SIX

Financing Small-Business Creation:
The Case of Chinese and Korean Entrepreneurs

S elf-employment is feasible in most lines of small business only if the potential entrepreneur assembles sufficient financial capital to buy the equipment and supplies needed to begin operations. Evans and Jovanovic (1989) demonstrate that capital constraints effectively kill the plans of numerous potential small-business owners. Those with high net worth are more likely than others to enter self-employment (chapter 2).

The number of Asian-owned small businesses operating in the United States has grown spectacularly in recent years (chapter 3), and this growth has largely been immigrant driven (Bates 1994a). Koreans rank first and the Chinese second in self-employment among Asians. Where did the financial capital come from to finance such rapid business formation? This chapter examines how self-employment entry was financed by Chinese and Korean immigrants who started businesses between 1979 and 1987.

The conventional wisdom suggests that immigrant Asian entrepreneurs in the United States benefit from their high propensity to help each other. Social histories of early Chinese and Japanese immigrants on the West Coast indicate that their poverty, combined with discrimination in the labor market, often drove them into self-employment (Light 1972). Despite their humble economic circumstances, cooperative self-help institutions made small-business creation feasible:

"Immigrants to the United States from southern China and Japan employed traditional rotating credit associations as their principal device for capitalizing small business" (Light 1972, 23). The notion that poor immigrants, with the help of group solidarity, could bootstrap their way to economic success by operating small businesses continues to be widely accepted (Bonacich and Light 1988; Aldrich and Waldinger 1990). If appropriate social networks do help Asian immigrants start their own businesses, the question becomes why indigenous minorities do not do likewise: "The logic of Asian-American business development raises questions about the absence of parallel development among American blacks" (Light 1972, 6).

This study found that since 1979, Korean- and Chinese-immigrant-owned firms began operations with an average initial capitalization of $57,191, nonminority start-ups with $31,939, and firms created by Asian Americans with $43,186. The mean Korean or Chinese firm began with a financial investment that was 79.1 percent higher than nonminority start-ups and 55.5 percent higher than Asian American-owned new firms.

Start-up capital came from both equity and debt sources, and greater equity investments tended to make debt capital more accessible (Bates 1990b). Rotating credit associations (RCAs) provide debt. Equity comes almost entirely from family wealth. Less than 2 percent of small-business start-ups attract equity from outside investors (Bates and Bradford 1992). The Korean and Chinese firms relied more heavily on equity capital to finance their businesses than did Asian American and nonminority firms. For the groups under consideration, mean equity at start-up was:

Korean and Chinese	$31,472
Nonimmigrant Asian	$22,932
Nonminority	$14,195

Debt provided 45.0 percent of the start-up capital that financed Korean- and Chinese-immigrant-owned firms. The largest debt source was loans from financial institutions. Debt was not easily accessible: per dollar of equity investment, Korean and Chinese owners raised less debt than nonminority borrowers.

Irrespective of loan source, immigrant Koreans and Chinese generated relatively few dollars in loans per dollar of equity invested in a small business. Friends and family provided even less leverage than financial institutions. Controlling for traits of owners and firms, even

African American owners borrowing from friends and family generated significantly more debt capital than did the Koreans and Chinese. Facing reluctant banks and tightfisted family and friends, the Koreans and Chinese nonetheless exhibit the highest mean firm capitalization at start-up: $57,191. With an equity investment that is 2.2 times larger than the amount invested at start-up by nonminority cohorts ($31,472 versus $14,195), limited debt availability did not necessarily handicap the typical young firm owned by Korean or Chinese immigrants.

Scholarly literature tends to misrepresent the realities of how aspiring Korean and Chinese entrepreneurs finance their entry into small business. Ivan Light sums up: "Obtaining loan capital poses an obstacle for all small business ventures, but the problem is especially severe for immigrant or ethnic minority entrepreneurs, who lack credit ratings, collateral, or are the victims of ethno-racial discrimination. Rotating credit associations reduce the severity of this financial obstacle" (Light, Kwuon, and Zhong 1990, 35). Light's statement may be literally correct, yet people often interpret such statements to mean that nontraditional credit sources (family, friends, RCAs) are the main sources of financing for small businesses created by Asian immigrants. This is incorrect: equity capital is the most important source; loans from financial institutions rank second. Although not terribly significant in the aggregate, nontraditional types of credit are important for the smaller-scale, less profitable, more failure-prone operations.

SOCIAL CAPITAL AND CLASS RESOURCES

Ivan Light and others suggest that the economic attainment of Asian immigrants in the United States is inextricably linked to the structure of their communities. The entrepreneur is seen as a member of supportive kinship, peer, and community groups that assist new firms by providing financing and serving as loyal customers and employees (Aldrich and Waldinger 1990). RCAs are thought to typify the process whereby supportive peer and community groups assist firms by providing loans.

Light (1972) and Bonacich and Light (1988) have argued that Asians (Chinese and Koreans specifically) entering business have benefited from their participation in RCAs, associations commonly set up by groups that shared some important common trait, such as having come from the same village in their homeland. The members of an RCA were likely to be well acquainted, quite irrespective of their association membership. Capital-access constraints on small-business formation were overcome by these associations, where each member made regular cash contributions to create a pool of savings that members could borrow for such purposes as starting a small business (Light 1972).

One problem with this vision of the RCA as a social resource is that there is little concrete evidence that they are a major force in financing Asian-owned businesses (Waldinger 1986). However, Light, Kwuon, and Zhong (1990) report that at least 11 percent (and perhaps as many as 30 percent) of garment manufacturers in Los Angeles received loans from RCAs. Yoon (1991a) collected data on the financing sources used by 199 Korean merchants to capitalize their current businesses. While 27.6 percent used loans from Korean RCAs (called *Kye*), other popular debt sources were loans from kin (34.7 percent) and banks (27.1 percent). Yoon's survey covered only merchants operating in minority neighborhoods in Chicago and was not representative of the Korean business community at large. Small samples focusing on specific business groups do suggest the use of RCAs, but data describing the start-up financing of broader Asian-immigrant entrepreneur groups have been unavailable to date. Despite this paucity of data, the conventional wisdom still claims that Asian immigrants have created their own institutional arrangements for generating loans to capitalize small businesses.

The CBO database, compiled by the U.S. Bureau of the Census in 1992, contains comprehensive data on the sources of debt capital used to finance small-business formation.[1] Table 6.1 summarizes the traits of firms and owners for a large, representative nationwide sample of immigrant Korean and Chinese small businesses and comparison groups of Asian American- and nonminority-owned firms. All of these firms, formed between 1979 and 1987, were still operating in 1987. (The CBO database is explained, in detail, in the appendix, "Databases and Variable Definitions.")

Table 6.1 highlights the substantial class resources (human and financial capital) that Korean and Chinese immigrants have invested in their small businesses. In addition to the higher levels of financial capital, Korean and Chinese owners are much more likely to be college graduates than nonminority and Asian American business owners. Despite their higher human- and financial-capital investments and the longer hours they worked in the small business, Korean- and Chinese-immigrant-owned firms are less profitable than other similar firms.

Table 6.1

Traits of Selected Asian- and Nonminority-Owned Young Firms
Operating in 1987 (Firms Formed since 1979 Only)

	Immigrant Korean and Chinese	Asian American	Nonminority
Firm's traits			
Gross sales, 1987 (mean)	$127,188	$119,678	$154,274
Number of employees (mean)	1.5	0.9	1.5
Total financial capital			
(mean)[a]	$57,191	$43,186	$31,939
Equity capital (mean)[a]	$31,472	$22,932	$14,195
Debt capital (mean)[a]	$25,719	$20,254	$17,744
Percent of firms still			
operating, 1991	81.9%	80.5%	76.9%
Owner's traits			
Percent with less than			
four years of high school	13.2%	10.0%	10.4%
Percent college graduates	53.2%	46.4%	37.7%
Owner-labor input (mean)	2,210	1,906	1,960
Before-tax profits, 1987			
All firms (mean)	$15,740	$17,835	$15,838
Owners working full-time			
in the business (mean)	$18,308	$23,260	$21,611

Source: U.S. Bureau of the Census, Characteristics of Business Owners (CBO) database, 1992.

Note: Variables are defined in the appendix, "Databases and Variable Definitions," pp. 270–3.

[a]Invested in the firm at entry.

Looking solely at the firms in table 6.1 that used debt capital, Korean and Chinese owners had the lowest debt. Average loan sizes were:

Korean and Chinese	$50,997
Asian American	$56,398
Nonminority	$53,443

The Korean and Chinese owners were also more likely than others to borrow money to invest in their businesses; percentages of firms using debt capital to finance formation were:

Korean and Chinese	53.4%
Asian American	40.4%
Nonminority	37.2%

Part of this greater propensity to borrow is rooted in the unique business distribution of Korean and Chinese firms. These firms are heavily concentrated in retailing, while young Asian American and nonminority firms are more frequently in the skill-intensive services. Table 6.2 reveals that retailing businesses are heavily capitalized and more frequent borrowers than skilled-service firms at start-up. In each of these business sectors, however, Koreans and Chinese are more likely to use debt capital than other similar groups. For all firms borrowing, table 6.3 describes major debt sources, average loan sizes, and the leverage obtained from each important type of lender.

Considering average loan size as well as borrowing frequency by source, financial institutions provide the largest amount of debt to finance business start-ups. Dominance of debt from financial institutions typifies all of the groups—immigrant Koreans and Chinese, Asian Americans, and nonminorities. The pattern of relying heavily on family and financial institutions for debt capital typifies all groups: family consistently ranks second in terms of amount of debt provided. This borrowing pattern does not support the conventional wisdom that RCAs are a major source of credit for immigrant Asian small businesses. Multiple-source borrowing is particularly common among Korean and Chinese entrepreneurs: 21.5 percent of bank loan recipients also borrowed from family sources; 14.5 percent of bank borrowers also received loans from friends. Multiple-source borrowing from family and friends typifies a distinct subset of Korean and Chinese immigrants—the firm owners who did not attend college.

Overall, start-ups by Korean and Chinese immigrants exhibit the most distinctive borrowing pattern. Family borrowing is actually more frequent than bank borrowing, even though the latter source provides the most loan dollars overall (reflecting larger loan sizes). Family and former owners are roughly equal in terms of the dollar amount of debt raised, while friends are a distant fourth for Korean and Chinese owners. This group has difficulty leveraging their equity investments: note that Koreans and Chinese have both the highest mean equity investments and the lowest debt amounts of any group under consideration. Considering all firms and all sources of capital, Koreans and Chinese are the least reliant on debt and the most reliant on the owner's equity investment.

While the data in table 6.3 are inconsistent with the hypothesis that RCAs are a major source of credit for financing business entry, they may nonetheless be a factor in some instances. Since RCAs are not

Table 6.2

Capitalization of Firms in Selected Businesses
(Firms Formed since 1979 Only)

	Immigrant Korean and Chinese	Asian American	Nonminority
Retail			
Total financial capital (mean)	$70,014	$68,885	$51,828
Percent using borrowed capital	66.1%	58.1%	48.0%
Percent in this line of business	40.5%	20.9%	16.4%
Skill-intensive services			
Total financial capital (mean)	$33,783	$30,542	$24,952
Percent using borrowed capital	30.5%	22.4%	24.3%
Percent in this line of business	24.7%	36.4%	31.5%

Source: U.S. Bureau of the Census, Characteristics of Business Owners (CBO) database, 1992.

Note: Variables are defined in the appendix, "Databases and Variables," pp. 270–3.

aSkill-intensive services include business and professional services, finance, insurance, and real estate.

listed as an option on CBO questionnaires, businesses using this source may check "friends" or "other" as the credit source. While "other" was an infrequent choice, Korean and Chinese immigrants did indicate that friends were a loan source for 21.7 percent of all borrowers; corresponding figures for nonminority firms were 6.4 percent: Asian owners were roughly three times more likely to finance business entry with loans from friends than were nonminorities. Greater borrowing from friends (some of which may represent RCAs) is consistent with the hypothesis that social resources available from group support networks disproportionately benefit Asian-immigrant firms. Yet the two major sources of capital (the owner's equity capital and loans from financial institutions) provided over $46,000 to the average young Korean- or Chinese-immigrant-owned firm.

Considering the entire Korean and Chinese sample (including non-borrowers), debt from friends was a source of initial capitalization for

Table 6.3

Debt Sources (Firms Formed since 1979 Only)

	Immigrant Korean and Chinese	Asian American	Nonminority
Major debt sources			
Percent borrowing from			
Family	41.2%	37.6%	26.8%
Friends	21.7%	21.9%	6.4%
Financial institution	37.4%	52.6%	65.9%
Former owner	17.8%	8.4%	6.1%
Loan size by source (mean)			
Family	$34,787	$39,137	$35,446
Friends	$36,198	$34,255	$30,907
Financial institution	$75,267	$67,299	$56,784
Former owner	$67,535	$64,557	$97,225
Leverage (total debt for all borrowers divided by total equity for all borrowers)			
Family	1.16	2.07	2.32
Friends	0.96	2.06	2.03
Financial institution	1.43	2.23	3.10
Former owner	1.28	1.97	3.69

Source: U.S. Bureau of the Census, Characteristics of Business Owners (CBO) database, 1992.

11.6 percent of the start-ups. The striking thing about using friends as a debt source is the small amount of leverage achieved by Korean and Chinese borrowers: whereas nonminorities borrowing from friends received loans that were, on average, 2.03 times the borrower's equity, Koreans and the Chinese borrowing from friends raised $0.96 in debt per dollar of equity. In all debt categories, Koreans and Chinese had less success than any other group in leveraging their equity. These firms stand out as well capitalized because of their large investments of owner's equity, rooted in substantial accumulations of household wealth. Loans from friends are a minor source of new firm capitalization.

EXPLAINING THE SIZE OF LOANS

Past studies have shown that having maximum access to debt is directly associated with being highly educated and investing a substantial sum

Table 6.4

Access to Bank and Nonbank Debt among Borrowing Firms (Firms
Formed since 1979 Only)

	Bank borrowers	Nonbank borrowers*
Immigrant Korean and Chinese		
Debt (mean)	$75,267	$36,516
Equity (mean)	$52,656	$36,089
Percent who attended graduate school	31.1%	14.3%
Asian American		
Debt (mean)	$67,299	$44,313
Equity (mean)	$30,174	$35,801
Percent who attended graduate school	34.0%	14.1%
Nonminority		
Debt (mean)	$56,784	$46,991
Equity (mean)	$18,299	$21,623
Percent who attended graduate school	17.6%	14.6%

Source: U.S. Bureau of the Census, Characteristics of Business Owners (CBO) database, 1992.

Note: Variables are defined in the appendix, "Databases and Variable Definitions," pp. 270–3.

*Includes borrowing from family, friends, former owners, or miscellaneous sources such as government agencies.

of equity capital into one's business (Bates 1990b; Bates 1991).
Financial institutions tend to skim off the most attractive loan recipients among Korean and Chinese entrepreneurs (table 6.4):

	Bank borrowers	Nonbank borrowers
Debt (mean)	$75,267	$36,516
Equity (mean)	$52,656	$36,089
Percent who attended graduate school	31.1%	14.3%

All groups of bank borrowers receive larger loans than nonbank
borrowers, partly because the loan recipients usually have larger
equity investments and higher educational attainments, and partly
because financial institutions commonly leverage each equity dollar
more highly than do family and friends. It follows that the lower loan
sizes typifying Korean and Chinese borrowers are rooted partially in

the fact that they rely more on nonbank sources than other borrowers. Within the Korean and Chinese group, bank loans often flow to the highly educated owners, while those who have not attended college are heavily dependent upon friends, family, and former owners for loans. Considering the total financial capital raised by all of the firms described in table 6.4, the ratio of all debt to all equity capital is 2.75 to 1 for nonminorities and 1.18 to 1 for Korean and Chinese immigrants.

All of the characteristics of loans, firms, and borrowers above suggest that financial institutions are a better loan source because more loan dollars are forthcoming from them. This hypothesis (financial institutions provide more loan dollars than other sources) is tested in an OLS regression model where the loan amount is the dependent variable (table 6.5).

Past studies have shown that small-business start-ups with access to debt capital are commonly those well endowed with equity capital as well as owner's traits associated with firm viability (Bates 1990b). Owners who are college graduates investing large amounts of equity into small businesses enjoyed greater loan access than other groups of owners (Bates 1993b). OLS regression equations (summarized in table 6.5) explain dollar amounts of debt used to finance small-business start-ups owned by the Korean and Chinese immigrants, Asian Americans, and nonminorities. Four types of independent variables explain loan amounts: the owner's equity capital investment, the owner's human capital traits, the loan source, and the owner's demographic traits; firm traits are control variables.

Considerations of supply by the lender and demand by the borrower are relevant to the size of the loan. Strong borrowers should get large loans, where the borrower's strength is measured by the owner's human- and equity-capital investments in the business at start-up, and the lender's aversion to weak borrowers should limit their access to loans. While table 6.5 explains loan amounts for all borrowing firms, later OLS regression exercises separate borrowers by type of lender. Family and friends, in particular, may be guided by motivations unlike those of financial institutions. The loan amount and equity capital variables used in the econometric exercises are expressed in dollar amounts. (Units of measurement for other explanatory variables are defined fully in the appendix, "Databases and Variable Definitions.")

In the regression equations in table 6.5, loan sizes for all groups are heavily influenced by equity capital: Korean and Chinese borrowers

Table 6.5

OLS Regression: Explaining Loan Amounts
(Firms Formed since 1979 Only)

	Regression coefficient (standard error)		
	Immigrant Korean and Chinese	Asian American	Nonminority
Constant	−5,220.78	−61,267.20[a]	−2,687.33
	(13,798.97)	(27,350.67)	(9,469.01)
Education			
High school	1,467.84	6,862.10	8,336.75
	(10,628.53)	(21,444.95)	(7,323.24)
College, 1–3 years	−13,520.59	25,482.14	20,855.12[a]
	(10,915.61)	(21,507.40)	(7,724.02)
College graduate	−5,711.36	34,945.71	33,548.37[a]
	(9,974.62)	(22,437.11)	(8,260.36)
Graduate school	13,340.80	44,957.74[a]	26,366.69[a]
	(10,793.23)	(22,863.37)	(8,330.06)
Managerial experience	9,960.98	−4,035.09	14,426.66[a]
	(6,845.19)	(11,459.72)	(4,679.52)
Bought ongoing firm	−1,554.98	12,622.03	11,274.50[a]
	(6,606.99)	(12,390.98)	(4,955.94)
Married	3,207.05	1,810.34	4,850.44
	(8,581.55)	(12,506.17)	(5,439.03)
Gender	9,960.98	−4,035.09	14,426.66[a]
	(8,916.39)	(12,271.87)	(5,164.12)
Equity capital	1.05[a]	1.26[a]	1.27[a]
	(.02)	(.04)	(.03)
Loan source:			
Family	2,947.09	15,740.71	−14,023.80[a]
	(6,595.46)	(11,396.57)	(5,199.23)
Friends	−7,131.66	4,878.78	−13,524.21
	(7,244.11)	(14,971.25)	(8,656.05)
Bank	22,026.32[a]	44,299.76[a]	8,866.35[a]
	(6,823.50)	(12,242.10)	(4,644.16)
Former owner	24,338.37[a]	14,252.60	30,577.52[a]
	(8,593.55)	(19,645.63)	(9,317.59)

Continued on next page

[a]Statistically significant at the 5-percent level.

Table 6.5—*Continued*

	Regression coefficient (standard error)		
	Immigrant Korean and Chinese	Asian American	Nonminority
N	1,515	866	5,882
R^2	.604	.588	.325
F	176.4	93.7	131.0

	Variable Means		
	Immigrant Korean and Chinese	Asian American	Nonminority
Education			
High school	.196	.201	.309
College, 1–3 years	.179	.231	.237
College graduate	.296	.240	.178
Graduate school	.206	.246	.166
Managerial experience	.275	.406	.376
Bought ongoing firm	.387	.261	.277
Married	.858	.771	.817
Gender	.770	.749	.790
Equity capital	$42,280	$32,842	$19,433
Loan source:			
Family	.412	.376	.268
Friends	.217	.219	.064
Bank	.374	.526	.659
Former owner	.178	.084	.061

Source: U.S. Bureau of the Census, Characteristics of Business Owners (CBO) database, 1992.

Note: Variables are defined in the appendix, "Databases and Variable Definitions," pp. 270–3.

[a]Statistically significant at the 5-percent level.

receive an extra $1.05 debt per equity dollar, well below the $1.26 and $1.27 debt increments associated with each equity dollar invested by Asian Americans and nonminorities. Loan sizes associated with various loan sources behave similarly for all of the groups in table 6.5: among immigrant Koreans and Chinese receiving bank loans, for example, the mere fact that the loan was extended by a bank was associated with a $22,026 increase in loan amount, other factors being constant. Financial institutions extend larger loans (table 6.5), while friends and family do not extend loans significantly larger than those made by the excluded group—miscellaneous loan sources.[2]

The greatest difference in loan size determination involves human-capital variables: college-educated nonminorities and those with managerial experience consistently received larger loans than other nonminority borrowers, other things being equal. Among Korean and Chinese immigrants, in complete contrast, none of the human-capital variables had a significant impact on the loan amount. Asian American borrowers represent a middle ground: human-capital variables were generally insignificant, but the most highly educated owners did receive an incremental $44,957 in loan dollars, relative to the excluded group (owners not completing high school). Lenders, it appears, do not recognize the human capital of Koreans and Chinese seeking to finance the creation of a small business. This finding complements the observation by Kim, Hurh, and Fernandez (1989) that American employers often do not recognize the education and work experience that immigrants accumulated in their native countries. Min (1984a) claims that college-educated Koreans often confront serious language barriers that hamper their prospects, especially in jobs requiring contact with the public (see chapter 4). Thus, Asian immigrants may be denied the opportunity to use their training and professional skills, a key cause of small-business formation (chapters 4 and 5). Their inability to leverage their human capital when they finance the creation of small businesses can also act as a barrier to self-employment among Asian immigrants in cases where owners do not have significant household wealth.

In summary, the regression exercises in table 6.5 indicate that the largest loans accrue to the Korean and Chinese immigrants investing the greatest equity capital and those borrowing from financial institutions. In sharp contrast to nonminorities, Koreans and Chinese are unable to leverage their strong human capital. Loans from former owners, furthermore, are significantly larger than loans from other nonbank sources. These findings are consistent with the hypothesis that loan dollars accruing to Korean- and Chinese-immigrant owners are held down by their heavy reliance on family and friends as debt sources. Table 6.3 indicated that Koreans and Chinese actually receiving loans from financial institutions were less highly leveraged than other groups of borrowers, suggesting that differences in bank treatment may further reduce their reliance on debt. This hypothesis can be tested by reestimating the OLS regression model explaining debt in table 6.5, including only those firms receiving loans from financial institutions, for a pooled sample of borrowers (table 6.6). Binary variables identifying Korean- and Chinese-immigrant borrowers and Asian American borrowers are introduced in the regression analysis of loan sizes extended by financial institutions in table 6.6. The OLS model explaining loan size for borrowers from financial institutions can then be compared to a companion OLS model analyzing borrowers receiving loans from family and friends.

Nonminority borrowers dominate table 6.6, because the firms being analyzed are weighted to represent their relative frequency among U.S. small businesses.[3] The key finding is that Korean and Chinese immigrants borrowing from financial institutions do not get significantly smaller loans than nonminority borrowers. But their small-business start-up loans are significantly smaller, other things being equal, when they also borrow from family or friends: the applicable table 6.6 regression coefficient indicates a loan size penalty of $25,321.86 for the Korean or Chinese immigrant relative to a nonminority borrowing from family or friends.

While table 6.6 clearly demonstrates that Korean and Chinese immigrants receive small loans from family and friends, the reasons for this parsimonious behavior are unclear. Table 6.7 investigates this issue: OLS regressions are used to explain loan sizes received by two groups of borrowers receiving loans from family or friends—Korean and Chinese immigrants and African Americans entering self-employment.[4] African American borrowers did get smaller loans on average than Korean and Chinese immigrants ($15,593 versus $32,065) but this difference is rooted in differences in owners' endowments (particularly less equity capital).[5]

Analysis of the subset of Korean and Chinese immigrants borrowing from family and friends reveals that their low loan sizes were rooted in the small amount of incremental debt generated by each dollar of equity capital invested. Coefficients of equity variables in tables 6.6 and 6.7 show that a dollar of equity is associated with a debt increment of $1.25 for the broader group borrowing from family and friends. For

Table 6.6
OLS Regression Explaining Loan Amounts to Immigrant Chinese or Korean, Nonminority, and Asian American Firms (Firms Formed since 1979 Only)

	Regression equations	
	Regression coefficient (standard error)	
	Loans from financial institution	Loans from family or friends
Constant	10,651.11	−21,292.25
	(9,624.20)	(12,156.5)
Education		
High school	5,835.18	6,500.31
	(7,674.59)	(7,657.06)
College, 1–3 years	24,378.48[a]	12,690.68
	(8,343.53)	(7,890.79)
College graduate	32,900.85[a]	30,345.30[a]
	(8,895.11)	(8,190.08)
Graduate school	34,352.31[a]	21,147.34[a]
	(9,289.30)	(8,733.25)
Managerial experience	4,031.44	5,919.65
	(5,131.01)	(4,477.47)
Bought ongoing firm	18,044.46[a]	10,008.08[a]
	(5,328.78)	(4,882.18)
Married	7,016.21	2,787.91
	(6,150.63)	(4,696.87)
Gender	−3,350.38	2,418.78
	(5,836.91)	(4,808.79)
Asian American	−12,560.85	2,590.86
	(26,557.90)	(15,822.04)
Korean or Chinese immigrant	−26,363.14	−25,321.86[a]
	(21,937.57)	(11,171.28)
Equity capital	1.24[a]	1.25[a]
	(.03)	(.05)
Loan source:		
Family	−10,600.13	7,073.61
	(6,572.83)	(8,535.14)

Continued on next page

[a]Statistically significant at the 5-percent level.

Table 6.6—*Continued*

	Regression equations	
	Regression coefficient (standard error)	
	Loans from financial institution	Loans from family or friends
Friends	673.09	933.86
	(12,670.25)	(7,329.64)
Bank	—	9,368.91[a]
	—	(4,291.63)
Former owner	50,186.97[a]	38,453.61[a]
	(11,767.53)	(9,073.63)
Retail firm	−9,250.18	4,584.88
	(5,671.62)	(5,074.34)
Skill-intensive firm	−15,436.04[a]	2,955.05
	(6,308.57)	(3,542.74)
N	4,713	2,598
R^2	.248	.256
F	96.9	52.3
	Mean values, explanatory variables	
Education		
High school	0.303	0.301
College, 1–3 years	0.223	0.24
College graduate	0.176	0.221
Graduate school	0.178	0.155
Managerial experience	0.391	0.357
Bought ongoing firm	0.273	0.231
Married	0.840	0.768
Gender	0.806	0.777
Asian American	0.007	0.015
Korean or Chinese immigrant	0.011	0.031
Equity capital	18,863.76	15,720.64

[a]Statistically significant at the 5-percent level.

Table 6.6—*Continued*

	Mean values, explanatory variables	
Loan source:		
Family	0.141	0.858
Friends	0.034	0.222
Bank	—	0.332
Former owner	0.041	0.053
Retail firm	0.248	0.251
Skill-intensive firm	0.241	0.216

Source: U.S. Bureau of the Census, Characteristics of Business Owners (CBO) database, 1992.

Note: Variables are defined in the appendix, "Databases and Variable Definitions," pp. 270–3.

Korean and Chinese borrowers, the corresponding debt increment is $0.67. African Americans financing new businesses by borrowing from family and friends generated $0.83 in debt per dollar of equity, other factors remaining constant (table 6.7). While lack of equity may hold down loan size, African Americans are clearly suffering no disadvantage relative to Korean or Chinese immigrants when they leverage that equity by borrowing from family and friends.

The Korean- and Chinese-immigrant-owned firms analyzed in table 6.7 are particularly concentrated in retailing: 58.9 percent ran retail operations versus 40.5 percent of all Korean and Chinese firms (table 6.2). In fact, average profits in retailing are low relative to those from other lines of small business. Thus, their heavy concentration in a low-yielding field could account for the small loans of Koreans and Chinese who borrow from family and friends. Yet the regression exercise in table 6.7 shows that starting a retail business produces no loan size penalty, and starting a high-yielding, skill-intensive business produces no loan size increase. The type of business started and loan size show no clear-cut relationship for either Koreans and Chinese or African Americans borrowing from family or friends.

CONCLUSIONS

Empirical studies to date have commonly sought to explain variations in the rates of self-employment among immigrant groups (Borjas

Table 6.7

OLS Regression Explaining Loan Amounts to African American and Immigrant Chinese or Korean Firms Borrowing from Family and Friends (Firms Formed since 1979 Only)

	Regression equations	
	Regression coefficient (standard error)	
	Korean- or Chinese-owned firms	African American-owned firms
Constant	−28,615.90[a]	−13,417.98
	(13,434.70)	(9,333.31)
Education		
High school	8,658.10	1,224.47
	(8,422.06)	(5,617.54)
College, 1–3 years	5,772.69	8,095.68
	(8,721.24)	(6,213.18)
College graduate	2,517.80	2,145.45
	(7,784.84)	(7,023.30)
Graduate school	14,160.90	14,809.59[a]
	(9,278.84)	(7,656.49)
Managerial experience	10,686.57[a]	4,056.49
	(5,485.50)	(4,451.78)
Bought ongoing firm	502.34	5,809.09
	(5,522.52)	(5,261.24)
Married	13,214.09[a]	−1,317.51
	(7,435.06)	(4,347.61)
Gender	−6,271.37	−868.30
	(5,661.95)	(4,045.63)
Equity capital	.672[a]	.832[a]
	(.04)	(.07)
Loan source:		
Family	14,799.34	14,867.66[a]
	(7,830.59)	(6,607.61)
Friends	8,157.39	8,652.77
	(7,082.56)	(5,995.29)
Bank	26,679.48[a]	12,475.69[a]
	(6,709.76)	(4,442.48)
Former owner	9,764.52	5,438.37
	(8,629.92)	(9,751.79)

[a]Statistically significant at the 5-percent level.

Table 6.7 — *Continued*

	Regression equations	
	Regression coefficient (standard error)	
	Korean- or Chinese-owned firms	African American- owned firms
Retail firm	5,901.27	700.93
	(5,476.36)	(4,777.44)
Skill-intensive firm	−10.26	−2,157.17
	(9,768.24)	(5,606.49)
N	770	592
R^2	.350	.250
F	27.0	14.8
	Mean values, explanatory variables	
Education		
High school	.206	.344
College, 1–3 years	.169	.220
College graduate	.288	.133
Graduate school	.189	.140
Managerial experience	.287	.263
Bought ongoing firm	.369	.162
Married	.854	.739
Gender	.755	.670
Equity capital	30,602.38	7,553.41
Loan source:		
Family	.716	.746
Friends	.429	.379
Bank	.207	.271
Former owner	.107	.041
Retail firm	.589	.228
Skill-intensive firm	.115	.196

Source: U.S. Bureau of the Census, Characteristics of Business Owners (CBO) database, 1992.

Note: Variables are defined in the appendix, "Databases and Variable Definitions," pp. 270–3.

[a]Statistically significant at the 5-percent level.

1986; Evans 1989; Kim, Hurh, and Fernandez 1989), while descriptive studies often focus on owners' traits and the operating environment of immigrant firms (Min 1986–87; Fratoe 1988; Bonacich and Light 1988). Out of this literature has emerged the conventional wisdom that entrepreneurship among Asian immigrants has been substantively promoted by RCAs and supportive social networks.

The small businesses started by Korean and Chinese immigrants examined in this chapter generated lower sales and profits than similar nonminority-owned small businesses, despite their larger investments of human and financial capital. The majority of start-up capital for all small-business borrowers came from financial institutions (debt) and family wealth (equity). Firms receiving smaller loans often borrowed from family or friends. Controlling for traits of firm and owner, loans from family and friends were shown to be smaller than loans from financial institutions for nonminority, Asian American, and Korean- and Chinese-immigrant borrowers. Looking solely at firms borrowing from family and friends, loans extended to Korean and Chinese borrowers were significantly smaller than loans of comparison groups. African Americans borrowing from family and friends received $0.83 in debt per dollar of equity versus $0.67 for Korean and Chinese immigrants (controlling for owner and firm traits).

The lower loan sizes to Korean and Chinese immigrants are caused, in part, by their heavier reliance on loans from family and friends (table 6.3). Size of start-up capitalization is linked positively to subsequent firm size, profitability, and survival prospects (Bates 1994b; Bates 1993b). This pattern is consistent with Yoon's observation that Korean-owned firms in Chicago using nontraditional types of credit were smaller, less profitable, and more failure prone (1991a). In fact, small businesses started by Vietnamese immigrants rely more heavily on loans from family and friends than small businesses owned by any other major Asian group.[6] Relative to their Asian cohorts, Vietnamese nationwide run the smallest firms, earn the lowest returns from self-employment, and go out of business most often (chapter 3; Fratoe 1986). Self-employed Asian Indians, in contrast, rely most heavily on loans from financial institutions to finance new businesses. Relative to their Asian-immigrant cohorts, Asian Indians have the highest mean self-employment income and go out of business least often (Fratoe 1986; table 3.4). However, these patterns do not necessarily imply that borrowing from family and friends undermines firm viability.

The high levels of start-up capital typifying Korean- and Chinese-immigrant-owned firms reflect their heavy reliance on equity capital to finance new small businesses. Retail firms headed by owners who are not college educated are one area in which loans from family and friends are a major source of capital for Korean and Chinese small businesses. Proliferation of such marginal firms, indeed, appears to be an outcome of the propensity for Koreans and Chinese to use nontraditional sources of start-up capital. This issue is explored, in detail, in chapter 10, where I compare firms operated by African Americans and those operated by Korean and Chinese immigrants.

NOTES

1. Firms analyzed in this study are weighted to be representative of small businesses operating in the United States in 1987 that generated revenues in 1987 of at least $5,000 and that filed a small-business income-tax return (proprietorship, partnership, or corporation) with the Internal Revenue Service in 1987. Thus, many of the firms under consideration have no employees and are run by those whose main labor-force status was employee. (See the appendix, "Databases and Variable Definitions," for additional details.)

2. Control variables identifying retail and skill-intensive services are not reported in table 6.5 because they had no impact on the results.

3. The CBO very heavily oversampled minority-owned firms and firms having paid employees, necessitating the use of weights, so the weights attached to CBO observations by Census Bureau statisticians are used in this study. (See the appendix, "Databases and Variable Definitions," for additional details.)

4. African American-owned firms were selected for inclusion in the CBO database using the same procedures applied to nonminority- and Asian-owned firms (Nucci 1992).

5. Mean values of variables appearing in OLS regression tables sometimes differ slightly from corresponding values appearing elsewhere. Item nonresponse makes samples used in regression analyses slightly smaller than the corresponding samples used for generating the summary statistics in tables 6.1, 6.2, 6.3, and 6.4.

6. This calculation is based on CBO database samples of firms created between 1979 and 1987.

CHAPTER SEVEN

Traditional and Emerging Lines of Black-Owned Small Businesses

The nature of the black business community is profoundly different today than it was in the 1960s. Its size and scope have expanded, and business diversity has flourished; highly educated entrepreneurs are the norm in many lines of business, and bank credit is more widely available (Bates 1993b). As growth in the African American business community increasingly derives from participation in broader markets, inner-city black communities are often left out. Their exclusion reflects basic shifts in the kinds of opportunities attracting black entrepreneurs. In light of the reorientation of emerging black enterprise toward racially diverse or largely nonminority clienteles, choice business locations are increasingly found outside of minority neighborhoods.

Scholars and journalists often view black business owners as the walking wounded among entrepreneurs (D'Souza 1995). Those who depict the black business community as weak typically assume that black-owned businesses are located in minority communities. The target clientele, by assumption, is made up of urban African Americans. The assumption that black businesses generally serve a ghetto clientele is partly due to the influential writings of Andrew Brimmer. A member of the Board of Governors of the Federal Reserve System, Brimmer wrote on black entrepreneurship had a broad impact because he was the highest ranking black economist serving in government in the late

1960s and 1970s. According to Brimmer (1966), the typical black firm lacked the technical, managerial, and marketing competence needed to compete successfully in the business world.

Caplovitz, in his 1967 study of retail businesses operating in central Harlem, found that white business owners were better educated than black owners. Furthermore, whites were much more likely to have had managerial or sales experience before becoming self-employed. Black business owners operated small establishments and were typically less successful than their white cohorts.

Black businesses existed in niches where whites were reluctant—or unwilling—to compete for black customers. The resultant segregation provided protected markets that directly benefited black enterprise. "Behind the wall of segregation which cut Negroes off from many public services, there grew up a whole new area of opportunity. Behind this wall of protection emerged the Negro physician, the Negro lawyer, and above all, the Negro businessman" (Brimmer 1968, 34). In fields where black customers had relatively free access to mainstream retail establishments, black-owned businesses were typically nonviable. Desegregation, according to Brimmer, merely undermined black businesses. Specifically, the erosion of segregation and discrimination was giving blacks greater access to public accommodations, and white firms were catering to buyers increasingly without regard to race. As the tariff wall fell, Brimmer asserted, most black firms would face increasingly hard times. Government assistance to the black business community, by implication, was a strategy doomed to fail.

A later study by Brimmer suggested that the potential of black enterprises to create jobs, even making optimistic assumptions, was minimal. Brimmer's job creation estimates assumed that no jobs would be created by black firms in construction, manufacturing, or transportation. "This omission was not accidental; rather it resulted from the fact that there are few Negro-owned firms competing in these types of businesses" (Brimmer and Terrell 1971, 304–6).

Scholars critical of black business viability, including Andrew Brimmer, were not surprised when the efforts of the Small Business Administration (SBA) to provide long-term credit to minority-owned businesses produced high rates of loan delinquency and default. The SBA targeted self-employed blacks through its Economic Opportunity Loan (EOL) program. Before 1968, virtually all SBA loans to minority borrowers were EOLs, and in the five fiscal years 1969–73, 24,422 of the 36,782 SBA loans to minorities were EOLs (Bates 1984).

Reflecting its origins in the War on Poverty, the EOL program was designed to help low-income people who either owned or wanted to establish small businesses in traditional fields. Having a high personal income and/or evidence of past or present aptitude for business was grounds for being denied a loan. The EOL program was designed to serve minorities who were unlikely candidates for success in business; the high default rate followed directly from the underlying philosophy of the loan program. Default rates among black borrowers forming new firms in inner-city Boston, Chicago, and New York exceeded 70 percent (Bates and Bradford 1979).

Brimmer's pessimistic view of the black business community has not withstood the test of time. One fundamental flaw in his analysis was the assumption that the emergent black firms of the 1970s would be replicas of the existing species; he failed to consider the possibility of evolution and progress. Brimmer's observation that segregation and discrimination had protected black business, although not without insight, was a one-sided interpretation of the history of black entre-preneurship in America. His protected-markets thesis failed to explore causal relationships between racism and the stunted state of the black business community. Among the more important causal relationships he ignored was the fact that black firms frequently lacked access to financial capital (Bates 1973). Discrimination in the labor market made it difficult for potential entrepreneurs to generate the initial equity investment needed to start a business, partially explaining the small number of firms and the limited variety of businesses in the black busi-ness community. Limited educational and training opportunities simi-larly thwarted many potential black business owners.

Black-owned shoeshine stands had always had access to mainstream markets. In recent decades, African Americans in a wide variety of businesses—from business services to construction—have successfully penetrated markets that had traditionally been inaccessible. In truth, the erosion of discrimination ushered in a new era of opportunity for black entrepreneurs.

THE TRADITIONAL BLACK BUSINESS COMMUNITY

One of the oldest ways for blacks to become self-employed in urban areas was to sell personal services to upper-class whites. In fields like catering and barbering, blacks often held substantial market positions, even in northern cities (Kusmer 1976). In *The Philadelphia Negro*, W.E.B. Du Bois (1899) observed that blacks owned the city's leading catering firms. Yet by the early twentieth century this tradition was declining. "The Negro caterer has slowly been losing ground, probably through loss of personal contact with the fashionable group whose first thought used to be for the Negro when 'service' of any kind was to be done" (Fleming and Sheldon 1938).

Large-scale migration of black Americans from the rural South to the urban North during and after World War I complicated traditional white-black relations in many cities. Before the war, urban blacks were employed predominately in traditional service occupations, often serving white customers as porters, waiters, domestics, and the like. The stereotypical black service worker was courteous, efficient, and nonthreatening (Fusfeld and Bates 1984). Migrants flowing into cities from the rural South to fill factory jobs during World War I were often seen as country bumpkins by established black residents. As migrants continued to arrive in large numbers, older blacks feared that the unsophisticated ways of the new arrivals would disturb relationships between urban blacks and whites. To established city residents, black and white alike, the rural newcomers seemed noisy, dirty, and too numerous. "The Negro migrant was strange; soon he became the object of ridicule. Ultimately he was feared" (Weaver 1948, 29).

Rising black-white antagonism, typified by the outbreak of twenty-six major race riots in U.S. cities in 1919, marked the beginning of the end for black businesses that relied on affluent white clients. Lieberson's explanation of ethnic stratification postulates that discrimination affects African American and Asian entrepreneurs differently. White perceptions of other racial groups—servile versus threatening, courteous versus surly—are the crux of the matter. Whites, according to Lieberson, view particular jobs as suitable for minorities to perform in service to whites—serving meals, shining shoes, ironing shirts, and other tasks. These tasks, however, vary in status and working conditions. Asians, who rank higher in the ethnic queue, have a better chance of occupying niches serving white customers (in restaurants, laundries) than do blacks: Asian entrepreneurs, therefore, find it much easier to penetrate the white market than do black business owners. The more desirable the job, the greater the likelihood that it will be performed by someone who is not an African American (Lieberson 1980).

Rapid growth of the black business community in the early twentieth century coincided with large-scale migration of black Americans to urban areas, and the targeted clientele commonly shifted from white to black as embryonic ghetto communities expanded and antagonism between whites and blacks increased. That this antagonism was a driving force behind rapid black business expansion is clearly illustrated by the rise of life insurance companies.

The year 1898—marked by a race riot and a white-supremacist election campaign—was something of a low point in North Carolina race relations. The growing intensity of Jim Crow served as a catalyst for the creation of North Carolina Mutual, the black-owned life insurance company established in Durham in 1898. After the publication of Frederick Hoffman's *Race Traits and Tendencies of the American Negro* in 1896, major life insurance companies often refused to cover blacks. Black solidarity also appealed widely in this hostile milieu, with economic self-sufficiency an important part of that appeal. North Carolina Mutual's motto, "a company with a soul and a service," reflected its message that investment in the Mutual was not merely an individual economic decision but a moral act of cultural solidarity. The Mutual's strategy was the forerunner to a pattern of business creation and expansion that would generate tremendous growth of a new sort in America's twentieth-century black business community.

The aftermath of World War I saw the development of a dynamic, rapidly growing African American business community. Abundant wartime industrial jobs swelled urban black populations and eased financial constraints for many black entrepreneurs. The wave of race riots in Chicago, Washington, and many other cities in 1919 roused urban blacks to a high state of racial consciousness. Coming together for mutual help and protection, they built and supported their own enterprises. A "buy black" sentiment prevailed, and many businesses were financed by churches and fraternal lodges, whose members would be loyal patrons of the newly formed firms. Church support for individual black firms was so decisive in some areas that the religious denomination of the entrepreneur would determine the clientele patronizing the business.

A conspicuous example of increasing racial consciousness was the widespread development of newspapers owned by African Americans and serving the African American community. A black-owned printing industry arose as a complement to the rapidly growing number of publications. Capitalizing on racial sentiment and financing from high wartime incomes, black businesses formed in every line of commerce and industry.

Particularly in the northern industrial cities, the events of World War I permanently altered the pace and character of life for African Americans. The economic expansion resulting from the war effort created an enormous demand for labor, but the traditional source of manual labor for manufacturing—European immigrants—was closed off by the war. Deprived of its supply of foreign labor, industry was forced to seek workers from the domestic agricultural hinterlands. Northern mills, foundries, and assembly plants sent recruiting agents to the South, urging blacks and whites alike to come to the great industrial cities. Chicago, for example, experienced a 148 percent increase in black population between 1910 and 1920 (from 44,103 to 109,458), along with a 21 percent increase in white population.

Intense competition for housing was a predictable consequence. Black-white competition for housing created antagonisms that paralleled those that emerged in the labor market right after the war. The return of soldiers seeking jobs coincided with the fading of war-induced prosperity. This tense milieu produced the race riots of 1919. Some of these race riots took place in the South, but the largest outbreak of violence occurred in northern cities. In Chicago, earlier periodic bombings and attacks on blacks who ventured into white communities were merely a prelude to the great riot during which five days of violence caused mainly by white gangs took at least 38 lives, caused over 500 injuries, destroyed much property, and left over 1,000 people homeless.

As growing spatial separation reduced contact between the races, black institutions expanded and flourished. Partly by choice and partly as a means to avoid white rejection and possible conflict, African Americans increasingly patronized their own churches, stores, and places of amusement. The decline of normal and spontaneous black-white interactions tended to lessen racial tolerance and mutual understanding. The "buy black" sentiment was an expression of racial solidarity in an increasingly hostile, racially intolerant urban environment.

Aspiring black leaders in the urban North sought to channel heightened black consciousness in various directions. A. Philip Randolph warned blacks not to "depend on white men and white women to work out the problem. We have too long relied on white people. . . . You have got to get it yourself" (Randolph, 1919, cited in Stein 1986, 47). While black socialists such as Randolph judged unions to be the most effective vehicle for racial power, Marcus Garvey and others stressing a "race first" ideology attempted to tie black community militancy to the development of black business. The Black Star Line, a transatlantic steamship enterprise Garvey proposed, typified racial independence in business. Enterprises like the Black Star Line would, according to Garvey, "make it possible for the youth of the race to find suitable employment . . . and remove the need for our high school and college graduates seeking jobs among the whites" (Garvey 1920, cited in, Stein 1986, 85). In the turmoil of 1919, many black professionals, intellectuals, and small businessmen supported Garvey's "race first" strategy as a way to anchor the new racial consciousness in large-scale businesses.

Large-scale businesses, financed and operated by African Americans or any other group, require considerable financial capital and expertise. Garvey's unsuccessful Black Star Line possessed neither: neither Garvey nor any members of his board of directors had practical experience in shipping. The failure of the Black Star Line notwithstanding, the growth of the black business community in the 1920s was rapid. Black professionals, often moving north along with their clients, saw their practices and income rise as segregation increased. After 1920, black businessmen were commonplace in urban black communities. While previously concentrated in a few fields, African Americans were now participating in many lines of business in black residential areas. Black progress was particularly apparent in life insurance: 32 firms employed 6,000 agents and controlled assets of over $18 million in 1928 (Harmon, Lindsay, and Woodson 1929). By 1930, an estimated 70,000 black-owned businesses were operating in the United States, a 700 percent increase over 1900 (Pierce 1947). The 1920s were the golden years for the urban black business community.

That community was vibrant in many southern as well as northern cities. The Hayti district of Durham, North Carolina, for example, had become by the 1920s home to a substantial and widely diversified black business community. Commercial activities were concentrated on two main streets, ensuring a high level of pedestrian traffic for retailers. Black-owned banks encouraged development by providing business and real-estate loans. In addition to the many types of retail operations, the district included black-owned and -operated hotels, restaurants, personal and professional services, finance, insurance, real-estate, and repair businesses, a library, and trade schools.

The Great Depression destroyed much of the ground gained during the previous decade. Black retailers were hit hard. White ghetto merchants had always enjoyed greater access to financial capital and trade credit, and this advantage often proved decisive in the early 1930s. The viability of the black retailer had often been predicated upon the loyalty of the black consumer; during hard times, this loyalty weakened. Black merchants, failing in droves—cried that they were being abandoned by their race. Black consumers responded that they were being exploited by the self-serving racial appeals of the black merchant. Economist Abram Harris wrote that "what the Negro businessman wants is to monopolize and exploit the market the black population provide" (1936, 184).

Drake and Cayton (1962) summarized the local small-business community operating in 1938 in the heart of Chicago's Black Belt (table 7.1): nearly 90 percent of the retail stores in this area were white-owned, with black strongholds reduced to niches in the personal services. Only in beauty parlors, barber shops, and funeral parlors did black-owned business monopolize the local market in the center of the nation's largest urban black community.

The 1940s were not a noteworthy period for black business development, but 1944, under the sponsorship of Atlanta University, did see the first large-scale quantitative study of the black business community undertaken. Joseph Pierce's survey of 3,866 black firms in twelve cities revealed a clear picture of the state of urban black enterprise. Six lines of personal services and retailing dominated the sample: beauty parlors and barber shops—1,005, eating places—741, food stores—293, cleaning and pressing shops—288, shoeshine stands and repair shops—183, funeral parlors—126 (1947, 33–35). Only 3 percent of the firms surveyed had received start-up financing from commercial banks.

For a subsample of firms operating in nine cities, Pierce collected information on the financial capitalization of the business, the age of the business, and operational problems of business ownership as expressed by the owners themselves. The median value for initial business capitalization was an incredibly low $549. This paucity of financial capital was responsible for the smallness of the black-owned businesses described by Pierce. The median initial capitalization for all sampled retail firms was $544, and the median age of the firm was 5.3 years. The median age of firms operating in service businesses was 7.1 years, and for the six most common lines of black enterprise, funeral parlors were the oldest (22.6 years), while shoeshine stands and repair shops were the youngest (3.2 years). When asked to rank the most significant obstacles to progress in business operation among blacks, the

Table 7.1

Business Types by Owner's Race in the Chicago Black Belt, 1938

	Ownership (number of firms)		
	Black	White	Percent black-owned
Retail	19	150	11.2
Food stores	3	45	6.3
Clothing	8	49	14.0
Furniture	0	14	0
General merchandise	1	16	5.8
Other	7	26	21.2
Personal services	41	36	53.2
Laundries, cleaners	6	16	27.3
Tailor	5	9	35.7
Barber shop	12	0	100
Beauty parlor	11	0	100
Funeral parlor	4	0	100
Other	3	11	21.4

Source: Drake and Cayton, 1962, *Black Metropolis* (New York: Harper and Row, 450–51).

entrepreneurs identified lack of financial capital as their single greatest barrier. Other commonly mentioned obstacles were lack of African American patronage and trained personnel.

Outstanding among the few large-scale lines of black business, black-owned life insurance companies weathered the Great Depression. By 1942, they carried nearly $500 million in insurance, an increase of almost 40 percent since 1928.

The history books have little to say about the black business community of the 1950s, which is indicative of the lack of progress. Large-scale urban renewal programs had a devastating effect on black commercial districts in some large cities. In Durham, North Carolina, for example, Hayti's commercial core was slated for blanket demolition in the late 1950s to make way for interstate highway construction and redevelopment (Butler 1991). Investment in Hayti's substantial black business district came to a standstill when demolition plans were drawn up, and businesses began to disburse. Approximately one hundred black-owned firms were demolished; most never reopened. The destruction of Hayti as a compact, coherent shopping area altered shopping habits and contributed to further loss of sales among the remaining black establishments.

A 1964 survey of black businesses in Philadelphia revealed a pattern of small firms concentrated in personal services and retailing: the most common were beauty parlors and barber shops, which accounted for 35 percent of Philadelphia's black-owned firms, and restaurants for 11 percent. Black firms were concentrated in the same lines of business reported by Pierce in 1944, and mean growth in sales had barely outpaced inflation (Foley 1966). The traditional black business community in many urban minority communities never recovered from the Great Depression.

THE EMERGING BLACK BUSINESS COMMUNITY

The growing lines of black business are dominated today by large-scale firms that often serve a racially diverse clientele. Increasingly, these enterprises sell to other businesses, including large corporations, and to government. Firms operating in the broad marketplace are commonly run by black entrepreneurs who have attended college. Areas of particularly rapid growth include the skill-intensive services: finance, business services, and various professional services. These areas are commonly called emerging lines of black enterprise because the presence of African American owners has been minimal historically. Furthermore, the mode of operation—frequent use of paid employees, catering to a nonminority clientele—tends to differentiate firms in the emerging lines from the traditional black business community.

The markets accessible to black-owned businesses have broadened significantly in recent years. While increased loan availability typified efforts to promote black business in the 1960s, the use of procurement dollars and setasides targeted to minority firms by corporations and government became a major force promoting business growth in the late 1970s.

Growth of black-owned firms in the business services industry typifies the process of expansion taking place in emerging lines of black enterprise. Total employment among black enterprises nationwide operating in the business services niche has grown explosively, from 12,432 paid employees in 1982 to 32,636 employees in 1987 to 72,130 employees in 1992 (U.S. Bureau of the Census 1991; U.S. Bureau of the Census 1996). The underlying causes of this growth are the underlying causes of rapid expansion generally in the emerging lines of black enterprise. Two traits powerfully delineate the emerging fields that are rapidly expanding their aggregate sales and employee numbers from the traditional fields where growth is either weak or entirely lacking. The growing lines of black-owned business have most often attracted highly educated and skilled owners, more so than the stagnant fields. The growth sectors, furthermore, are much more oriented toward serving a racially diverse clientele—including corporate and government clients. Traditional neighborhood personal service and mom-and-pop retail businesses, in contrast, serve a predominantly minority clientele. Not all of the growth sectors have been dominated by college-educated owners. Construction has been a growth area in which firm owners are commonly not college educated. Yet construction has been very heavily oriented toward serving mainstream markets, particularly government clients (Boston 1997).

Historically, African American-owned firms have not been involved in the contracting and procurement activities of government agencies and authorities. While the majority of the population in Atlanta, Georgia, in 1973 was African American, black-owned firms received only .01 of 1 percent of the city's procurement business in that year. Atlanta was a pioneer in seeking to expand the presence of minority businesses in public procurement: during the first full year of the city's Minority Business Enterprise (MBE) program, the minority share of contracting and procurement rose to 19.9 percent. By 1988, the minority share had reached 34.6 percent (Boston 1992). Penetration of the public marketplace has permitted minority businesses to grow and diversify, and MBE programs have drawn increasing numbers of qualified minorities into entrepreneurship.

A multibillion-dollar market has clearly opened up: by 1987, over 10 percent of the minority-owned firms operating nationwide sold goods or services to state or local government (Bates and Williams 1995). Black construction businesses, for example, derived over half their revenue outside of the minority community in 1987. Employment in the affected sectors has soared; most of the employees are minorities (Bates 1993b). Challenges to the constitutionality of MBE programs, however, threaten to reverse the broadening of markets served by black-owned enterprises. Minority business setasides are being cut back due to the judicial constraints imposed by the Supreme Court's rulings in *Richmond v. Croson* (1989) and *Aderand v. Pena* (1995).

Emerging businesses are progressing rapidly, but still face problems small businesses have to contend with in general and several additional obstacles that disproportionately affect black firms. One factor that continues to retard black business growth is the lack of equity capital available for investment in small firms.

Personal wealth is traditionally a major source of capital for creating and expanding small businesses. The lack of personal wealth in the black community discourages entry into self-employment and handicaps black business start-ups (chapter 2). Data describing family wealth in 1984 indicate that black households had a median net worth of $3,397 versus $39,135 for white households: for every dollar of wealth in the median white family, the median black family had nine cents (Jaynes and Williams 1989). While only 8.6 percent of white households had zero or negative net worth, 31 percent of black households held absolutely no wealth whatsoever. Wealth in the form of business equity was most common among black households whose income exceeded $24,000. Business equity was held by 3.5 percent of black upper-middle-income households ($24,000–$48,000) and by 14.0 percent of black high-income households ($48,000 plus). In contrast, the fraction of white households owning business equity surpassed that of black households at every income level. At the upper-middle and high-income levels, respectively, 11.0 percent and 21.5 percent of the white households held wealth in the form of small-business equity. The greatest disparity in business equity holdings derives from the fact that higher income white households are relatively more numerous than higher income black households.

In the 1990s, as earlier, black business creation has been concentrated in areas where formation requires relatively little financial capital. Lacking assets and therefore borrowing capacities, blacks are too often ill-equipped to exploit economic opportunities.

Low levels of personal wealth also restrict business viability because commercial banks lend most freely to those who possess significant amounts of equity capital to invest in their businesses. And the second and third most important sources of debt capital for small business—family and friends respectively (Bates 1991)—are limited because of the low net worth of black households in general. Thus, the financial capital constraints facing black-owned businesses are unlikely to ease completely until average net worths rise. The low net worths typifying black households will be alleviated, at best, over a period of many years.

Access to credit has risen for black firms in recent decades. However, credit access is not approaching parity with that of white businesses. Black college graduates have experienced improved credit access, but black-owned firms as a group are less likely to get loans than white-owned firms, and when they do, the loans are smaller than those going to their white counterparts (Ando 1988; Bates 1991).

Although traditional businesses remain numerous within the black business community, data from the U.S. Bureau of the Census reveal a clear trend toward more skill-intensive lines of business. In 1960, nearly 30 percent of self-employed blacks ran personal service firms, and fewer than 10 percent operated in skill-intensive areas such as finance, insurance, real estate, and business and professional services. Among black-owned firms that began operations between 1976 and 1982, 25 percent were in these skill-intensive services; only 10.3 percent of the business start-ups were in personal services. Among the black businesses started between 1982 and 1987, 31.2 percent were in the skill-intensive services. Thirty years ago, blacks in skill-intensive areas were concentrated in several specialties: medicine, law, and insurance. Today, common lines of business include these fields as well as consulting, advertising, engineering, accounting, employment agencies, computer programming, and so forth. The data on black business reflect trends toward business diversity that are vitally important for comprehending the trajectory of black entrepreneurship.

The U.S. Bureau of the Census periodically publishes rough counts of the number of minority-owned businesses operating nationwide, broken down by business and by race-ethnicity. These data suffer from inconsistencies and are too crude to support sophisticated statistical analysis (Bates 1993b; see also, the appendix, "Databases and Variable Definitions"). Nonetheless, they are adequate to document some of the gross changes that have reshaped the black business community nationwide. Firm formations in traditional lines of retailing have lagged, particularly in recent decades. In 1972 and 1992, the number of black-owned food stores and restaurants (the nation's largest retail fields in 1972) were:

	1972	1992
Food stores	12,271	8,466
Eating and drinking establishments	15,154	13,832

While the number of black-owned firms in these traditional fields declined outright from 1972 to 1992, skill-intensive firms in finance, insurance, real estate, and business services showed very rapid growth. Numbers of black firms operating nationwide were:

	1972	1992
Finance, insurance, and real estate	8,001	40,924
Business services	10,846	76,988

In these two areas, where most of the owners were college educated, aggregate numbers of black-owned businesses increased six-fold over twenty years. Business services, the fastest growing line of black business, stands out as less reliant on a minority clientele than any other major group in the black business community.

COMPARING TRADITIONAL AND EMERGING LINES OF BLACK ENTERPRISE

The dual trends of growth and decline that typify the community of black-owned businesses are rooted in the fundamentally different attributes of traditional and emerging enterprises. Beyond catering to a minority clientele, traditional firms tend to be small, have high failure rates, and generate few jobs because owners often have little education and low skill levels. Emerging firms, in contrast, are most commonly started by better educated owners—many of whom have attended college for four or more years—whose financial investment in their businesses is high relative to those observed in traditional fields. These larger financial investments and higher levels of education and skill tend to create firms that are larger, have lower failure rates, and generate more jobs than do their traditional counterparts.

The dichotomy between traditional and emerging firms is interesting, but, in fact, the black business community does not split neatly in two. Traditional and emerging firms both break down into those with high human and financial capital and those with low human and financial capital. In fact, hybrid cases are common. The number of firms in transportation—trucking, most commonly—has grown rapidly. Black owners in this niche have rarely attended college. However, buying a truck (or trucks) commonly requires significant investments of financial capital: black-owned trucking firms, therefore, tend to be financially capital-intensive endeavors owned by people with a high-school diploma at most. Many of the skill-intensive services, in contrast, are owned by college graduates, but they are started with no or very little financial capital.

A study based upon SBA loan application data supported the dichotomy between traditional and emerging business quite nicely (Bates 1978):

	Traditional firms	Emerging firms
Gross sales revenues (mean)	$53,190	$81,219
Total tangible business assets (mean)	$23,795	$32,179

Yet SBA loan applicants are not representative of the black business community overall; the applicant pool is skewed by the nature of available SBA loan programs. The above study used loan application data for firms seeking SBA guarantees against loan default—the 7(a) program in which emerging firms were overrepresented—as well as firms seeking direct loans from the SBA's EOL program—traditional firms were overrepresented in this applicant pool. EOL loans are targeted to low-income applicants, while 7(a) loans are not.

Table 7.2 reports CBO data describing representative nationwide samples of young black-owned businesses that began operation between 1979 and 1987. Traditional fields include firms operating in retailing and personal services, while emerging firms are all other business groups. The emerging firms stand out in terms of their higher firm profitability and higher proportion of college-educated owners: 33.2 percent of emerging black-owned businesses are headed by college graduates versus 23.4 percent of traditional firms. Particularly striking in table 7.2 is the lag in average profitability reported by college-educated owners operating in traditional fields—in 1987 before-tax profits for full-time owners were $12,866 versus $21,027 for owners in the emerging group.[1]

Yet the traditional business group does have strong traits: mean sales and firm capitalization figures for the traditional firms are higher than corresponding means describing the emerging business group. Further, the emerging firms discontinued operations at a somewhat higher rate than traditional businesses: 27.3 percent of the former versus 23.1 percent of the latter had shut down by late 1991. Neither the traditional nor the emerging black business group emerges as clearly superior in terms of the owner's human- and financial-capital investments or the survival and profitability of the business.

Table 7.2

Small Black-Owned Businesses Reporting Business Type and Operating in 1987 (Firms Formed since 1979 Only)

	Traditional	Emerging
Firm's traits		
Gross sales, 1987 (mean)	$78,290	$60,573
Total financial capital (mean)*	$17,840	$13,048
Percent serving predominantly		
minority clientele	64.5%	37.7%
Percent of firms still operating, 1991	76.9%	72.7%
Owner's traits		
Percent with less than four years		
of high school	17.5%	20.1%
Percent college graduates	23.4%	33.2%
Annual owner-labor input in		
hours (mean)*	1,693	1,846
Before-tax profits, 1987 (mean)		
All firms	$7,846	$13,161
Firms with college-educated owners	$6,036	$13,900
Firms with college-educated owners		
working full-time in the business	$12,866	$21,027
Firms with owners working full-time		
in the business	$13,264	$18,236

Source: U.S. Bureau of the Census, Characteristics of Business Owners (CBO) database, 1992.

Note: Variables are defined in the appendix, "Databases and Variable Definitions," pp. 270–3.

*at time of entry into self-employment

Logistic regression equations explaining firm survival help delineate traditional from emerging lines of black business (table 7.3). These survival analyses broadly mirror the logistic regression exercises delineating surviving from defunct Asian-immigrant-owned firms (chapters 3 and 4). The dependent variable in the logistic regression exercise in table 7.3 is whether the business operating in 1987 was still functioning in late 1991: positive coefficient values are associated with firms that were still operating in 1991 and negative coefficient values with those that had closed. (Complete definitions of explanatory variables are presented in the appendix, "Databases and Variable Definitions.")

Table 7.3

Logistic Regression Explaining Survival of Black-Owned Firms, 1987–91 (Firms Formed since 1979 Only)

	Regression coefficient (standard error)		Variable Mean	
	Traditional	Emerging	Traditional	Emerging
Constant	1.364a (.971)	−2.666a (.539)	—	—
Education				
High school	−.302 (.237)	.251a (.122)	.328	.239
College, 1–3 years	−.524a (.240)	.504a (.128)	.277	.242
College graduate	−.551a (.271)	.424a (.142)	.137	.163
Graduate school	−.275 (.299)	.642a (.143)	.102	.185
Managerial experience	−.387a (.172)	.017 (.097)	.218	.255
Bought ongoing firm	−.259 (.185)	.227 (.171)	.182	.067
Married	.128 (.157)	−.027 (.088)	.704	.715
Age	.025 (.042)	.125a (.024)	44.381	42.768
Age^2	−.0002 (.0005)	−.001a (.0002)	2,089.9	1,950.5
Gender	−.200 (.143)	.177a (.088)	.501	.715
Owner-labor input	.024a (.006)	.025a (.004)	17.193	18.762
Number of employees	.094a (.047)	.100a (.033)	.975	.700
Capital	.059a (.019)	.030a (.010)	6.882	6.215
Leverage	−.015 (.012)	.003 (.008)	2.540	1.737
Entered				
1984 or 1985	−1.110a (.233)	−.315a (.118)	.235	.222
1986	−1.684a (.242)	−.618a (.119)	.166	.195
1987	−1.711a (.217)	−.792a (.108)	.291	.290
Minority clientele	.215 (.140)	−.026 (.079)	.564	.398
N	1,387	3,735		
−2 Log L	1,307.7	4,035.0		
Chi-squared	163.1	297.5		

Source: U.S. Bureau of the Census, Characteristics of Business Owners (CBO) database, 1992.

Notes: Variables are defined in the appendix, "Databases and Variable Definitions," pp. 270–3.

aStatistically significant at the 5-percent level.

Logistic regression results identify strikingly different survival patterns for traditional and emerging black business groups. Being college educated is strongly positively associated with firm survival among owners of emerging businesses, but the opposite typifies traditional firms:

Education	Traditional business	Emerging business
College, 1–3 years	−.524	.504
College graduate	−.551	.424
Graduate school	−.275	.642

Rather like Asian-immigrant owners (chapter 4), being college educated is positively linked to firm closure for many African American owners of traditional businesses. All the measures of the owner's human capital for traditional firms point toward a common pattern: greater education and experience predict firm discontinuance. Owners of traditional firms with managerial experience before self-employment are significantly less likely to see their firms survive than other owners. This pattern is absent among owners of emerging firms. The age proxy for work experience does not behave as expected among owners of traditional firms either: owners in their prime self-employment years (their forties) are no more likely than others to see their businesses remain in operation. The exact opposite pattern prevails among owners of emerging firms.

Beyond the measures of human capital, explanatory variables in the exercises in table 7.3 behaved similarly for the traditional and emerging firms. The larger-scale, better-capitalized firms headed by full-time owners were more likely to remain in operation than others. Serving a minority clientele, as opposed to competing in the broader economy, had no significant impact on survival prospects, although traditional firms served the minority niche much more heavily than did the emerging lines of black-owned business. Again, reminiscent of the Asian-immigrant experience, entering self-employment by buying an ongoing firm did not promote business survival among black owners. Finally, the youngest firms were much more likely to have discontinued operations by 1991 than the older, more established firms.

The failure of traditional black businesses to retain well-educated owners bodes poorly for the future of this group. The profit statistics in table 7.2 suggest that returns in this niche are no higher for college-educated owners than they are for those whose formal schooling ended with high school. Table 7.4 uses OLS regression equations to explain the log of the dollar amount of 1987 profits for the traditional and emerging groups of young black-owned businesses. These OLS regressions use the data and explanatory variables described in the logistic regression section of this chapter. Is there really no systematic payoff to college education in traditional fields? The answer is no (table 7.4).

College-graduate owners of firms in the emerging fields, in contrast, generate significantly higher returns, other things being equal. Management experience does translate into higher profits for both the traditional and emerging groups but, as the logit exercise in table 7.3 indicated, traditional black businesses do not retain experienced managers. All of the statistical evidence suggests that black business owners in traditional fields are finding that their college credentials are earning little in the way of financial returns. Moving from self-employment to salaried employment is a pragmatic response to this reality.

A noteworthy finding in the analysis of firm profitability in table 7.4 is that traditional and emerging black firms that cater to a minority clientele are significantly less profitable than those competing in the broader, racially diverse economy. Emerging firms in business services, construction, transportation, manufacturing, and wholesaling are most likely to serve a racially diverse or largely nonminority clientele. Interestingly, this breakout includes two business groups—construction and transportation—in which few of the owners have attended college. Clearly, serving a racially diverse clientele is not a trait narrowly linked to owners with college degrees. Construction and transportation, in fact, are the two black business groups that are most active in public-sector procurement. The unique problems facing firms in this market will be analyzed in chapter 11.

The portrait of profitable firms emerging from the analysis in table 7.4 is one of full-time owners working in businesses that do not serve a predominantly minority clientele. Normally stable relationships between the firm's profitability and the owner's financial capital and education are inconsistent, varying for traditional and emerging firms.[2] More detailed inquiry into the nature of the black business community, pursued in chapters 8 through 11, seeks to pin down the behavior and the trajectory of black-owned businesses.

Table 7.4

OLS Regression Explaining the Log of Before-Tax Profits for Black-Owned Businesses Operating in 1987 (Firms Formed since 1979 Only)

	Regression coefficient (standard error)	
	Traditional	Emerging
Constant	8.645[a] (.120)	8.801[a] (.076)
Education		
High school	.130 (.089)	.017 (.057)
College, 1–3 years	−.028 (.093)	.031 (.059)
College graduate	.014 (.108)	.167[a] (.062)
Graduate school	.118 (.125)	.341[a] (.063)
Managerial experience	.222[a] (.072)	.131[a] (.043)
Bought ongoing firm	−.180[a] (.078)	.018 (.074)
Married	−.111 (.062)	.034 (.039)
Gender	.099 (.059)	.124[a] (.040)
Owner-labor input	.024[a] (.003)	.028[a] (.002)
Capital	.034[a] (.008)	.004 (.005)
Leverage	.001 (.005)	.009[a] (.004)
Entered		
1984 or 1985	−.085 (.074)	−.051 (.049)
1986	−.181[a] (.087)	−.148[a] (.052)
1987	−.283[a] (.078)	−.297[a] (.048)
Minority clientele	−.171[a] (.057)	−.169[a] (.037)
N	764	2,334
R^2	.202	.192
F	12.6	36.8

Source: U.S. Bureau of the Census, Characteristics of Business Owners (CBO) database, 1992.

Notes: Variables are defined in the appendix, "Databases and Variable Definitions," pp. 270–3.

[a]Statistically significant at the 5-percent level.

CONCLUSIONS

Traditional lines of black-owned business stand out for their limited ability to attract and retain college-educated owners. The emerging fields are clearly the areas of growth in the black business community, and they are a diverse lot. Past studies have described emerging lines of black-owned businesses as larger scale, better capitalized, and more apt to be headed by college graduates than traditional fields (Bates 1993b). This broad generalization, in fact, stretches the outer boundaries of accuracy, tending to mask growth fields, such as construction, where college-educated owners are the exception and financial-capital requirements for starting firms are often minimal. The emerging fields of black enterprise do stand out for their greater emphasis on serving a racially diverse and largely nonminority clientele. But the firms in the emerging group are highly diverse themselves and not easily stereotyped regarding the owner's financial-capital investment or educational background. Further inquiry into the present-day black business community will be pursued in chapters 8 and 9.

NOTES

1. Full definitions of variables and descriptions of samples appear in the appendix, "Databases and Variable Definitions."

2. The statistical insignificance of capital for emerging firms in table 7.4 typifies the instability inherent in profitability regressions. The causes of this instability were discussed in chapter 3.

CHAPTER EIGHT

The Owner's Human Capital and Market Accessibility: Factors Shaping the Black Business Community

Black-owned businesses are shaped by broad, discontinuous social forces. Distinctive epics characterize African American experiences in the United States: slavery and the social milieu of the antebellum South shaped black entrepreneurship in the nineteenth century (Bates 1973). Urbanization, northern migration, and the growing intensity of segregation that followed World War I shaped a black business community in the 1920s that was profoundly different from its nineteenth-century predecessor (chapter 7). Finally, a lessening of segregation and discrimination in recent decades has generated an entirely new growth dynamic in the black business community of the 1990s. The lessening of discriminatory barriers and how they shape black business opportunities will be investigated in this chapter.

Creation of viable small businesses commonly entails involvement of talented and capable entrepreneurs who have access to financial capital to invest in their business ventures and access to markets for the products of their enterprises (Bates 1993b). Black-business progress in the 1980s and 1990s has been strongly rooted in the human-capital gains of the entrepreneur: the depth of expertise and experience of black entrepreneurs has expanded substantially. Whereas the median black business owner in 1960 had less than eight years of formal schooling, the median entrepreneur in the 1980s was college educated.

Access to markets has expanded profoundly: a narrow focus on serving a black clientele typified the traditional black business community in 1960; today, emerging lines of black enterprise compete in the mainstream economy, serving households, business clients, and government customers. While human-capital gains and expanded market access are key factors explaining the growth of black enterprise, financial-capital constraints limit gains in the number, size, and scope of black-owned business.

The trajectory of the black business community—larger-scale, more diverse businesses—is causing a narrowing of the gap in self-employment earnings reported by blacks and whites (Bates 1987). Nonetheless, parity with nonminority businesses is not close at hand. The emerging as well as the traditional sector of the black business community lags behind nonminority small business; firms owned by African Americans tend to be smaller, less profitable, and more prone to failure than those operated by nonminorities. The difficulties experienced by self-employed blacks in breaking into larger emerging lines of business, such as manufacturing, are a reflection of constraints that are deeply rooted in U.S. society.

Chapter 7 analyzed the traditional-emerging dichotomy that typifies black entrepreneurship. In this chapter, consequences of trends in the human capital of owners and market accessibility will be traced to show their impact on the nature of the present-day black business community.

BLACK BUSINESS DEVELOPMENT: THE OWNER'S HUMAN CAPITAL

For African Americans entering self-employment nationwide in the period 1979–87, 54.2 percent had attended college, while only 18.9 percent of the entrants had not graduated from high school. Among the high-school dropouts, business creation was most common in a traditional field, the beauty parlor. College graduates most commonly entered the skilled services.

Table 8.1 reviews nationwide statistics comparing young black and nonminority firms (those formed between 1979 and 1987). Group differences in mean gross sales—$64,526 for blacks versus $154,274 for nonminorities—stand out more than differences in the owner's educa-

Table 8.1

Nationwide Comparison of Small Businesses, 1987 (Firms Formed since 1979 Only)

	Black	Nonminority
Firm's traits		
Gross sales, 1987 (mean)	$64,526	$154,274
Total financial capital at start-up (mean)	$14,226	$31,939
Percent of firms still operating, 1991	73.6%	76.9%
Number of employees (mean)	0.7	1.5
Owner's traits		
Percent with less than four years		
of high school	18.9%	10.4%
Percent college graduates	30.2%	37.7%
Annual owner-labor input in		
hours (mean)	1,803	1,960
Before-tax profits (means)		
All firms	$11,726	$15,838
Firms with owners working full time		
in the business	$17,014	$21,611
Annual owner-labor input in hours	2,846	2,832
Equity capital	$9,590	$15,560
Profits, less 10% equity return,		
divided by hours worked	$5.64	$7.08

Source: U.S. Bureau of the Census, Characteristics of Business Owners (CBO) database, 1992.

Note: Variables are defined in the appendix, "Databases and Variable Definitions," pp. 270–3.

tional background. Indeed, fewer black college graduates own businesses than whites—30.2 percent as opposed to 37.7 percent.

Lines of business in which Asian immigrants concentrated were responsible for some of the gaps in their business performance relative to nonminorities: the firms owned by Asian immigrants were smaller and less profitable, on average, than white-owned firms started in the period 1979–87. Their heavier concentration in retailing particularly depressed the relative profitability of the young firms owned by Asian immigrants. Table 8.2 summarizes black-white business distributions for all young firms as well as for those headed by college graduates. Differences in business distribution are present in the statistics in table

Table 8.2

Nationwide Distribution of Firms Operating in 1987 (Firms Formed since 1979 Only)

	Black	Nonminority
All Firms		
Retail	16.6%	16.4%
Personal services	11.5%	6.8%
Business services	13.2%	12.0%
Professional services	12.0%	10.4%
Other services	9.5%	13.0%
Finance, insurance, and real estate	6.0%	9.1%
Construction	9.9%	12.8%
Manufacturing	2.2%	3.3%
Transportation	10.9%	4.6%
Wholesaling	1.5%	3.8%
Miscellaneous and unknown	6.7%	7.9%
Firms Formed by College-Educated Owners		
Retail	15.6%	14.9%
Personal services	9.9%	5.2%
Business services	15.2%	15.0%
Professional services	17.1%	15.2%
Other services	10.0%	12.8%
Finance, insurance and real estate	9.5%	11.8%
Construction	6.5%	7.9%
Manufacturing	1.7%	3.0%
Transportation	6.9%	2.2%
Wholesaling	1.7%	4.1%
Miscellaneous and unknown	5.9%	7.9%

Source: U.S. Bureau of the Census, Characteristics of Business Owners (CBO) database, 1992.

8.2, but they are rarely stark. Personal-service firms are particularly interesting because this business group generates lower mean sales and profits for both blacks and nonminorities than any other line of business; blacks are overrepresented in this lowest-yielding field. Transportation (largely trucking) is another area in which black firms are overrepresented.

Differences in areas of concentration persist when firms owned by college graduates are examined separately: blacks are still overrepresented in personal services and transportation. Furthermore, 7.1 percent of the nonminority owners who have attended college operate wholesaling or manufacturing firms versus only 3.4 percent of their black counterparts. These two fields stand out as having the highest gross sales of all small-business lines, and manufacturing firms report higher average profits than any other small-business field. That black businesses are heavily overrepresented in the smallest, least profitable line of business—personal services—and are underrepresented in the largest lines—manufacturing and wholesaling—holds up for young firms headed by black owners, whether college educated or not. Clearly, merely eliminating educational disparities would not close the large sales gaps between black-owned and white-owned firms.

Does the owner's education noticeably affect the firm's performance? The answer is clearly yes. Other studies show that black firms headed by college-educated owners are larger and much more profitable than similar firms whose owners did not attend college (Bates 1985; Bates 1993b). Table 8.3 shows these same patterns: the black college-educated owners report mean sales of $77,164, which exceeds the corresponding figure of other black owners—$49,590—by 55.6 percent. Among owners working full time (those who spent at least 2,000 hours working in their small business) in 1987, those with college backgrounds reported profits averaging $19,384, which is 35.8 percent higher than mean profits for other owners. Larger firms and higher profits are traits that typify the firms of the better educated black owners. However, focusing solely on the set of black, college-educated owners does not close the gaps in size, profits, and capitalization between white- and black-owned firms. The group of all young firms owned by nonminorities reported higher sales, higher capitalization, higher survival rates, and higher profits, on average (table 8.1), than the group of young firms owned by college-educated blacks (table 8.3).

Underrepresentation of blacks in the largest small-business fields, manufacturing and wholesaling, persists no matter how one sorts the data. Looking solely at young firms of black college graduates with $50,000 or more in start-up capital, one finds that 3.4 percent of their firms are in manufacturing and wholesaling, which is no higher than the corresponding percentages in table 8.2 for the broadly defined black firm groups. Among this elite of well-capitalized black firms, 62 percent operate in the skill-intensive services, particularly professional services.

Table 8.3

Nationwide Comparison of Small Black-Owned Businesses by Owner's Educational Background, 1987 (Firms Formed since 1979 Only)

	No college	College
Firm's traits		
Gross sales, 1987 (mean)	$49,590	$77,164
Total financial capital at start-up (mean)	$10,867	$17,069
Percent of firms still operating, 1991	73.2%	73.9%
Number of employees (mean)	0.5	0.9
Owner's traits		
Percent with less than four years of high school	41.2%	0
Percent college graduates	0	55.8%
Annual owner-labor input in hours (mean)	1,831	1,779
Before-tax profits (mean)		
All firms	$11,420	$11,963
Firms with owners working full-time in the business	$14,276	$19,384
Annual owner-labor input hours	2,826	2,841
Equity capital	$8,320	$11,815
Profits, less 10% equity return, divided by hours worked	$4.76	$6.41

Source: U.S. Bureau of the Census, Characteristics of Business Owners (CBO) database, 1992.

Note: Variables are defined in the appendix, "Databases and Variable Definitions," pp. 270–3.

BLACK BUSINESS DEVELOPMENT:
MARKET ACCESS IN THE BLACK COMMUNITY

A comparison of the industry distribution of young black-owned firms with those formed before 1979 (old firms) reveals long-term trends in the nation's black business community. The number of personal-service firms declined most dramatically as shown in the comparison between young and old businesses in table 8.4: while personal-service firms made up 16.4 percent of black-owned businesses in operation since before 1979, they constituted only 11.5 percent of the younger small businesses. Business services and finance, insurance, and real estate accounted for 13.9 percent of old and 19.2 percent of young black-owned businesses. Recall that personal services rely more heavily on a

Table 8.4
Nationwide Distribution of Black-Owned Firms by Firm's Age, 1987

	Old firms	Young firms
Retail	14.8%	16.6%
Personal services	16.4%	11.5%
Business services	9.0%	13.2%
Professional services	12.0%	12.0%
Other services	10.6%	9.5%
Finance, insurance, and real estate	4.9%	6.0%
Construction	10.8%	9.9%
Manufacturing	2.3%	2.2%
Transportation	11.3%	10.9%
Wholesaling	1.1%	1.5%
Miscellaneous and unknown	6.8%	6.7%

Source: U.S. Bureau of the Census, Characteristics of Business Owners (CBO) database, 1992.

Note: "Old" firms were those started before 1979, while "young" firms were those started between 1979 and 1987.

minority clientele than any other line of black enterprise, while the business services rely least on minority households. Clearly, the decline of the black business community's traditional clientele has had a powerful effect on the shape of firm creation, growth, and survival.

In the urban ghetto that typified America forty years ago, many residents held jobs that paid well. The managerial and professional classes, the working class, underemployed poor, and the underclass all lived in the ghetto. It was race—not poverty—that defined the ghetto, which was comprised of both slum and nonslum areas. In recent decades the inner-city ghetto has lost some of this heterogeneity (O'Hare et al. 1982). Higher-status black residents, members of the professional and managerial classes, have moved to suburban neighborhoods, draining the traditional inner-city black business community of many of its affluent customers (Boyd 1990a) and leaving behind a poorer inner-city ghetto that, by the 1970s, had actually lost population in many eastern and midwestern urban areas. A related serious contributor to the poverty of urban ghettos today is the drain of labor, which has grown in intensity in recent years. The ghetto's chief resource is labor, but its best workers have been leaving by way of the educational system and the high-wage economy. Drawn by opportunities outside of poor urban areas, many of the most intelligent, capable, and imaginative young people have moved into the economic main-stream, where rewards are greater and opportunities wider. Meanwhile, the ghetto gets poorer; its isolation and loss of talent and capital only grow worse (Bates 1989).

Middle-income earners and working-class households still living in inner-city ghettos have shown less inclination to shop in those envi-rons. The suburban mall has captured a growing share of the purchases of central-city residents, and older shopping districts in central cities have become less competitive. This is especially true in ghetto areas that are losing more affluent households.

A shrinking middle class, a rising incidence of remaining residents shopping outside of the community, and a growing poverty rate typify most traditional ghettos in the United States. This is not an environ-ment that is conducive to small-business creation and expansion. Instead, disinvestment is the norm. These trends have certainly not encouraged banks to reverse their longstanding aversion to lending in inner-city minority communities (Bates 1993b).

Neighborhood-oriented black-owned firms serving a minority clien-tele are unlikely to alter the local landscape. Fundamentally, the state of these enterprises reflects the economic circumstances of the clientele. Weak internal markets reflect the fact that poor people possess minimal purchasing power. Declining local markets and lack of access to finan-cial capital seldom attract skilled and experienced entrepreneurs.

The traditional black-owned mom-and-pop business continues to be common in most low-income, inner-city African American communi-ties. This sort of enterprise often means working poverty for its owner rather than economic development, yet government loans are fre-quently targeted to precisely these firms (Bates 1997). A problem char-acteristic of loan programs that target marginally viable firms is that many of the borrowers do not repay their loans. The SBA successfully covered up the fact, for nearly a decade, that the majority of all EOL loans to minority borrowers ended in default (Bates 1984; chapter 7). Of those businesses repaying their loans, many closed down because of their inability to make a living running tiny firms in the ghetto. The EOL program, its credibility destroyed by massive ineffectiveness, was terminated in 1984.

In the wake of the Rodney King riots of 1992, the SBA reestablished a modern variant of the EOL program so that ravaged urban areas such as South Los Angeles could once again get federal loans. But, again, these programs targeted nonviable firms with no potential to generate the sort of economic development desperately needed in inner cities. The U.S. Commission on Minority Business Development (1992) concluded that federal government loan assistance to minority businesses "perpetuates their relegation to areas of business endeavor that are among the most crowded and least profitable" (24).

The modern generation of these assistance efforts are most commonly called "micro-loan" programs. One of the first such programs, the Self-Employment Investment Demonstration (SEID), was a national project designed to turn welfare recipients into small-business owners. Implemented in 1986, SEID participants in five states received training and loans to set them up in business (Raheim and Foster 1995).

SEID's effectiveness was evaluated in 1994 by investigators from the University of Iowa's School of Social Work, using a random sample of 120 SEID participants who had started businesses. Of the 96 firms still operating in 1993, average business age was 31.5 months. In 1993 these 96 businesses generated gross mean revenues of $21,231, less expenses of $18,220, leaving a net average profit of $3,011. The median firm was much less successful, generating gross revenues of $8,000; median profits were not reported. Of the 96 owners, 34 reported that they were withdrawing money from their businesses for household expenditures (Raheim and Foster 1995). Even so, the lead evaluator of SEID concluded that "micro-enterprise development offers a viable alternative to consumption-based income maintenance social welfare programmes," (Raheim 1996). Clearly, this conclusion was not based on mean ($3,011) or median (amount unknown) firm profitability; rather, it was based on unspecified, seemingly subjective criteria. The criterion most often stressed was that "AFDC and food stamps receipt was significantly reduced among this sample of SEID participants" (Raheim and Foster 1995, xiv). In fact, the success of micro-loan programs is not commonly judged by the loan recipient's ability to use self-employment as a way out of poverty. Program goals, more commonly, are to revitalize communities, empower women, reduce welfare roles, or raise the self-esteem of the program's participants (Bates and Servon 1996; Clark and Huston 1993).

These modern interpretations of self-employment as working poverty—the entrepreneur's self-esteem notwithstanding—do nothing to alter the harsh reality that small-business ownership in ghetto communities often generates poverty-level incomes for its owners. The three elements of viable small-business creation (human capital, financial capital, and market access) are difficult to pull together in the ghetto milieu: markets are weak, skilled and experienced entrepreneurs tend to look elsewhere for opportunities, and financial capital is hard to assemble. Availability of tiny amounts of debt capital, whether through EOL loans or micro-loans, does little to alter this bleak reality; successful business creation commonly requires more than one of the three elements of firm viability. Strong human capital, in particular, is required for viability in self-employment: financial capital and human capital inputs are complements, not substitutes.

Efforts to encourage small-business creation to serve weak and declining markets in inner-city minority communities are ongoing. One of the most instructive of such efforts was undertaken by South Shore Bank of Chicago in 1973. South Shore Bank, a division of Shorebank Corp., was established to demonstrate that a regulated bank-holding company could stabilize a neighborhood (Chicago's South Shore) declining from disinvestment following racial change. One of Shorebank's initial programs was to lend money to local small businesses and to recruit "attractive retail and service businesses to 71st Street (the local 'Main Street') to meet resident shopping needs" (Houghton 1995, 6). Shorebank's rationale for building the community's small-business base was quite explicit: "Resident demand for local jobs and local wealth creation opportunities must be met. Local residential communities will always require local jobs to maintain the fabric and amenities of the communities" (Houghton 1995, 3).

In 1973 Shorebank established a four-person department dedicated to responding aggressively to the demand for loans of $5,000 to $500,000 by both new and existing South Shore businesses. By 1983, the year Shorebank discontinued this program, the bank had made 204 loans to local small businesses. Shorebank had conducted a fascinating ten-year experiment: a redlined African American community enjoyed the presence of a bank that aggressively lent to local businesses, particularly targeting black-owned local retail and service firms operating on the community's main commercial strip. South Shore, during this period, could not be characterized as an impoverished community: it was largely working class, and a substantial number of its residents were white-collar workers employed in the central business district. Why was the loan program halted?

According to Mary Houghton, president of Shorebank Corp., "the low success rate of businesses financed and lack of community benefits persuaded the bank to discontinue the program," (1995, 5). After 1983, the bank declined most requests for start-up financing and for business loans of less than $50,000. Franchise financing for minority entrepreneurs was emphasized, using SBA-guaranteed loans, but this successful lending strategy did not focus on the South Shore community. Shorebank concluded that its ten-year small-business lending effort had "no positive impact on the main shopping street," (Houghton 1995, 6).

What went wrong? Of the three key elements of business viability, the availability of financial capital was clearly enhanced: did this lure skilled and experienced entrepreneurs to the local retail and consumer service market? Shorebank analyzed a sample of sixty-six businesses borrowing more than $25,000 to address this issue. Their main conclusion was that the owner's management competence was the single most important cause of business success or failure. According to Houghton, "the traditional shopping streets in South Shore did not attract experienced entrepreneurs who could use a loan of this size effectively. Too often the bank stretched to finance entrepreneurs who were out of their depth in an already weak market situation. It became clear that the costly, labor-intensive effort of providing banking services to volatile young businesses was not going to create successful businesses, transform 71st Street, or meet the shopping needs of local residents. Residents took cars and buses to attractive shopping centers with superior prices, variety, and amenities" (1995, 7). Not every loan was a failure. Of the sixty-six business borrowers studied, Shorebank concluded that thirty-five were successful. Retailing had the lowest success rate—48 percent of borrowing firms—and services, at 57 percent, the highest.

The shopping habits of South Shore residents broadly mirrored those of central city residents. Major purchases were most frequently made at stores outside of the South Shore neighborhood; purchases at large suburban shopping malls were quite common. Like older central-city neighborhood shopping districts in general, South Shore's commercial strip was in a state of long-run decline. Selection, convenience, price, amenities: the small South Shore merchant often had difficulty competing. Increasingly, the local commercial strip was used only for small purchases of convenience items. Availability of bank loans does not alter the reality of weak and declining markets facing many of the traditional black-owned businesses that operate in urban neighborhoods.

In older, viable inner-city neighborhoods like Chicago's South Shore, there is one important market that cannot easily get up and go elsewhere. Old buildings require maintenance, repair, and periodic renovation if viability and stability are to be maintained. Shorebank discovered that black-owned construction companies represented a profitable niche for bank lending. The rental rehabilitation market was particularly attractive. Availability of bank credit, in turn, served to expand the pool of small firms doing building rehab work. The typical borrower was a local black resident who employed other local residents. Many of the rehab firms maintained ownership of the buildings they had redone, thereby increasing local ownership of the rental housing stock. The fit between the bank's loans and a successful business strategy was right. Owners of over a dozen black-owned, local rehab operations are millionaires today as a result of the business growth enabled by ready access to Shorebank's loan funds.

Traditional lines of black enterprise went nowhere in South Shore during the 1970s and 1980s, availability of bank credit notwithstanding. Yet bank credit helped an emerging line of black business—the construction firm—to grow rapidly in a niche where its presence had traditionally been small. Decline in traditional markets and growth in new markets: this is the story of black business development in South Shore, and it is the crux of business growth nationwide. Black-owned construction firms grew very rapidly in the 1970s and 1980s. Their most important new market was public-sector procurement, particularly in state and local government.

BLACK BUSINESS DEVELOPMENT: ACCESS TO THE GOVERNMENT-PROCUREMENT MARKET

Big city black mayors were responsible for the initial opening up of the government-procurement market to minority-owned businesses. Following the lead of Atlanta (chapter 7), many cities headed by black mayors aggressively sought to steer city contracts to minority-owned businesses in the 1970s. Case studies show that black mayors place a high priority on municipal contracting with minority-owned businesses. Promoting black-owned businesses was ranked as "very important" by 86 percent of black elected officials (Jaynes and Williams 1989). To date, however, there has been no empirical study directly linking black mayors to the overall health of black business. The evidence presented below will demonstrate that black mayors affect the size and scope of the black business community: political power generates economic benefits.

City governments have at their disposal numerous ways of promoting minority business development. Their most powerful tool is the setaside—a piece of legislation or an executive order requiring that a specified percentage of procurement expenditures go to minority businesses. Mayors often initiate programs to aid minority enterprises without the benefit of formal legislation; executive orders mandating increased purchases from minority business have been commonplace. A complementary approach frequently undertaken entails appointing procurement officials whose mandate is to assist minority businesses in securing government contracts.

Long-term tenure expands a mayor's ability to promote preferential procurement policies. Procurement decisions are often decentralized, with special districts controlling government expenditures in many areas. It takes time to place proponents of preferential procurement and minority business setaside programs into positions of authority. Between 1973 and 1980, "the black share of administrators rose from 13 to 35 percent in Atlanta and from 12 to 41 percent in Detroit" (Eisinger 1984, 252). New market opportunities resulting from such realignments in local political control benefited existing black-owned businesses and encouraged new firm formation (Bates 1993b).

The mere presence of a successful black business community, by itself, does not demonstrate the positive impact of a black mayor. A substantial black business sector may predate a mayor, and the tenure of a mayor might be influenced by the vibrancy of the black business sector. Thus, direct evidence that black political power in city hall assists black-owned firms can only be derived by studying businesses formed after a mayor is in office.

I used two methods to determine empirically the effect of black mayors on the black business sector. First, using aggregate data, I examined the sales and rate of entry by black-owned firms across cities with and without black mayors and across time in cities that elected a black mayor between 1982 and 1987. If the presence of black mayors benefits black businesses, then both the sales and the rate of entry by black-owned firms should be higher in cities with black mayors than in cities without black mayors.

The findings reported below indicate that the aggregate sales of black-owned firms were significantly higher in the 1980s in cities with black mayors than they were in cities without black mayors, all else remaining constant. Additional analyses using firm-level data from the Census Bureau's CBO database suggest that large black-owned firms in emerging lines of business, such as wholesaling and construction, benefited disproportionately from the setasides and procurement activities of mayors in comparison with small, traditional black-owned firms, such as those in personal services.

The analyses in tables 8.5 through 8.8 show that sales by black firms and business-creation rates among blacks were higher in cities with black mayors during the 1980s than they were in cities without black mayors. The size and scope of the black business community are directly measured by the total volume of sales and the net number of new black-owned businesses.

In order to analyze the effect of black mayors on the black business community, I also had to control for other factors that may have influenced the demand for and supply of output by black-owned businesses. One determinant of both total sales and net number of black-owned firms is the overall market demand for the output of black-owned businesses. The two empirical proxies for aggregate market demand used here are, first, personal income, measured by total wages from all sources within the relevant metropolitan statistical area (MSA), and, second, local government expenditures. As discussed above, government officials can promote minority business development by directing procurement expenditures toward black-owned businesses. If a certain percentage of procurement expenditures is earmarked for black-owned firms through setasides, then black-owned businesses will benefit directly from higher local government expenditures. Another determinant of the size and scope of black businesses is the availability of employment. While over 75 percent of all black-owned businesses have no employees other than the owner, self-employment is likely a substitute for other employment opportunities. So the MSA unemployment rate acts as an inverse proxy for employment opportunities: a higher unemployment rate means fewer employment opportunities, which should also mean an increase in the number of black-owned firms.

Among cities with one hundred or more black-owned businesses in 1982 and 1987, there were twenty-two African American mayors in 1982 and twenty-six in 1987. Eight African American mayors were newly elected between 1982 and 1987, while four incumbents were defeated during the period.

METHODOLOGY

I estimated an ordinary least squares regression model explaining the aggregate sales of black businesses to assess the effect of black mayors

Table 8.5

Analysis of Cities with and without Black Mayors, 1982 and 1987:
Differences in Variable Means (Excluding Cities without 1982 sales)

	Black Mayor[a]	No Black Mayor[b]	*t* statistic[c]
1982			
Number of black firms	4,639	1,558	1.87
Firms per 1,000 people	2.5	1.8	2.55
Population (in thousands)	1,604	889	1.47
Sales of black firms			
(in millions)	$168.2	$59.1	3.00
Personal income in MSA			
(in millions)	$20,546	$10,902	1.47
Unemployment rate			
in MSA	8.8%	9.5%	0.80
Local government			
expenditures (in millions)	$647.5	$470.6	0.58
1987			
Number of black firms	6,420	1,648	3.03
Firms per 1,000 people	2.9	2.1	2.51
Population (in thousands)	2,127	842	2.62
Sales of black firms			
(in millions)	$277.4	$58.3	3.20
Personal income in MSA			
(in millions)	$31,467	$11,512	2.68
Unemployment rate			
in MSA	6.6%	7.5%	1.43
Local government			
expenditures (in millions)	$981.2	$533.2	1.22

Sources: Data from: *The Survey of Minority-Owned Businesses* (U.S. Bureau of the Census, 1991); *Local Area Personal Income* (U.S. Department of Commerce, 1989 and 1990); *City Government Finances* (U.S. Department of Commerce, 1985 and 1990); *Employment and Earnings* (U.S. Bureau of Labor Statistics, 1982 and 1987); *Black Elected Officials: A National Roster* (Joint Center for Political and Economic Studies, 1987).

[a]$N=17$

[b]$N=122$

[c]Tests the null hypothesis that ($X_{\text{black mayor}} = X_{\text{no black mayor}}$), where X_i is the value of the variable for each subsample.

on the size and scope of the black business community. The applicable variables explaining aggregate sales are defined below:

"Sales" is the 1982 and 1987 aggregate sales by black businesses in selected large cities with one hundred or more black-owned firms;

Table 8.6

Analysis of Cities with and without Black Mayors, 1982–87: Paired
Difference in Means Tests

	No Black Mayor, 1982–87[a]	Incumbent Mayor, 1982–87[b]	Lost Black Mayor, 1982–87[c]	Gained Black Mayor, 1982–87[d]
Net change: number of black firms	301 (3.09)	1,297 (3.30)	395 (2.69)	918 (2.68)
Net change: number of black firms per 1,000 people	0.29 (4.95)	0.69 (4.76)	1.0 (13.96)	0.35 (4.12)
Population (in thousands)	6.4 (9.82)	6.4 (3.26)	4.5 (1.17)	2.6 (2.39)
Net change: sales of black firms (in millions)	$47.2 (7.33)	$50.6 (4.69)	$54.4 (5.12)	$63.7 (1.46)
Personal income (in millions)	$18.4 (16.40)	$24.5 (6.40)	$19.5 (5.28)	$18.4 (6.72)
Local government expenditures	$19.1 (6.12)	$20.1 (2.80)	$120.6 (0.99)	$5.45 (1.01)
Unemployment rate	−1.8 (5.31)	−2.8 (3.85)	−0.8 (1.16)	−3.7 (10.16)

Sources: Data from: *The Survey of Minority-Owned Businesses* (U.S. Bureau of the Census, 1991);
Local Area Personal Income (U.S. Department of Commerce, 1989 and 1990); *City Government
Finances* (U.S. Department of Commerce, 1985 and 1990); *Employment and Earnings* (U.S. Bureau
of Labor Statistics, 1982 and 1987); *Black Elected Officials: A National Roster* (Joint Center for
Political and Economic Studies, 1987).

[a]$N=115$

[b]$N=14$

[c]$N=3$

[d]$N=7$

Note: The null hypothesis tested is $(X_{87} - X_{82})= 0$, where X_t is the value of the variable in 1987
and 1982; t-statistics are given in parentheses.

"demand" is proxied by personal income or government expenditures; "personal income" is nonfarm personal income in 1982 and
1987 by MSA (U.S. Bureau of Economic Analysis 1989, 1990, table
4); "government expenditures" is total municipal government expenditures for the fiscal year, including all fiscal years that closed within
the twelve months ending 30 June 1983 and 30 June 1988 for the
1982 and 1987 samples, respectively (U.S. Bureau of the Census
1985, table 5; U.S. Bureau of the Census, 1990, table 5; Moulder
1987; Desantis 1990); "unemployment rate" is the unemployment

Table 8.7

OLS Regression Estimates of Total Sales by Black-Owned Businesses
(Excludes Cities without 1982 Sales)

| | Regression coefficient (standard error) | | | |
| | Model 1 | | Model 2 | |
	1982	1987	1982	1987
Intercept	−21,025	−50,168[a]	66,855[a]	76,551[a]
	(16,820)	(17.006)	(28,090)	(27,242)
Personal income	0.007[a]	0.007[a]	—	—
	(0.000)	(0.000)		
Government expenditures	—	—	0.046[a]	0.048[a]
			(0.005)	(0.004)
Unemployment rate	−146	2,947	−4,193	−5,792
	(1,622)	(1,965)	(2,814)	(3,291)
Mayor—1982	43,250[a]	86,875[a]	108,297[a]	167,423[a]
	(15,283)	(17,410)	(26,096)	(29,424)
New mayor	59,348[a]	31,376	178,127[a]	170,445[a]
	(23,366)	(26,147)	(42,922)	(43,704)
N	138	138	138	138
R^2	0.83	0.86	0.50	0.58
P-value	0.0001	0.0001	0.0001	0.0001

Sources: Data from: *The Survey of Minority-Owned Businesses* (U.S. Bureau of the Census, 1991);
Local Area Personal Income (U.S. Department of Commerce, 1989 and 1990); *City Government
Finances* (U.S. Department of Commerce, 1985 and 1990); *Employment and Earnings* (U.S. Bureau
of Labor Statistics, 1982 and 1987); *Black Elected Officials: A National Roster* (Joint Center for
Political and Economic Studies, 1987).

[a]Statistically significant at the 5-percent level.

rate for the MSA during January 1982 and January 1987 (U.S. Bureau
of Labor Statistics 1982, 1987, table D-1);[1] "mayor—1982" equals
one if there was a black mayor in 1982, zero otherwise; "new mayor"
equals one if there was a black mayor in 1987 but not in 1982, zero
otherwise. "Personal income" is included to control for overall purchasing power in the metropolitan area.

Total sales in the black-business community ("sales") should be
directly related to total personal income in the MSA, all else remaining constant. Government expenditures is the upper limit of govern-

ment resources that could potentially be transferred to all businesses. Because I assume government procurement dollars to be an important source of revenue for the black business community, sales should rise with government expenditures. The unemployment rate is an indirect measure of the opportunity cost of self-employment. Many small businesses are started because there is a shortage of employment at the lowest wage the entrepreneur will accept. Therefore, total sales should be positively related to the unemployment rate in the metropolitan area. Finally, the model includes dummy variables for whether there was a black mayor in 1982 ("mayor—1982") and for whether there was a new black mayor in 1987 ("new mayor"), since I expect black mayors to benefit the black business community by allocating more government procurement dollars to them than would otherwise occur.

Since it is as likely that the black business community will grow if the mayor is black as it is that the presence of a large black business community makes it easier to elect a black mayor, I estimated separate regressions for the years 1982 and 1987 and observed differences in the coefficients for the mayoral dummy variables across the two subsamples. If black mayors promote black business development, then the sales and number of black businesses in cities with a black mayor in 1982 should have increased relative to black business communities without a black mayor in 1982.[2]

I also tested the differences in the estimated coefficient for whether there was a new black mayor in 1987 for regressions estimated separately for the 1982 and 1987 subsamples.

Finally, I examined cross-sectional differences in the means of the variables measuring the size and scope of the black business community in table 8.5, and I reported differences in population, total personal income, and government expenditures.

RESULTS

On average, the number of black businesses and their total sales in cities with black mayors were significantly larger than the number and sales of black businesses in cities without black mayors. In 1982, the mean number of black businesses was 4,639 in cities in which a black mayor presided compared to 1,558 in cities with no black mayor. Moreover, the differences were not due to the city's size: the mean number of firms per 1,000 people was also significantly higher in cities with black mayors. Total sales by black businesses in 1982 averaged $168 million in cities with black mayors compared to $59 million in cities without black mayors.

A similar pattern was evident in 1987. In cities with black mayors, the mean number of black businesses was 6,420, and their average total sales were $277 million. In cities that had no black mayor in 1987, the mean number and total sales of black businesses were 1,648 and $58 million, respectively. Again, the fact that black mayors typically preside over larger cities does not explain the higher concentration of black businesses in cities with black mayors: the mean number of firms per 1,000 people was also greater in cities with black mayors. (These differences are statistically significant at conventional levels.)

Data on the characteristics of the cities studied reveal that in 1982 and 1987 black mayors presided over larger cities, as measured by population, than their white counterparts. Cities in which a black mayor presided also had higher average aggregate personal incomes. Differences in government expenditures and the percentage unemployed were insignificantly different in both sample years.

More revealing is the comparison of changes in the number and total sales of black businesses for cities with and without black mayors. Table 8.6 reports the results of paired differences in means tests (1982 versus 1987) for each city. The sample is divided into four subsamples: (1) cities with no black mayor, 1982–87; (2) cities in which a black mayor presided during the entire period 1982–87; (3) cities in which a black mayor was not reelected between 1982 and 1987; and (4) cities in which a black mayor was newly elected between 1982 and 1987.

The percentage change in total sales and the mean net number of new firms should be greater in cities with an incumbent black mayor over the entire period, 1982–87, than in cities with no black mayor over the period; if black mayors benefit black businesses, then the mean percentage change in total sales and the net number of new firms in cities in which black mayors were either newly elected or not reelected should be greater than in cities with no black mayor over the period but less than in cities with an incumbent for the entire sample period (table 8.6). In the cities with incumbent black mayors (Subsample 2) there was a net increase of 1,297 new black businesses between 1982 and 1987, but only 301 new black businesses in cities with no black mayor (Subsample 1). Over the same period, the number of firms per 1,000 people increased by 0.69 in cities with an incumbent black mayor compared to 0.29 in cities with no black mayor. There was a concomitant small increase in the average total sales of black businesses in cities with an incumbent black mayor of roughly $51 million, compared to $47 million for cities with no black mayor.

Fewer new black businesses were formed in cities in which a black incumbent mayor was not reelected between 1982 and 1987 (Subsample 3) than in cities in which a black mayor was newly elected during the period (Subsample 4). Moreover, the increases in numbers of black businesses for these two subsamples were greater than in the no-black-mayor group (Subsample 1) but less than in the incumbent-black-mayor group (Subsample 2). The number of firms per 1,000 people in both Subsamples 3 and 4 was greater than in Subsample 1 (cities with no black mayor), as expected, but the number of firms per 1,000 people was larger than expected in Subsample 3 (cities whose black mayors were not reelected). Sales by black businesses in Subsamples 3 and 4 increased. However, the increase in sales in the gained-black-mayor group (Subsample 4) was greater than the increase in the incumbent-black-mayor group (Subsample 2). One explanation for the larger sales in the gained-black-mayor subsample is that this group includes some disproportionately large cities, such as Philadelphia, Chicago, and Baltimore.

Table 8.7 examines the effect of black mayors on the size and scope of the black business community, controlling for the general economic condition of the cities. Two alternative models were estimated in the ordinary least squares regressions. In model 1, personal income proxied for market demand. In model 2, local government expenditures proxied for market demand. Separate regressions were run for both 1982 and 1987 for each empirical specification.

With few exceptions, the explanatory variables were statistically significant, either positively or negatively, as expected. One exception was the unemployment rate for the MSA: the regression coefficient estimate was statistically insignificant in both models for both years. Apparently, after controlling for other relevant factors, a shortage of employment opportunities did not significantly affect total sales by black-owned firms.

Personal income in the MSA was positively and significantly related to total sales by minority-owned businesses. It was highly significant in model 1. However, little money out of personal income goes to the purchase of products sold by black-owned firms: an increase in personal income of $100,000 was associated with an increase in total sales to black-owned businesses of only $700.

As expected, municipal government expenditures were also an important determinant of total sales by black-owned businesses. The estimates for model 2 suggest that total sales of the black business community increased by $4,600 to $4,800 for every $100,000 increase in local government expenditures.

When personal income is the measure of market demand (model 1) the estimated coefficient for cities in which a black mayor presided in 1982 is positive and statistically significant ($t = 2.83$). Thus, the total sales of the black business community in cities with black mayors in 1982 were $43.3 million greater than were the sales of black businesses in cities with no black mayor in 1982. This result could be due either to the black mayor's ability to promote black business development or to the political influence of a large black business community. By 1987, the sales of black businesses in cities with black mayors exceeded the total sales of black firms in cities without black mayors by $86.9 million. Thus, the black business community with black mayors gained an incremental $43 million relative to cities with no black mayor between 1982 and 1987.

The results using model 2 also suggest that sales in the black business community in cities with black mayors increased relative to sales in cities with no black mayor. The estimated coefficient for "mayors —1982" in 1982 is 108,297 compared to 167,423 in 1987, indicating that the total sales of the black business community in cities with black mayors grew by over $59 million more than in cities with no black mayor between 1982 and 1987. Together, these estimates provide strong evidence that black mayors promote the growth of black businesses.

Regarding "new mayor," 1982 sales by black-owned businesses in cities that elected a black mayor before 1987 were $59.3 million greater than sales in cities that had no black mayor in 1982 and did not elect one by 1987. As expected, this indicates that a large, viable black business community may facilitate the election of black mayors.

Surprisingly, model 1 suggests that by 1987 the total sales of the black business community in cities with newly elected black mayors decreased relative to sales of the black business community in cities with no black mayor. The applicable regression coefficient, however, is not statistically significant. A qualitatively similar result is indicated by the estimates in model 2. Compared to cities with no black mayor, cities that elected a black mayor by 1987 had sales by black-owned businesses that were $178.1 million higher in 1982 but only $170.5

million higher in 1987. The change in estimated regression coefficients for "new mayor" between 1982 and 1987 suggests that the black business community did not directly benefit from the election of a black mayor by 1987. One interpretation of this result is that such mayors did not have enough time to adopt policies or to realize the benefits of the policies they did adopt in the short time that they had held office.

Although the evidence on total sales is suggestive, the results could be accounted for by substantial growth in the size of a few firms. So the results do not warrant the conclusion that black mayors create an environment conducive to the development of the black business community as a whole. To address this issue, I estimated the impact of black mayors on net new business formations (defined as the number of black businesses in 1987 minus the number of black businesses in 1982).

Table 8.8 reports estimates of a regression equation in which the change in the number of black businesses between 1982 and 1987 is explained by the change in personal income ("ΔIncome") and change in the unemployment rate ("ΔUnemployment"), and the dummy variables "mayor—1982" and "new mayor." As before, I also estimated the results for a second model in which the change in local government expenditures proxied for the change in aggregate demand.

The results are consistent with the notion that black mayors promote the development of the entire black business community: the number of black businesses grew by 765 in cities with a black mayor during 1982 and 1987, according to model 1's estimate, and by 860 according to model 2's estimate for cities with black mayors in 1982. The regression coefficient estimate for "new mayor" suggests that the number of black businesses grew at a more rapid rate in cities that elected a black mayor between 1982 and 1987, although the coefficient estimates are statistically insignificant.

Overall, the regression results indicate that, in cities with black mayors in 1982 and 1987, both total sales and number of black-owned firms increased relative to the sales and number of black-owned firms in cities with no black mayor.[3]

ANALYSIS AT THE LEVEL OF THE FIRM

Having provided citywide evidence that black businesses benefit from black mayors, I now shift the analysis to focus on individual black-

Table 8.8

OLS Regression Estimates of Changes in Numbers of Black-Owned Businesses, 1982–1987 (Excludes Cities without 1982 Sales)

	Regression coefficient (standard error)	
	Model 1	Model 2
Intercept	40 (174)	323 (121)[a]
ΔPersonal income	16.21[a] (8.36)	—
ΔGovernment expenditures	—	−1.21 (2.16)
ΔUnemployment rate	20 (28.17)	−0.75 (25.00)
Mayor—1982	765[a] (282)	860[a] (288)
New mayor	657 (421)	599 (428)
N	138	138
R^2	0.07	0.05
p-value	0.0086	0.0372

Sources: Data from: *The Survey of Minority-Owned Businesses* (U.S. Bureau of the Census, 1991); *Local Area Personal Income* (U.S. Department of Commerce, 1989 and 1990); *City Government Finances* (U.S. Department of Commerce, 1985 and 1990); *Employment and Earnings* (U.S. Bureau of Labor Statistics, 1982 and 1987); *Black Elected Officials: A National Roster* (Joint Center for Political and Economic Studies, 1987).

[a]Statistically significant at the 5-percent level.

owned businesses. This section will identify the characteristics of firms that benefit most from black mayors, using data compiled in the CBO database described in earlier chapters.

Tighter constraints on sample size limit the analysis to twenty-eight large MSAs. Of these twenty-eight MSAs, ten had a black mayor in 1982: Atlanta, Birmingham, Detroit, Gary, Los Angeles, Newark, New Orleans, Oakland, Richmond, and Washington, D.C.

Chapter 7 indicated that it is the emerging lines of black business that are most capable of exploiting expanded market opportunities created by setasides and other governmental transfers. A majority of black-owned firms do not benefit directly from procurement programs targeted at minorities either. The emerging firms (including wholesaling, construction, skilled-services, and manufacturing) are most capable of benefiting from preferential procurement efforts, whereas preferential procurement programs are irrelevant to most traditional businesses (including retailing and personal services). Thus, all traditional businesses—personal services and retail—are excluded from the following analysis. Firms in agriculture, mining, and forestry and firms that could not be assigned to a business group are also excluded. The final sample includes only firms in manufacturing, wholesaling, other services, transportation, and construction.

Analysis shows that the average black-owned business in an emerging field was clearly larger in the ten urban areas with black mayors presiding than were similar firms in the eighteen other urban areas. Mean sales and average number of employees were $160,022 and 4.3 for black-owned firms in the cities with black mayors versus $105,361 and 2.3 for black-owned businesses in cities without black mayors (Bates 1993b). An alternative explanation for the result that average firm size is larger for black businesses in cities with black mayors is that a large, viable black business community increases the likelihood that a black mayor will be elected. One way to avoid favoring the first explanation is to examine data on firms formed after the black mayor took office. Table 8.9 presents the results of this comparison. Firms formed in cities with black mayors were larger in terms of sales and number of employees than their cohorts in the other eighteen areas. Blacks starting businesses in cities with black mayors were more likely to be college graduates and made larger initial financial-capital investments in their firms. Evidence from several sources falls into a consistent pattern: black mayors encourage the creation and expansion of black businesses.

The conventional wisdom among scholars is that the overrepresentation of black Americans in government jobs causes a corresponding underrepresentation in self-employment. Boyd claimed in 1990 that affirmative action is more strictly enforced in the public sector than in private industry and, thus, that "blacks have a strong incentive to seek government jobs and eschew self-employment as a pathway to upward mobility" (1990b, 127). Kotkin (1986) claimed that growing black employment in the public sector raised the opportunity costs of self-employment and drew potential black entrepreneurs away from independent enterprise. Analyzing census data samples for 1980 and controlling for age, occupational background, and other traits, Boyd found in 1990 that black employment in government had a negative effect on black entrepreneurship: "A one percent increase in the percentage of blacks working in the public sector lowers the estimated odds of black

Table 8.9
Summary Statistics for Black-Owned Firms Formed 1976–1982

	Cities with black mayors	Cities without black mayors
Firm's traits		
Gross sales, 1982		
(mean)	$53,793	$35,953
Number of employees		
(mean)	0.8	.04
Owner's traits		
Percent of college		
graduates	38.3%	33.8%
Total financial capital		
(mean)	$25,432	$18,915

Source: Timothy Bates, *Banking on Black Enterprise* (Washington, D.C.: Joint Center for Political and Economic Studies, 1993, chapter 6).

self-employment by a factor of 0.97" (1990b, 265). The findings of this chapter completely contradict this. As Eisinger (1984) has noted, the black share of administrators rose from 13 to 35 percent in Atlanta following the election of a black mayor. Was black self-employment in Atlanta undermined by these gains in public-sector employment? No: the black business community of Atlanta has flourished since 1973 (Boston 1997).

Lack of opportunities in business certainly has pushed black Americans onto other career paths in the past. Indeed, that is why in 1938 73 percent of black Americans with college degrees were preachers or teachers (Holsey 1938). But occupational patterns rooted in a lack of opportunities can change substantially when new doors open. Black mayors in big cities such as Atlanta indeed opened those doors during the 1970s and 1980s; black self-employment flourished. Clearly, a lack of opportunities thwarts black entrepreneurship, not a lack of interest.

NOTES

1. I used the state unemployment rate when the unemployment rate for the metropolitan area was not available.

2. Formally, I tested the null hypothesis $b_{3,82} = b_{3,87}$ against the alternative hypothesis $b_{3,82} < b_{3,87}$. Rejection of the null hypothesis in favor of the alternative hypothesis is consistent with the argument that black businesses benefited from presiding black mayors.

3. This analysis of black business formation and growth in cities with and without black mayors was coauthored by Darrell Williams.

CHAPTER NINE

Access to Financial Capital: Factors Shaping the Black Business Community

T here are three primary ways in which limited access to financial capital shapes the present-day black business community. First, some potential entrepreneurs never take the plunge because they are unable to assemble the financial capital necessary to launch their businesses. This discouraged-entrepreneur phenomenon is most pronounced in capital-intensive lines of small business, such as manufacturing. Second, since the amount of financial capital invested at start-up is a powerful determinant of firm size among the small businesses that actually do begin operations, a lack of financial capital often translates into extremely small black-owned businesses (Bates 1993b). Third, since small firms often generate insufficient revenues to pay the bills and provide the owners with a decent livelihood, extremely small, poorly capitalized black-owned businesses often close after a few years of operation, in turn, lowering the self-employment rate in the African American community. These outcomes of limited access to capital—discouraged entrepreneurs, extremely small firms, and the resultant small-business closure—are likely to persist for many decades because they are firmly rooted in the overall lack of wealth among black households. Reducing financing barriers could substantially increase the size and scope of the black business community.

Patterns of start-up capitalization typifying black- and Asian-immigrant-owned businesses formed between 1979 and 1987 reveal stark differences that profoundly shape firm viability:

	Black businesses	Asian-immigrant businesses
Financial capital at start-up (mean)	$14,226	$53,550
Percent of firms started with equity capital of $25,000+	5.0%	25.6%
Percent of firms using borrowed funds to finance start-up	28.8%	46.2%
Percent of firms started with zero capital	28.9%	16.2%
Leverage (start-up debt divided by equity)	1.03	1.00

Where do these huge differences in capitalization come from? Debt, on average, accounts for just over 50 percent of the aggregate capitalization of black business start-ups nationwide, about the same as the share of debt financing in the capitalization of Asian-immigrant-owned firms. The crux of differences in start-up financing lies in household wealth. Asian households nationwide are almost six times more likely than black households to be in the $100,000+ net-worth group: 4.2 percent of black and 25.0 percent of Asian households were in this high-wealth category (chapter 2).

Human- and financial-capital endowments are the prerequisites for success in most lines of self-employment. For people lacking the requisite skills and capital, self-employment entry rates are low (chapter 2). For those lacking appropriate human and financial capital who start a business nonetheless, business failure and self-employment exit rates are high (chapters 2, 3, and 7). It is the financial-capital gap, more than the human-capital gap, that produces the lower rates of self-employment entry and higher rates of small-firm closure of blacks relative to Asian immigrants, Asian Americans, and nonminorities.

Progress among black Americans entering self-employment has been most pronounced in the emerging lines of business, and no area has grown more rapidly than the skill-intensive services, where college-educated owners are the norm. Small-business creation is often feasible with minimal financial-capital outlays in these service niches. Underrepresentation of black business today is most pronounced in the capital-intensive lines—manufacturing and wholesaling.

OVERCOMING FINANCIAL-CAPITAL BARRIERS

Average capitalization of black-owned businesses is $14,226, and median capitalization is under $10,000. These start-up capitalization figures are low. What do they really mean? First of all, they show that self-employment is often a part-time endeavor. Recall that the firm samples cited in this book define *small business* as any firm reporting gross revenues of $5,000 or more in 1987. Table 9.1 provides detailed information about the financial-capital structure of black- and nonminority-owned firms that began operating during the 1979–87 period.

The figures in table 9.1 describe black business start-ups as more likely to begin operations with zero capital and less likely to borrow funds than white firms. Zero-capital start-ups are common in construction and service businesses, and most are tiny with no employees.

Also, a lower proportion of the aggregate capitalization of black firms is debt: capitalization is 55.6 percent debt for white-owned firms versus 50.7 percent for black-owned firms. Aggregate leverage (debt divided by equity) is 1.25 for white-owned firms versus 1.03 for black-owned firms (table 9.1). Among young firms nationwide that used financial capital at start-up, 55.0 percent of the nonminority operations used equity financing only, while 45.0 percent used equity and debt. The corresponding figures for black-owned firms were 59.9 percent and 40.5 percent, respectively.

A comparison of firms borrowing to finance start-up sheds light on the capital-gap issue:

	Firms formed after 1979 that borrowed to finance start-up	
	Nonminority	African American
Financial capital at start-up (mean)	$74,237	$35,842
Debt (mean)	$51,700	$25,073

Mean revenues in 1987 for the two groups of firms described above were $268,373 for white firms and $112,459 for black firms. Average sales revenues among the nonborrowers, in contrast, were $94,650 and $45,156, respectively, for the white- and black-owned businesses. No matter how the data are sorted and grouped, the black businesses show much lower average sales revenues than the white businesses.

Table 9.1

Start-up Capitalization among Small Businesses by Race-Ethnicity of Owner (Firms Formed since 1979 Only)

	Nonminorities	African Americans
Firm's traits		
Gross sales, 1987 (mean)	$154,274	$64,526
Total financial capital at start-up (mean)	$31,939	$14,226
Debt capital at start-up (mean)	$17,744	$7,216
Equity capital at start-up (mean)	$14,195	$7,010
Percent still operating in 1991	76.9%	73.6%
Capital Structure		
Leverage at start-up (debt divided by equity)	1.25	1.03
Percent of firms started with zero capital	23.7%	28.9%
Percent of firms using borrowed funds to finance start-up	34.4%	28.8%
Percent of firms borrowing $5,000 or more at start-up	23.6%	15.5%
Percent of firms started with equity capital of $25,000 or more	9.6%	5.0%
Owner's traits		
Percent college graduates	37.7%	30.2%

Source: U.S. Bureau of the Census, Characteristics of Business Owners (CBO) database, 1992.

Measuring the effects of various characteristics of firms and owners on sales revenues is difficult: they are inextricably linked to one another and operate simultaneously. So I used a multiple linear regression analysis with the CBO data to disentangle these influences and measure their effects. The regression analysis shows that of all the traits of owners and firms under consideration—the owner's education, managerial experience, contribution of labor, the age of the firm, the type of operation, and so forth—what most decisively explains the low sales of black firms is the low investment of financial capital. This conclusion is complemented by the finding that better-educated owners invest larger amounts of financial capital (Bates 1993b). Poorly capitalized, extremely small firms are more likely to go out of business than larger, better-capitalized operations.

Another way of highlighting the significance of the capital gap is to examine capital-intensive lines of small business. The following figures for manufacturing and wholesaling—the two most capital-intensive lines of small business—describe actual start-up financing for young black- and white-owned firms with paid employees that were operating in 1987:

	Manufacturing and wholesaling firms formed after 1979	
	Nonminority	African American
Gross sales, 1987 (mean)	$1,005,884	$394,208
Financial capital at start-up (mean)	$92,935	$37,571
Percent of firms started with equity capital of $25,000+	26.6%	13.1%
Debt (mean)	$54,452	$18,420
Equity (mean)	$38,483	$19,151
Leverage (mean)	1.41	0.96

Smaller young firms are much more likely to go out of business than larger young firms (Bates and Nucci 1989; Evans 1987). Table 9.2 shows that, among the young African American firms still active in late 1991, mean 1987 sales were $76,971, while 1987 sales averaged $29,819 for those that had gone out of business. (Table 9.2 describes the same firms as table 9.1, tracked to late 1991. The firms that closed down over the 1987–91 period are described separately from the firms that were still active in late 1991.)

A lag in firm size, rooted in low initial capitalization, predictably results in reduced survival prospects: this applies to all owners but is particularly applicable to African American owners because of their strikingly low mean initial capitalization. Note, further, that the surviving firms described in table 9.2 are more active borrowers and more highly leveraged than the discontinued small businesses. The firms that borrowed, on average, were larger and more successful.

To summarize, capitalization differences are enduring causes of disparities between black- and white-owned small businesses: Poorly capitalized firms generate low sales volumes; tiny firms often generate insufficient net revenues to provide a decent livelihood for the owner;

Table 9.2

Start-up Capitalization among White- and Black-Owned Small Businesses by Race-Ethnicity of Owner: Active versus Discontinued Firms, 1991 (Firms Formed since 1979 Only)

	Nonminority		African American	
	Active	Closed Down	Active	Closed Down
Firm's traits				
Gross sales, 1987 (mean)	$185,458	$50,602	$76,971	$29,819
Total financial capital at start-up (mean)	$36,301	$17,437	$16,454	$8,013
Debt capital at start-up (mean)	$20,414	$8,866	$8,563	$3,459
Equity capital at start-up (mean)	$15,886	$8,571	$7,891	$4,554
Capital Structure				
Leverage at start-up (debt divided by equity)	1.29	1.03	1.09	0.76
Percent of firms started with zero capital	20.2%	35.7%	26.1%	36.6%
Percent of firms using borrowed funds to finance start-up	37.2%	24.6%	30.1%	25.4%
Percent of firms borrowing $5,000 or more at start-up	26.3%	14.6%	16.7%	12.3%
Percent of firms started with equity capital of $25,000 or more	11.3%	3.8%	5.5%	3.4%
Owner's traits				
Percent college graduates	40.2%	29.5%	30.5%	29.4%

Source: U.S. Bureau of the Census, Characteristics of Business Owners (CBO) database, 1992.

and poorly capitalized, tiny firms disproportionately go out of business during the early years of operation.

Given the greater viability of firms that borrow, one might conclude that a greater availability of loans would produce increases in black business viability independent of other characteristics of firms or owners. But as was shown in chapter 8, this is often untrue. Debt cannot overcome deficiencies in the owner's human capital. Just as debt and equity are complements, so are the owner's human and financial capital. While the college graduate with a decade or more of relevant business experience may indeed benefit from greater debt access, evidence suggests that most potential borrowers with low incomes and without high-school degrees might not (Bates 1993b).

WHY IS NET WORTH SO LOW AMONG BLACK HOUSEHOLDS?

Studies of wealth among blacks and whites invariably cite enormous differences in the average household net worth of families whose incomes and educational backgrounds are similar (Blau and Graham 1990; Oliver and Shapiro 1995). Data on family wealth holdings, discussed in chapter 7, indicated that black households in 1984 had a median net worth of $3,397 versus $39,135 for white households (Jaynes and Williams 1989). Oliver and Shapiro (1995) reported nationwide mean household-net-worth figures of $95,667 for whites and $23,818 for blacks in 1988; median figures were $43,800 for whites and $3,700 for blacks. Households reporting high net worths typically have high incomes, own their own homes, and are headed by college graduates (Oliver and Shapiro 1995). None of this sheds light on why high-income, homeowning, black college graduates report vastly lower average net worths than similar whites. This section will explain these large differences, paying particular attention to high household wealth linked to self-employment entry (chapter 2).

Oliver and Shapiro fine-tuned their analysis by examining households in the $25,000–$50,000 income bracket; all of these households are headed by college graduates. In this middle-income group, mean household net worth nationwide was $74,922 for whites, $17,437 for blacks. Oliver and Shapiro then re-sorted the data to focus solely on households that held wealth in the form of small-business equity. Among white households, 10.9 percent owned all or part of a small business, and the median worth of this asset was $25,239. Only 2.4 percent of black households owned small-business net assets (median value of $10,000). Whatever subset of the population focused on, wealth-holding differences between whites and blacks were enormous.

Income differences, of course, are a major factor in explaining differences in wealth holdings between racial groups. The SIPP database that I used to analyze self-employment entry in chapter 2, I use again in this section to examine wealth differences between blacks and whites in a way that controls for income differences. I have ruled out an aversion to saving among blacks—hypothetically rooted in conspicuous consumption—as a cause of large-scale differences in wealth accumulation. Hamermesh (1982) and Alexis (1971) found that the savings rates typifying blacks exceed those of whites, while Galenson (1972) found that savings rates for blacks and whites were identical. No systematic study of the propensity to save suggests that savings behavior, by itself, is a cause of differences in household wealth accumulation. Blau and Graham (1990) conclude that differences in wealth among blacks and whites having identical incomes are largely rooted in racial differences in inheritance and other intergenerational transfers.

Table 9.3 reports OLS regression equations separately estimated for black and white households that explain the log of the dollar amount of household net worth. Drawn from the SIPP database, these households are representative of households nationwide that are made up of adults aged 21 to 60. Household income emerges as the most important single determinant of household wealth for blacks as well as whites. (Precise definitions of the dependent and explanatory variables in table 9.3 appear in the appendix, "Databases and Variable Definitions.") Beyond the similar income-wealth relationship, differences between blacks and whites are most stark when the relationship between age and net worth is examined. When income, education, and other factors are controlled for, the findings show that wealth accumulates steadily as white people grow older, but this positive relationship between age and net worth is entirely absent for blacks.[1] This finding is consistent with Blau and Graham's conclusion (1990) that whites are more likely than blacks to inherit wealth.

Also noteworthy are the racial differences in the values of the intercept terms (table 9.3). These differences suggest that white households, on average, hold substantially higher wealth than blacks who are otherwise identical regarding the explanatory variables in table 9.3—income, education, age, home ownership, and so forth. Blau and Graham attribute such differences to gifts—"transfers in the form of, for example, money for college, a down payment on a house, or a share in a family-owned business" (1990, 325). Gifts and inheritances are much more likely to be forthcoming if one's parents have significant wealth. As Oliver and Shapiro note, "Among our white interviewees with living parents, most had an idea of what they would inherit. Stacie is in line for $100,000. Perhaps this sum contributes to her optimistic,

Table 9.3

OLS Regression Explaining Household Net Worth for Owners
Aged 21 to 60

Regression equations	Regression coefficient	
	Nonminority households	Black households
Intercept	−4.464[a]	−6.369[a]
Education		
High school	.445[a]	.261
College, 1–3 years	.589[a]	.680[a]
College graduate	.704[a]	.798[a]
Graduate school	.615[a]	.950[a]
Age	.059[a]	−.018
Age^2	−.0003[a]	.001
Household income	.992[a]	1.022[a]
Owns home	3.422[a]	4.872[a]
Kids	−.329[a]	−.593[a]
MSA	.093[a]	−.090
N	21,381	2,693
R^2	.427	.539
F	1,589.9	284.7
	Mean values, explanatory variables	
Education		
High school	.38	.36
College, 1–3 years	.24	.22
College graduate	.11	.06
Graduate school	.11	.05
Age	38.0	37.0
Age^2	1,574	1,495
Household income	$34,891	$22,673
Owns home	.71	.49
Kids	.50	.62
MSA	.73	.84

Source: U.S. Bureau of the Census, Survey of Income and Program Participation (SIPP) database, 1988.

Note: Variables are defined in the appendix, "Databases and Variables," pp. 268–70.

[a]Statistically significant at the 5-percent level.

self-assured, and independent attitude with regard to the debts and challenges she faces. Among the white families we interviewed, everyone has inherited or will inherit hard assets" (1995, 155–56). Most of the black respondents, in contrast, did not expect inheritances.

Home ownership emerges from the results of the regression exercises in table 9.3 as a very important source of net worth accumulation. Differences in black and white rates of home ownership point out how wealth accumulation patterns can differ substantially among households reporting similar incomes. Oliver and Shapiro (1995) reported the following home ownership rates for 1988:

Household income	White households	Black households
$25,000–34,999	61.5%	45.4%
$35,000–49,999	76.5%	66.8%
$50,000+	85.4%	75.0%
All	63.8%	41.6%

These differences are also partially rooted in the substantial intergenerational wealth-holding patterns typifying whites and blacks. "Many bankers suggested that young white couples are more likely than blacks to receive parental help in buying a first house. Given the superior financial position of middle-aged and older whites, it is not surprising that the parents of young white couples are more apt to be in a position to help. Conversely, SIPP informs us that the likelihood of similar parental assistance for young blacks is minimal" (Oliver and Shapiro 1995, 145). This same phenomenon, of course, is highly applicable to racial differences in parental help available to finance a small business.

The SIPP database used in table 9.3 is responsible for the comprehensiveness of Oliver and Shapiro's 1995 analysis of wealth, which has frequently been cited in this chapter. The SIPP data permit a degree of sophistication previously unobtainable in studies of differences between blacks and whites in self-employment entry, home ownership, and wealth accumulation generally.[2]

This book has shown that new-firm creation is commonly financed by the owner's equity, which is derived almost entirely from household net worth, and from investments (largely loans) from outsiders, such as financial institutions, friends, and family. Outside investors typically expect a substantial portion of the owner's own funds to be invested in the firm. The owner's investment of his or her own funds provides an incentive and ensures that there is sufficient collateral to protect outside investors. Thus, both directly and as an inducement to outside investors, the owner's equity and its source—household net worth— are key ingredients of business formation.

IVAN LIGHT'S POSITION: FINANCIAL CAPITAL IS NOT A BARRIER

According to Light and Rosenstein (1995), lack of household wealth, and hence small-business equity financing, is not a barrier to entrepreneurial ambitions: the notion that financial-capital barriers retard small-business start-up and operation is a "myth." Similarly, discriminatory lending practices by banks are not seen as a barrier. Light and Rosenstein acknowledge the existence of "destructive lending and investment policies of mainstream financial institutions," but assert that "Asian immigrants are acquiring capital despite these obstacles" (220).

The evidence on firm capitalization put forth by Light and Rosenstein in their 1995 book, along with similar evidence that appears in Light's earlier work, is hard to evaluate because its empirical underpinnings are unclear. This flaw, however, has not prevented Light's interpretation of financial-capital barriers from becoming widely accepted in contemporary social science literature (Meyer 1990). The capitalization patterns described in this chapter are broadly applicable to Asian-immigrant-owned firms, as shown in earlier chapters of this book. The analysis of rates of survival and discontinuance for white- and black-owned firms from table 9.2 is replicated for young Asian-immigrant firms in table 9.4; the results do not support Light and Rosenstein's position on capital barriers.

Broadly, the comparisons summarized in table 9.4 reveal that the same patterns that delineated stronger from weaker black-owned firms also apply to the firms of Asian immigrants. Table 9.4 documents that poorly capitalized, extremely small Asian-immigrant-owned firms are the ones that most often go out of business. The Asian-owned operations that had closed down by late 1991 resembled nonminority closures, but were somewhat smaller both in terms of mean start-up capital and 1987 sales. Average start-up capital among the survivors was nearly four times greater than for discontinued businesses ($62,246 ver-

Table 9.4

Start-up Capitalization among Asian-Immigrant-Owned Small Businesses: Active versus Discontinued Firms, 1991 (Firms Formed since 1979 Only)

	Asian-immigrant owner	
	Active	Closed down
Firm's traits		
Gross sales, 1987 (mean)	$138,996	$46,294
Total financial capital at start-up (mean)	$62,246	$15,914
Debt capital at start-up (mean)	$31,651	$5,330
Equity capital at start-up (mean)	$30,595	$10,584
Capital Structure		
Leverage at start-up (debt divided by equity)	1.03	0.50
Percent started with zero capital	14.0%	26.1%
Percent using borrowed funds to finance start-up	48.6%	35.9%
Percent of firms borrowing $5,000 or more at start-up	39.0%	19.2%
Percent of firms started with equity capital of $25,000 or more	28.6%	12.3%
Owner's traits		
Percent college graduates	57.2%	60.5%

Source: U.S. Bureau of the Census, Characteristics of Business Owners (CBO) database, 1992.

sus $15,914), and the sales of the latter group lagged far behind those of surviving firms. The closed Asian-immigrant firms stand out as having very low levels of debt and leverage, even though 35.9 percent of them (versus 24.6 percent of the nonminority closures) used borrowed funds to finance start-up. Like the small firms described previously, the surviving Asian-immigrant-owned small businesses were more likely to borrow and were more highly leveraged than the closed firms.

Light and Rosenstein (1995) support their position on the irrelevance of financial-capital barriers by noting that entrepreneurs often start firms with little or no financial capital investment. Because Light and Rosenstein analyze PUMS data, a data source that offers no information on either household net worth or small-business capitalization, the factual underpinnings of their position are unclear. On the assumption that Light's previous research documented the financial-capital barrier myth he hypothesizes, I reviewed his earlier study (Light, Kwuon, and Zhong 1990), "Korean Rotating Credit Associations in Los Angeles." This study implies that access to loan capital is a very real problem: "Obtaining loan capital poses an obstacle for all small business ventures, but the problem is especially severe for immigrant or ethnic minority entrepreneurs, who lack credit ratings, collateral, or are the victims of ethno-racial discrimination" (Light, Kwuon, and Zhong 1990, 35). But it does not necessarily contradict Light's position that one needs little or no capital to start a business.

The key source cited by Light and Rosenstein (1995) to support their position that firm formation requires little or no capital is a 1988 study by Fratoe. Since Fratoe's study relies on CBO data—the same data source used throughout this book—reconciling his findings with the facts in this study should be straightforward. According to Fratoe, "One of the most interesting facts disclosed by the CBO study is that the majority of all business owners initiated their enterprises with little or no financial capital" (1988, 39). Fratoe defines a "small business" as anyone who generated gross sales of at least $50 from self-employment in 1982 and filed a schedule C (proprietorship) form with his or her 1982 federal income-tax return. About 40 percent of proprietorships thus defined generated gross self-employment sales of less than $5,000 in 1982; that is, most proprietors were wage or salary earners who earned small amounts of self-employment revenue. Indeed, most of these casual small businesses with total sales of less than $5,000 were started with little or no financial capital.

Fratoe, Light, and I certainly agree that one needs little or no financial capital to generate gross self-employment revenues of several hundred, or even several thousand, dollars a year. But we disagree about whether this constitutes a small business. Throughout this study, casual self-employment activity has been delineated from small-business ownership: a $5,000-revenue cutoff has been applied whenever CBO data are used, and small businesses are defined as only those meeting the $5,000 cutoff (see the appendix, "Databases and Variable Definitions"). To Fratoe and Light, anyone who held a Tupperware party that produced sales of $100 is a small-business proprietor; in this book, the Tupperware seller was engaged in casual self-employment but had not started a small business.

A reasonable interpretation of Ivan Light's collective writings on self-employment is that financial capital is a barrier to starting a substantive small business, but Asian immigrants circumvent it by relying on RCAs to finance business start-up and operation (1972; Light, Kwuon, and Zhong 1990). Thus, financial capital is not a barrier to Asian immigrants because arrangements made among friends and acquaintances circumvent the problem. There are two serious difficulties with this position. First, the evidence from chapter 6 suggests that reliance on RCAs to finance business formation is minimal. Second, the scant evidence on RCAs and similar groups indicate that their lending practices might be more accurately described as loan sharking.

Breaking away from sociology's mainstream, Portes and Sensenbrenner (1993) detail specific ways in which the use of social capital actually hinders immigrant-owned small businesses operating in the United States. Their starkest criticism of informal community lending arrangements is the phenomenally high interest rates paid by small-business borrowers: "Nicholas had two active loans—one for $125,000 and the other for $200,000—only one of which was accompanied by some signed papers. He was paying a monthly interest of 2.6 percent" (Portes and Sensenbrenner 1993, 1334). My examination of loan interest rates paid by Korean business borrowers in New York City also revealed that RCAs were a phenomenally expensive credit source. According to one Korean-immigrant lender that regularly undercut the RCAs by offering lower-cost credit, "the high local demand for small business loans creates a situation whereby business persons belonging to the RCAs bid against each other for the right to borrow, and this bidding often drives business loan charges into the 30–40 percent range" (Bates 1995a, 99). Another loan source specializing in financing dry-cleaning establishments in New York City dismissed RCAs as competitors, noting that they specialized in short-term loans carrying monthly interest charges of 3 percent or more (Bates 1995a).

Light, Kwuon, and Zhong, in their study of Korean RCAs (called *kye*) operating in Los Angeles, offer indirect evidence of the costs incurred by small businesses borrowing from these organizations: "As recipients of usurious, tax-evading interest income, kye users do not wish to identify themselves to policemen or tax authorities . . . . Interest rates earned by kye members in the United States generally exceed 30 percent a year . . ." (1990, 41): deliciously high interest income to the lender is a usurious rate to the borrower.

All of the above indicates that small businesses borrowing from RCAs incur annual interest charges in excess of 30 percent. This high cost of business debt would explain why Asian-immigrant entrepreneurs prefer to get start-up loans from mainstream financial institutions. The usurious rates imposed by RCAs would also explain why Yoon observed that Korean-owned firms in Chicago borrowed from banks if possible, seeing the *kye* as a lender of last resort: strong firms borrow from banks; weak firms rely on the *kye*'s expensive credit: "Korean immigrants who are disadvantaged in bank loans because of their insufficient credit status can overcome a shortage of capital by using a kye" (Yoon 1991b, 195). At interest rates of 30 percent or higher, however, it is unclear whether the RCA customer has solved the capitalization problem: cost of credit may simply replace access to credit as the firm's most pressing financial problem. With or without the RCA, financial capital is a barrier to small-firm formation and survival. The evidence available to date does not support Light's hypothesis that financial capital is not a barrier. This issue will be pursued further in chapter 10.

CONCLUSION

Small businesses that finance their start-up, in part, with borrowed funds tend to be larger, more successful firms, and African American businesses are no exception. Among white-, Asian-immigrant- and black-owned firms summarized in table 9.5, the borrowers in every case reported mean 1987 sales that were more than double those of similar nonborrowers. Survival rates among the nonborrowers, in turn, consistently lag behind those of the firms using debt to finance their start-up. Using debt at start-up typifies stronger firms, and limited access to such debt, in turn, constrains the size and the scope of the black business community.

Past studies have consistently noted that blacks are less likely than whites to have their business loans approved (Ando 1988), and the loans they do receive from financial institutions are much smaller than those flowing to white business borrowers (Bates 1993b). Ando's 1988 study of bank-loan availability for established businesses found that only 61.7 percent of the short-term loan applications from black firms were accepted by banks versus 89.9 percent from white firms. Even when the borrower's level of credit risk was controlled for statistically, Ando found that black-owned businesses were much more likely to be denied bank loans than those owned by nonminorities.

Table 9.5
Start-up Capitalization among Small Firms: Borrowers versus
Nonborrowers (Firms Formed since 1979 Only)

	Borrowers	Nonborrowers
Gross sales, 1987 (mean)		
Black owners	$112,459	$45,156
White owners	$268,373	$94,650
Asian-immigrant owners	$167,725	$81,970
Percent of firms still operating, 1991		
Black owners	77.0%	72.2%
White owners	83.4%	73.4%
Asian-immigrant owners	85.4%	76.6%

Source: U.S. Bureau of the Census, Characteristics of Business Owners (CBO) database, 1992.

Note: Variables are defined in the appendix, "Databases and Variable Definitions," pp. 270–3.

Black-owned businesses seeking start-up capital also receive much smaller mean loans from banks than do white-owned businesses: the average black-owned business start-up borrowing from a financial institution (table 9.6) received a $31,958 loan, as opposed to $56,784 for the average white-owned business.

Yet differences in loan size, by themselves, do not indicate differential treatment. Owners of black firms successfully raising debt capital from financial institutions have, on average, less equity investment than white owners; they are less likely, furthermore, to be college graduates and to have managerial experience. Still, when these traits are controlled for statistically, black borrowers still receive fewer loan dollars than whites per dollar of equity capital invested in the business at start-up. Comparisons in table 9.6 indicate that financial institutions, on average, extend $3.10 in debt for each $1 of equity capital white owners have invested in their small business; the corresponding figure for blacks borrowing from financial institutions is $2.69. Closing that gap would benefit black business borrowers. The larger remaining gap, however, is in the underlying small-business equity investments that owners leverage when they receive bank loans: mean equity for white borrowers was $18,317 versus $11,880 for black borrowers. Gaps in financing are rooted more fundamentally in differences in equity capital among black- and white-owned firms than in different treatment of blacks and whites by banks. Household wealth—particularly regarding

Table 9.6
Debt Sources, Loan Sizes, and Leverage for Borrowers (Firms Formed since 1979 Only)

	Nonminorities	African Americans
Loan source		
Family	26.8%	21.2%
Friends	6.4%	11.3%
Financial institution	65.9%	59.1%
Former owner	6.1%	2.8%
Loan size by source (mean)		
Family	$35,446	$18,306
Friends	$30,907	$16,444
Financial institution	$56,784	$31,958
Former owner	$97,225	$54,188
Leverage (total debt for all borrowers divided by total equity for all borrowers)		
Family	2.32	2.22
Friends	2.03	2.15
Financial institution	3.10	2.69
Former owner	3.69	2.96

Source: U.S. Bureau of the Census, Characteristics of Business Owners (CBO) database, 1992.

Note: Variables are defined in the appendix, "Databases and Variable Definitions," pp. 270–3.

differences in intergenerational transfers of wealth—are holding back black business formation, growth, and survival. This barrier will fade only as the wealth of the black community grows.

NOTES

1. The wealth regression in table 9.3 must be interpreted with some caution. Three vitally important wealth determinants—education, income, and home ownership—are strongly related. The highly educated tend to earn high incomes; high income earners are more likely than others to be home owners. Such relationships among explanatory variables create some instability in regression coefficient values. It would therefore be risky, for example, to compare coefficients attached to household income for blacks and whites and conclude that blacks (coefficient = 1.022) accumulate more wealth per dollar of income than whites (coefficient = .992). I have avoided such comparisons in chapter 9, which stresses differences in regres-

sion coefficients, particularly for the ages of individuals, that do not suffer from problems of relatedness among variables. Definitions of variables are spelled out in the appendix, "Databases and Variable Definitions."

2. The SIPP wealth variable is a conventional measure of household net worth, that is, household assets (including deposits in financial institutions, other interest-earning assets, stocks and mutual fund shares, rental property, mortgages held by home sellers, equity in their own businesses, motor vehicles, and other financial assets) minus debts (including credit card and store debt, bank loans, and other unsecured debts). Note that assets such as one's home are measured net of secured debt. The wealth variable excludes assets such as personal clothing and home furnishings. It focuses on assets that are active rather than passive: home equity, for example, could serve as collateral to raise funds to enter self-employment, whereas personal clothing could not.

CHAPTER TEN

Entrepreneurship as a Route to Upward Mobility
among the Disadvantaged

Scholarly studies have failed to produce hard evidence that entrepreneurship in the United States today is an effective strategy for bootstrapping one's way out of poverty. Some scholars, nonetheless, assert that poor, hard-working minorities are doing just that. Yoon (1991b), for example, claims that small business has been a route for disadvantaged minorities to achieve upward social and economic mobility, but his study contains no analysis (or definition) of success or upward mobility. Claiming that businesses can be started without financial capital, Light and Rosenstein (1995) contend that "immigrants show us how the feat is accomplished"; further, "immigrants in general are less endowed with class resources of money and education than are the native born in general, but the immigrants nonetheless manage higher rates of self-employment than do the native born" (220). These claims are hard to assess, since they are often assertions. In fact, nationwide data from the U.S. Census Bureau document that immigrant business owners start their firms, on average, with significantly more financial capital than nonimmigrants and that they are also better educated, although not by a wide margin.[1] The findings summarized in this chapter, nonetheless, successfully identify a group of the self-employed that confirms Light's hypothesis: at least some immigrants without money or education are doing well in self-employment.

Analyses in previous chapters have shown that self-employment entrants are disproportionately well educated and affluent. More profitable firms prone to remain in operation generally are well capitalized and run by college-educated owners. Owners with the least human and financial capital have simply been aggregated into broader small-business groupings throughout this study. It is time to single them out: exactly who are these owners, and what sorts of businesses do they operate? Is the ubiquitous mom-and-pop retail store in fact a pathway to affluence for those willing to devote long hours to operating their own small business? The fact that most Asian-immigrant small-business owners are college-educated does not rule out investigation of such questions. Even if over 70 percent of the Korean-immigrant owners of retail stores are college educated, the residual less well educated group is large, and it is worthwhile to study their success in self-employment. The U.S. Bureau of the Census CBO database is certainly large enough to facilitate such an investigation.[2]

MINORITY-OWNED FIRMS STARTED WITH MINIMAL HUMAN AND FINANCIAL CAPITAL

Table 10.1 describes minority-owned businesses nationwide whose owners were not high-school graduates; all of these owners started firms between 1979 and 1987 with investments of under $5,000. Over half of these firms had immigrant owners, but most were Hispanic; Asian owners were rare overall in this small-business subset. Nearly half (46.9 percent) of the firms described in table 10.1 were started with no investment of financial capital whatsoever. Gross sales in 1987 were typically low, with 61.6 percent of the firms generating total revenues of under $20,000. Yet these firms were often vitally important contributors to household income; 46.7 percent of the owners reported that earnings from their small businesses were the major source of household income. Low household income was commonplace among this population of the self-employed: 48.8 percent of them reported household incomes from all sources of under $15,000. But it certainly was not universal. Self-employment among high-school dropouts starting firms on a shoestring is not synonymous with working poverty.

Firm longevity (table 10.1) was lower among the sparse human- and financial-capital group than among small businesses generally—70.8

Table 10.1

Traits of Minority-Owned Businesses Started with Minimal Human and Financial Capital (Firms Formed since 1979 Only)

Firm's traits	
Gross sales, 1987 (mean)	$33,054
Percent with gross 1987 sales under $20,000	61.6%
Number of employees (mean)	0.3
Percent with no paid employees	92.9%
Total financial capital at start-up (mean)	$1,354
Percent started with no financial capital	46.9%
Percent of firms still operating, 1991	70.8%
Owner's traits	
Annual owner-labor input in hours (mean)	1,664.7
Percent relying on business for 50 percent or more of household income	46.7%
Percent with total household income under $15,000	48.8%
Married	79.3%
Gender	77.9%
Black	30.0%
Hispanic	57.4%
Asian immigrant	8.4%
Other minority	4.2%
Business groups	
Retail	16.9%
Various services industries	35.5%
Construction	22.8%
Transportation	11.3%
Agriculture services, forestry	7.4%
Other	6.1%

Source: U.S. Bureau of the Census, Characteristics of Business Owners (CBO) database, 1992.

Note: Variables are defined in the appendix, "Databases and Variable Definitions," pp. 270–3.

percent of these firms were still operating in late 1991 versus 77.2 percent of all young firms nationwide (chapter 2 appendix). Recall that high-school dropouts were actually more likely to be associated with surviving firms than high-school graduates, other things being equal (chapter 2). This is because of opportunity costs: lacking the range of opportunities available to better-educated business owners, high-school dropouts who can manage to set up their own businesses often cling tenaciously to self-employment. Barriers to self-employment entry hold down the self-employment rate among high-school dropouts more than high firm failure rates.

Self-employment is not a lucrative activity for most of the high-school dropout entrepreneurs: 61.6 percent of the firms generated before-tax profits of under $10,000 in 1987. Yet a significant subset did well, with 9.7 percent of the firms netting $25,000 or more. What sort of individual, lacking a high-school diploma and financial resources, does well in small business? Looking solely at firms netting $10,000 or more before taxes in 1987, a clear-cut profile emerges. The successful person in this self-employment niche is most commonly a man working in construction.

People in construction nationwide, in fact, have the highest self-employment rate (over 22 percent) of any major business group in the United States (Devine and Mlaker 1992). The majority of those employed in construction work in a skilled craft, such as carpentry or plumbing, and it is the skilled craftsperson who is most apt to be self-employed. Among those described in table 10.1, Hispanics and blacks in construction were quite common, Asian immigrants (and women) were quite rare. Chapter 2's analysis indicated that self-employment entrants in construction were largely white males. The way work is allocated in construction tends to bar skilled minority construction workers—employees and self-employed—from practicing their crafts (Waldinger and Bailey 1991; Bates and Howell 1997). Discriminatory barriers limit nonimmigrant minority access to training in skilled crafts. Becoming a skilled sheet-metal worker is nearly impossible for minorities growing up in the New York City area (Waldinger and Bailey 1991).

In Mexico, Haiti, and Jamaica, however, there is no counterpart to the U.S. phenomenon of white male old-boy networks in construction that minimize access to skills for people outside the applicable networks, including most minorities. Thus, in 1987 skilled minority construction workers who were self-employed were often immigrants, including most Hispanics and over 40 percent of blacks with small construction businesses in the New York City area (Bates 1993a). Among the estimated 4,627 minority-owned construction firms operating in the New York City region that year, over 60 percent were immigrant owned, and 37.3 percent of the 4,627 owners had not completed high school.[3]

Thus, Light's hypothesis that immigrants lacking education and wealth can successfully penetrate the U.S. small-business realm does seem valid for construction workers who acquire their skills prior to immigration: many of them do pursue self-employment, and they stand out from other high-school dropouts with little wealth in that most generated $10,000 or more in net self-employment income.

But the self-employed immigrant in construction who lacks a high-school degree, while a counterexample, is nonetheless tangential. First of all, while possessing a skill, such as carpentry, is an important form of human capital, it is not one that is adequately measured by the available small-business databases. So, while this book may be flawed by incomplete measures of the human capital that befits one for self-employment, this is a database deficiency, not a failure of the underlying analyses. Second, discovering successfully self-employed immigrant high-school dropouts in construction is a diversion from this book's focus on Asian-immigrant and native-born black small-business owners. This niche is less available to African Americans because they are not immigrants, and self-employed Asian-immigrant high-school dropouts are so rare in construction that quantitative analysis is an impossibility, although the paucity of such business owners does reveal that construction is rarely a route to upward mobility among Asian-immigrant high-school dropouts without financial resources.

To return to the focus of this book, I would like to look at the 8.4 percent of the high-school dropout business owners described in table 10.1 who were Asian immigrants. In order to incorporate Asian immigrants into the analysis of those for whom self-employment was the road to upward mobility, it is necessary to look at the kind of businesses available to such owners. In fact, Asian immigrants who never attended college commonly run small-scale retail firms. Is ownership of a retail small business a path to upward mobility for disadvantaged Asian immigrants? Since running a mom-and-pop retail store is widely associated with Asian-immigrant entrepreneurship (Bonacich and Light 1988), it is investigated below.

SUCCESS IN RETAILING AMONG OWNERS WHO HAVE NOT ATTENDED COLLEGE

Retailing among self-employed Asian immigrants is most frequent among Koreans and the Chinese, so their success in retailing will be compared to that of African American and nonminority owners who have not attended college. (The focus on Korean and Chinese business owners facilitates comparisons with chapter 6's discussion of firm financing.) The findings, in fact, accurately describe immigrant experiences in retailing generally (see the appendix to this chapter). Among blacks and Korean or Chinese owners who have not attended college, financial returns to retail-firm operation are very low and quite similar. Yet Korean- and Chinese-owned firms stand out in terms of the sources and the amounts of their financing. By focusing on this relatively backward, unsuccessful subset of Asian-immigrant business owners, a pattern of using social capital to finance firm start-up emerges that conforms to popular stereotypes about capitalizing business formation without relying on mainstream financial institutions.

Relative to blacks and nonminorities, the immigrant Korean and Chinese owners of young retail firms described in table 10.2 are less likely to report household incomes exceeding $15,000, and they are more likely to rely heavily on self-employment earnings to support their households. Only 23.0 percent reported little reliance on self-employment income to support their households versus 46.9 percent and 39.9 percent of the blacks and whites owning retail operations. The incidence of household incomes below $15,000 among less well educated Korean and Chinese retail-firm owners was nearly as high as the 48.8 percent incidence reported by high-school dropout minority business owners in table 10.1. Yet these owners worked over 50 hours a week (on average) in their businesses (table 10.3) in 1987, and they invested a mean of nearly $53,000 in financial capital to launch their retail ventures; in contrast, blacks and whites on average invested $13,692 and $40,519, respectively, to start their retail firms.

The portrait of the typical less well educated Korean- or Chinese-immigrant owner of a retail store is one of heavy start-up investment, long hours of work, and low family income. Low household incomes are rooted in the low returns generated by small retail businesses—$12,978 before-tax profits in 1987 for the average Korean- or Chinese-owned firm. Low profitability comes most clearly into focus when it is broken down into the owner's returns on capital and labor invested in the retail operation. Among the Koreans and Chinese working full-time in their retail ventures (at least 2,000 hours in 1987), on average owners worked 3,254 hours, and their equity investment to launch the firm was $37,315. Attributing a 10 percent return to the owner's investment of equity capital ($3,732) and the balance of 1987 profits to labor, the average financial return to the owner per hour worked was $3.65 (table 10.3). (In cases where unpaid family members contribute to running the business, the owner's implicit wage of $3.65 per hour is leveraged

Table 10.2

Young Retail Firms with Owners Who Did Not Attend College (Firms Formed since 1979 Only)

	Immigrant Korean and Chinese	African American	Nonminority
Percent with total household income under $15,000, 1987	42.7%	39.6%	29.5%
Percent with total household income of $75,000, 1987	2.6%	1.9%	2.5%
Household income from self-employment under 10 percent	23.0%	46.9%	39.9%
Household income from self-employment 75 percent or more	45.4%	20.3%	30.9%

Source: U.S. Bureau of the Census, Characteristics of Business Owners (CBO) database, 1992.

upward, and the profit-per-hour figure for total family labor is lower than $3.65.) This is basically identical to the $3.66-per-hour return accruing to black retail-store owners who have not attended college, but well below the $5.13 an hour typifying white owners (table 10.3).

Three obvious facts about immigrant upward mobility and the experiences of Koreans and Chinese in self-employment are: (1) that Korean and Chinese immigrants are overrepresented in small-business operation, relative to the U.S. population overall; (2) that Korean and Chinese immigrants who own small businesses are heavily overrepresented in retailing, relative to all small businesses in the United States that were operating in 1987; and (3) that retailing offers lower profits to Korean- and Chinese-immigrant owners on average than small-business ownership in any other major business group. Despite working an average of 63 hours per week (3,254 hours per year) in the retail firm, the full-time Korean or Chinese owner barely makes a poverty-level income (table 10.3).

Oddly, sociologists commonly equate high rates of self-employment with immigrant success in small business. Yoon's well-documented

Table 10.3

Traits of Retail Firms Whose Owners Did Not Attend College, 1987
(Firms Formed since 1979 Only)

	Immigrant Korean and Chinese	African American	Nonminority
Firm's traits			
Gross sales, 1987 (mean)	$139,177	$83,624	$217,621
Total financial capital at start-up (mean)	$52,968	$13,692	$40,519
Number of employees (mean)	2.7	0.7	2.5
Percent of firms still operating, 1991	87.6%	78.3%	77.4%
Owner's traits			
Percent with less than 4 years of high school	54.7%	41.0%	26.4%
Annual owner-labor input in hours (mean)	2,634	1,849	2,131
Before-tax profits, 1987 (mean)			
All firms	$12,978	$8,076	$12,217
Firms with owners working full-time in the business	$15,610	$11,939	$17,451
Annual owner-labor input in hours (mean)	3,254	2,974	3,017
Equity capital (mean)	$37,315	$10,631	$19,769
Profits, less 10 percent equity return, divided by hours worked	$3.65	$3.66	$5.13

Source: U.S. Bureau of the Census, Characteristics of Business Owners (CBO) database, 1992.

Note: Variables are defined in the appendix, "Databases and Variable Definitions," pp. 270–3.

study of Korean firms operating in African American communities in Chicago is typical (1991b). Are the Korean- and Chinese-immigrant owners of retail operations described in table 10.3 successful? Among this group, 42.7 percent reported total household incomes under $15,000 in 1987 versus 29.5 percent of their nonminority cohorts. Their returns from self-employment should be seen, not as evidence of success, but as a reflection of the lack of opportunities available to Korean and Chinese immigrants in the U.S. labor market (chapters 4,

5; Borjas 1994). Heavy concentration in the lowest yielding business niche suggests that self-employment is often a state of underemployment in which immigrant store owners are trapped. What sort of interpretation of the widespread presence of subminimum wage returns to retail store owners permits Yoon to claim that disadvantaged minorities achieve upward mobility by running small businesses? Success in the context of self-employment is a concept sorely in need of elaboration.

FINANCING ENTRY INTO RETAILING

While evidence of upward mobility through retail-store ownership is sparse, the Korean and Chinese owners described in table 10.3 do stand out in one sense: discontinuance rates for their firms were only 12.4 percent overall for the 1987–91 period, whereas black and white retail-store owners saw their firms close at much higher rates—21.7 percent and 22.6 percent respectively. Furthermore, the closure rate from 1987 to 1991 among all young Korean- and Chinese-immigrant-owned firms was 18.1 percent (chapter 5), far higher than the rate at which cohort retail-store owners who had no college background discontinued operations.

A paucity of attractive alternatives would explain this very low closure rate among Korean and Chinese retail-store owners. Access to capital would too. When Light and Rosenstein (1995) asserted that two-thirds of all entrepreneurs in every ethnoracial category either required no capital or started their business without borrowing any capital, they certainly were not describing the experiences of retail stores owned by Korean and Chinese immigrants. Borrowing helped 67.1 percent of these firms get started (table 10.4). Borrowing among retail-store owners without a college education was more frequent than among young Korean and Chinese businesses generally, where a 53.4 percent borrowing rate typified the sample. Of the loan sources described in table 10.4, loans from financial institutions were most common among the nonminorities but least common among the Koreans and the Chinese.

It is likely that many of the Korean and Chinese immigrants who own retail firms would have been unable to assemble the requisite start-up capital in the absence of nontraditional debt sources. In terms of leverage, the indebtedness of the Korean and Chinese borrowers is low ($1.16 in debt per dollar of equity versus $2.10 among nonminorities).

Table 10.4

Debt Financing Patterns among Retail Firms Whose Owners Did Not
Attend College (Firms Formed since 1979 Only)

	Immigrant Korean and Chinese	African American	Nonminority
Percent of firms borrowing to finance start-up	67.1%	32.6%	43.2%
Capital structure of borrowing firms			
Debt (mean)	$31,782	$19,741	$42,531
Equity (mean)	$27,494	$9,246	$20,268
Leverage (debt divided by equity)	1.16	2.13	2.10
Loan size by source (mean)			
Family	$31,582	$16,033	$24,842
Friends	$29,906	$17,806	$13,766
Financial institution	$32,022	$25,709	$46,677
Former owner	$41,487	$25,712	$84,723
Percent borrowing from source			
Family	52.9%	24.6%	24.2%
Friends	22.9%	13.2%	7.2%
Financial institution	32.7%	59.3%	69.6%
Former owner	23.6%	8.4%	9.6%
Leverage (total debt divided by total equity for all borrowers)			
Family	0.97	1.49	1.15
Friends	0.72	1.83	1.31
Financial institution	1.87	2.50	2.65
Former owner	1.51	2.61	4.41

Source: U.S. Bureau of the Census, Characteristics of Business Owners (CBO) database, 1992.

Note: Variables are defined in the appendix, "Databases and Variable Definitions," pp. 270–3.

However, leverage is only one aspect of credit availability; the higher
overall incidence of borrowing by Korean and Chinese immigrants,
including those in the low-yielding retailing field, consistently delineates them from other groups. Firms that might not otherwise exist
are one outcome of their high propensity to borrow from friends and
family.

The Korean- and Chinese-owned firms that borrow (table 10.4) tend to be high equity investment–low leverage firms, the same pattern observed in chapter 6. The average Korean or Chinese retail firm started with an owner's equity capital investment of $27,494, nearly three times higher than the corresponding $9,246 figure invested by black owners. Each dollar of equity invested by black retailers who did not attend college generated $2.13 in debt, on average, among those using borrowed funds at start-up: the 2.13 leverage figure for black borrowers was nearly twice as high as the 1.16 leverage mean among Korean and Chinese immigrants. These differences between borrowers are stark: black retailers rely on low equity and high leverage, while Korean and Chinese owners have a high equity—low leverage financial structure.

Yet the Korean and Chinese firms described in table 10.4 do stand out for their much higher reliance on family and friends for loans. In the retail niche, black and white owners without college credentials continue to rely overwhelmingly on financial institutions for debt, while Korean and Chinese owners rely largely on nonbank sources. This marginal niche of low-profit retail firms is much less reliant on bank financing than the broader Asian-immigrant small-business community.

How do the low-yielding retail firms stay in business? Table 10.5 addresses this question by estimating a logistic regression equation to delineate small retail firms operating in 1987 and 1991 from firms operating in 1987 that had closed down by 1991. Positive regression coefficient values are associated with firms still operating in 1991 and negative coefficient values with those that had closed down. (Precise definitions of explanatory variables are spelled out in the appendix, "Databases and Variable Definitions.")

Asian-immigrant-owned firms stood out from nonminority- and black-owned firms in the econometric analyses of earlier chapters because the owners were much better educated and the firms were better capitalized and concentrated in less lucrative business niches. The Korean and Chinese owners analyzed here, like the white and black owners under consideration, are all in the same business—retailing—and all lack college credentials. All owners also suffer from the limited access to professional and managerial jobs that typifies people in the United States who have not gone beyond high school. Absent differences in business and education, four traits continue to distinguish the Korean- and Chinese-owned firms under consideration: (1) firms are

Table 10.5

Logistic Regression Explaining Survival of Young Retail Firms
Whose Owners Did Not Attend College, 1987–91 (Firms Formed
since 1979 Only)

	Regression coefficient	Regression coefficient standard error	Variable mean
Constant	−2.075[a]	.855	—
Education: high school	.334[a]	.163	.749
Managerial experience	−.579[a]	.160	.236
Bought ongoing firm	.542[a]	.157	.335
Married	−.274	.185	.821
Age	.175[a]	.038	44.080
Age^2	−.002[a]	.0004	2,090.9
Gender	.490[a]	.140	.638
Black	.199	.408	.027
Asian immigrant	.595	.516	.027
Owner-labor input	.000	.001	21.149
Number of employees	.053[a]	.022	2.560
Capital	.040[a]	.022	8.716
Leverage	−.049[a]	.009	3.677
Loan source: family, friends	.479[a]	.224	.145
Entered			
1984–85	−.417[a]	.207	.213
1986	−.866[a]	.211	.165
1987	−1.498[a]	.194	.285
Minority clientele	−.133	.168	.193

Source: U.S. Bureau of the Census, Characteristics of Business Owners (CBO) database, 1992.

Notes: Variables are defined in the appendix, "Databases and Variable Definitions," pp. 270–3.
$N = 1,582$; -2 Log $L = 1,480.8$; Chi-squared = 212.9.

[a]Statistically significant at the 5-percent level.

started with high capitalization; (2) capitalization reflects a mix of
high equity and low debt (i.e., low leverage) among borrowing firms;
(3) debt sources are disproportionately family members and other
nonbank sources; and (4) the average number of hours worked by
owners is much higher than that of black and white owners of retail
firms.

Factors associated with the much higher survival rates of Korean- and
Chinese-owned retail firms are, in fact, captured by three of the above

four traits.[4] Being a Korean- or Chinese-immigrant owner, per se, has no explanatory power for delineating surviving firms from defunct firms in the logistic regression exercise of table 10.5. Furthermore, the number of hours worked by owners does not delineate surviving businesses from those that discontinued operations by 1991. To the extent that table 10.5 identifies an advantage of Korean or Chinese firms, it is rooted in (1) large financial-capital investment, (2) low leverage, and (3) high indebtedness to family and friends. The first of these financial traits has successfully predicted firm survival consistently in past studies (chapters 2, 4; Bruderl, Preisendorfer, and Ziegler 1992). The importance of the second and third financial traits may be unique to this group of firms. High firm leverage is most often a trait of surviving firms (chapter 2), but it is sometimes found to be neutral (chapter 3) when other traits of firms and owners are controlled for. In this niche of retail firms with low profits, highly leveraged firms are more likely to go out of business than others.

Reliance on debt financing is a double-edged sword for marginal small businesses. The larger-scale, better-capitalized firms consistently have better survival prospects than others, and the results summarized in table 10.5 show that the young retail firms under consideration fit this pattern. Borrowing is an obvious way to become big and well capitalized, and the stronger firms tend to be the most active borrowers. In a low-yielding retail venture, however, an owner may be placed in the position of having to make large loan repayments to a bank while getting by on a household income that will not cover the basic necessities of life. Something has to give. If the owner of the marginal firm chooses to cover household expenses instead of repaying the bank, then default proceedings may lead to firm closure. This is why marginal small businesses consistently encounter difficulties servicing debt (Bates and Bradford 1979). Borrowing from family and friends may ease the dilemma for weak firms. Parents can be more patient than bankers when the business's cash flow is inadequate to cover the firm's obligations and the owner's need to make a living.

Being associated with lower leverage and smaller loan amounts, loans from family and friends are often used by weak borrowers as a fallback if loans from financial institutions are unavailable. But many of the retail firms under consideration have choked on high leverage and the consequent high loan repayment obligations that follow. Unlike small firms generally, the retail firms with high-school-educated owners clearly increase their chances of failure, other things being equal, when they become highly leveraged. In this niche, therefore, the unique low-leverage financing and heavy reliance on loans from family enhances survival among the Korean- and Chinese-owned firms. A firm financing structure normally thought to be inferior to bank borrowing is, for this immigrant business group, a pragmatic adaptation to the low-profit world of small-scale retailing. Heavy reliance on non-bank debt sources therefore appears to expand the pool of marginal Korean- and Chinese-owned firms in retailing.

CONCLUSIONS

The decision to enter self-employment was analyzed in chapter 4 from the perspective of disadvantage theory. Asian immigrants, according to Kim, Hurh, and Fernandez (1989), are often pushed into self-employment because their access to well-paying jobs as managers and professionals is blocked by employers who do not recognize the education and work experience that immigrants acquired in their home countries. The business owners analyzed in this chapter are not college educated and hence have little access to employment in high-wage, white-collar occupations. Barriers to self-employment entry, according to chapter 2's findings, hold down the business formation rates among the less educated generally, but construction stands out as the exception. This chapter has demonstrated that the least educated—those lacking high-school degrees—are overrepresented in construction self-employment; they are also disproportionately the highest earners among the high-school dropout self-employed. This finding, however, sheds minimal light on the self-employment behavior of the two groups this book has focused on; Asian immigrants and black Americans.

Among the least educated Asian immigrants, self-employment was widespread in retailing. Disadvantage theory offers little insight into this pattern of small-business concentration because white-collar employment is normally not an option for immigrants who have not attended college. Among the Korean and Chinese immigrants analyzed in table 10.3, owners of retail firms who worked full time in their business earned average profits in 1987 of $15,610. Does this represent success in self-employment? In fact, disadvantage theory in conjunction with the profit criterion—financial returns to owner time and money investment in the small business—summarized in table 10.3 provides a concrete success measure. Consider two scenarios facing a prospective Korean immigrant retail store owner:

1. *employee option:* expected hours of work and hourly wage, per year, are 2,200 hours at $5 an hour, yielding a labor income of $11,000.
2. *self-employment option:* expected hours of work and profit generated by an hour of work, per year, are 3,000 hours at $3.65 an hour, yielding a labor income of $10,950.

If hourly wage rates available as employees are an important determinant of the choice between employee and self-employed status, as disadvantage theory suggests, then it is valid and useful to compare those wage rates with the implicit hourly wage figure associated with self-employment ($3.65 an hour in the table 10.3 calculation). Access to wage work at $5 an hour, as shown in the above example, would make the likelihood of choosing self-employment much lower than if self-employed status offered $6 an hour. The self-employment option described above is not attractive.

Now, assume that the above self-employment option entailed investing $40,000 of the potential entrepreneur's savings into the small business, and this financial investment was expected to generate a 10 percent return, $4,000 per year. The self-employment option now yields a total return of $10,950 + $4,000 = $14,950. Would this make self-employment more attractive than employee status? Of course not. As an employee, one could invest the $40,000, earning, perhaps, a 10 percent expected yield: employee status and the return from financial investment would therefore yield $11,000 + $4,000 = $15,000, which is more than the $14,950 return from self-employment.

The above example explains why it is useful to break down business profits into component parts. To do otherwise is to obscure the nature of the choice between self-employed and employee status. As long as the returns for an hour of labor input favor the self-employment option, self-employment rates will tend to rise, and the opposite applies when employee status offers higher returns. Other factors may shape the self-employment decision: nothing in the above example requires that relative financial returns be the sole determinant, only that they be an important determinant. Furthermore, whenever potential employee wage income is compared to total self-employment returns in an analysis of the relative financial attractiveness of employee and self-employed status, apples are being compared to oranges. Yet sociologists routinely compare self-employment returns (on the owner's investments of labor and capital) with the wage returns on employee labor, as though they were measuring the relative financial attractiveness of these two alternatives; see, for example, Portes and Zhou (1996) and Light and Rosenstein (1995). These comparisons are not really valid except in the extreme case of zero owner financial investment.

The implication to be drawn from widespread self-employment in retailing among Korean and Chinese immigrants lacking a college education is that their prospects for working as employees are dismal. Severely limited employee options, in conjunction with the ability to invest substantial financial capital in small-scale retailing, delineate them from nonimmigrant potential entrepreneurs. Financial investment—both debt and equity—forthcoming from the Korean and Chinese retail firms described in this chapter vastly exceeded average start-up financing among black- and white-owned small retail operations. Borrowing extensively from family and friends, furthermore, delineated the Korean- and Chinese-owned business start-ups from those of whites and blacks. This unique borrowing pattern has undoubtedly served to expand the number of Korean- and Chinese-owned marginal retail firms operating in the United States.

NOTES

1. When CBO data describing young firms (entrants in the 1979–87 period) are broken down into two broad groups—immigrant- and nonimmigrant-owned firms—the immigrant-firm group reports mean capitalization at start-up exceeding $38,000; corresponding capitalization for the nonimmigrant-firm group was under $32,000. When young-firm survival is traced through 1991 for small businesses nationwide, as it was in the logit exercise in table 2.6, the immigrant trait (controlling for the owner's human capital, financial capital, and other traits) is strongly associated with firm discontinuance. The immigrant trait, per se, in linked to firm closure, but other characteristics of the firm, such as financial investment at start-up, offset the disadvantage of being immigrant owned.

2. Data analyzed in this chapter were selected, first, using two criteria: (1) 1987 gross sales revenues of $5,000 or more and (2) a small-business federal income-tax return being filed in 1987; second, specific criteria were used to focus analysis on owners who did not attend college. First, I analyzed only those owners who did not graduate from high school, but the resultant firm subgroup contained very few

Asian immigrants. To generate an Asian-owner sample of adequate size, I shifted the focus later in this chapter to retail-firm owners who did not attend college.

3. Among employed minority construction workers working in the same region, nearly 50 percent were immigrants in 1990 (Bates and Howell, 1997).

4. There were so few closures among the Korean- and Chinese-owned retail firms run by owners without a college education that the logit analysis in table 10.5 could not be replicated solely for this firm group.

APPENDIX: SURVIVAL AMONG YOUNG RETAIL FIRMS
WHOSE OWNERS DID NOT ATTEND COLLEGE

The analysis of survival among young retail firms whose owners did not attend college in table 10.5 is replicated in table A.2 with one modification. Instead of including only those Asian-immigrant owners who were Chinese or Korean, table A.2 uses all Asian-immigrant owners who fit the criteria: they lacked a college education and were in retailing. This modification adds 147 Asian-owned firms to the sample, providing a valuable increase in sample size to 1,729 firms. Most important, the number of Asian-owned firms that discontinued operations by 1991 rose by 17. The econometric exercises presented throughout this volume are based on such large samples that the issue of sensitivity to sample size is largely irrelevant. In the logit analysis in table 10.5, however, the number of discontinued firms was 156, and barely over 30 of these were Chinese- or Korean-owned. Reestimating this analysis using an expanded sample does not change the findings, but it does illustrate the robustness of the findings reported in table 10.5.

Table A.2

Logistic Regression Explaining Survival of Young Retail Firms
Whose Owners Did Not Attend College, 1987–91 (Firms Formed
since 1979 Only)

	Regression coefficient	Regression coefficient standard error	Variable mean
Constant	−1.960[a]	.739	—
Education: High school	.307[a]	.141	.749
Managerial experience	−.496[a]	.137	.235
Bought ongoing firm	.494[a]	.135	.334
Married	−.274	.161	.821
Age	.168[a]	.033	44.060
Age^2	−.002[a]	.0004	2,088.3
Gender	.556[a]	.121	.639
Black	.218	.356	.027
Asian immigrant	.511	.345	.040
Owner-labor input	.004	.005	21.191
Number of employees	.050[a]	.019	2.542
Capital	.043[a]	.019	8.730
Leverage	−.047[a]	.008	3.660
Loan source: Family, friends	.471[a]	.220	.144
Entered			
1984–85	−.401[a]	.180	.213
1986	−.882[a]	.184	.166
1987	−1.499[a]	.168	.285
Minority clientele	−.148	.145	.192

Source: U.S. Bureau of the Census, Characteristics of Business Owners (CBO) database, 1992.

Notes: Variables are defined in the appendix, "Databases and Variable Definitions," pp. 270–3.
$N = 1,729$; $-2 \log L = 1,619.3$; Chi-squared $= 228.8$.

[a]Statistically significant at the 5-percent level.

CHAPTER ELEVEN

The Government's Role in Assisting
Minority-Owned Businesses

Discussions in chapters 7 and 8 introduced the major loan and preferential procurement programs targeting minority-owned firms. Firm owners indicate that sales to government are particularly important to small business.[1] Among those operating in 1987, the following percentages of firms reported selling goods or services to federal, state, or local governments, government districts, authorities, and the like:

All small businesses	Percent of firms nationwide selling to government in 1987
White-owned	13.6%
Black-owned	9.9%
Asian-immigrant-owned	8.7%

The corresponding figures for firms started between 1979 and 1987 (young firms) were:

Young small businesses	Percent of firms nationwide selling to government in 1987
White-owned	13.2%
Black-owned	10.6%
Asian-immigrant-owned	9.2%

Targeting government procurement to small firms (particularly minority-owned businesses) is often justified on grounds of job creation (Bates, 1995d). The number of young firms with employees relying on government clients is indeed pronounced:

Young small businesses with employees	Percent of firms nationwide selling to government in 1987
White-owned	20.9%
Black-owned	17.5%
Asian-immigrant-owned	14.4%

Selling to government is serious business for small businesses in America, and it will be analyzed in detail in this chapter.

But first I will review nationwide data on assistance to minority-owned small businesses. The limited objectives of this chapter are to estimate the frequency with which black- and Asian-immigrant-owned firms were assisted, to identify the types of firms that received assistance, and to discern what sort of an impact governmental assistance had on minority-owned firms. As with previous chapters, young business start-ups will be scrutinized most thoroughly, and white-owned firms will be analyzed to provide a context for interpreting the significance of assistance to minority businesses.

ASSISTED FIRMS: THEIR TRAITS, THEIR FREQUENCY

In the process of constructing the CBO database, the Census Bureau asked tens of thousands of small-business owners (of whom roughly 60 percent were minorities) to identify the types of aid they had received from government and miscellaneous other sources: 113,615 firms nationwide reported being assisted by government, while 154,871 reported assistance from nongovernmental sources (Bates 1995d). (The owners' responses reflect their own judgments as to what constituted aid and who provided it [Bates 1995d].)

Among the young black-, Asian-immigrant-, and white-owned firms described in table 11.1, a surprisingly low 3.7 percent reported receiving assistance in the start-up or operation of their businesses. The assisted firms were somewhat larger and better capitalized than the unassisted firms, but the owners' traits and firm survival rates through

Table 11.1

Characteristics of Small Businesses Assisted and Unassisted by
Government, 1987 (Firms Formed since 1979 Only)

	All White, Black, and Asian-Immigrant-Owned Young Firms	
	Unassisted firms	Assisted firms
Firm's traits		
Gross sales, 1987 (mean)	$150,422	$167,503
Financial capital at start-up (mean)	$31,276	$52,320
Percent of firms still operating,		
1991	76.9%	77.6%
Owner's traits		
Percent college graduates	38.1%	37.1%
Percent with managerial experience	31.1%	23.3%
Annual owner-labor input in hours		
(mean)	1,948	2,263

	Distribution of Government Assistance	
	Federal assistance	State, local assistance
Racial designation of firm		
White-owned	93.6%	96.0%
Black-owned	4.5%	3.0%
Asian-immigrant-owned	1.9%	1.0%

Source: U.S. Bureau of the Census, Characteristics of Business Owners (CBO) database, 1992.

Note: Variables are defined in the appendix, "Databases and Variable Definitions," pp. 270–3.

1991 were generally similar. Only 0.7 percent of the firms reported
receiving assistance from the federal government, and only 0.8 percent
from state and local government. (All of these statistics are weighted to
be representative of young firms nationwide that were operating in
1987.[2]) Looking solely at the firms reporting governmental assistance,
black-owned firms are overrepresented, accounting for 4.5 percent of
the federally assisted group and 3.0 percent of the group assisted at the
state or local level. (Note that young black-owned small businesses
make up 2.4 percent of the small-firm universe nationwide.) In contrast, Asian immigrants accounted for 2.6 percent of firms generally,
but were only 1.9 percent of the group assisted at the federal level and
1.0 percent of the group assisted at the state or local level. Considering

assistance from all sources—federal, state, and local government and private sources—white-owned firms accounted for 94.4 percent of the assisted small businesses; shares accruing to black- and Asian-immigrant-owned firms were 3.0 percent and 2.6 percent respectively. Black overrepresentation notwithstanding, the important finding is that the overwhelming majority of small firms—whether white or minority owned—reported no assistance from government or the private sector whatsoever in starting up or operating their businesses.

Note that the source of assistance reported by a firm does not necessarily coincide with the funding provided by that source: governments most commonly contract with private organizations to provide small-business assistance. If all private assistance were really government supported, then nearly 5 percent of black businesses could be called "government assisted." Nonetheless, I am struck by the paucity of assistance reported.

The fact that about 13 percent of all young small businesses nationwide actually sell goods and services to the government illustrates a difficulty inherent in identifying assistance. Although government officials see their purchases from small vendors as "assistance," the firms' owners do not necessarily see their firms as having been assisted. Sales to government, instead, are seen as the outcome of the firm's considerable expertise and competitive pricing; clearly, this is not aid in the minds of most owners. The aid that owners identify is overwhelmingly managerial or through loan assistance. Table 11.2 identifies the black- and Asian-immigrant-owned firms that receive such aid.

The black- and Asian-immigrant-owned firms that identify themselves as aid recipients are clearly larger scale and better capitalized. They show higher survival rates over time than the unassisted firms, particularly among the black-owned businesses: 83.6 percent of the assisted businesses were still operating in late 1991 versus 73.0 percent of the unassisted black-owned firms.

Well over twice as many minority-owned firms nationwide sell goods and services to governmental clients than receive loan or managerial assistance. Table 11.3 describes the size and business distribution of young white-, black-, and Asian-immigrant-owned small businesses that sold to government clients in 1987. Median 1987 sales among these firm groups were, in all cases, less than $100,000, including sales to all customers, public and private. Nearly half of the young small firms selling to government dispense services, and most of these service providers are zero-employee operations that gross under

Table 11.2

Characteristics of Small Businesses Assisted and Unassisted by
Government by Owner's Race, 1987 (Firms Formed since 1979 Only)

	Black-Owned Young Firms	
	Unassisted firms	Assisted firms
Firm's traits		
Gross sales, 1987 (mean)	$62,281	$111,332
Financial capital at start-up (mean)	$13,245	$31,389
Percent of firms still operating,		
1991	73.0%	83.6%
Owner's traits		
Percent college graduates	29.3%	35.7%
Percent with managerial experience	22.3%	24.8%
Annual owner-labor input in hours		
(mean)	1,784	2,106
	Asian-Immigrant-Owned Young Firms	
Firm's traits		
Gross sales, 1987 (mean)	$119,207	$195,893
Financial capital at start-up (mean)	$52,289	$84,137
Percent of firms still operating,		
1991	81.2%	82.0%
Owner's traits		
Percent college graduates	58.0%	51.2%
Percent with managerial experience	28.9%	36.0%
Annual owner-labor input in hours		
(mean)	2,059	2,296

Source: U.S. Bureau of the Census, Characteristics of Business Owners (CBO) database, 1992.

Note: Variables are defined in the appendix, "Databases and Variable Definitions," pp. 270–3.

$100,000 per year; their mean government sales in 1987 averaged
under $30,000.

Relative to their numbers nationwide, both black- and Asian-
immigrant-owned young small businesses are underrepresented in
the ranks of government vendors. White-owned firms account for
96.0 percent of the small firms selling to government clients, while
black- and Asian-immigrant-owned firms account for 2.1 percent and
1.9 percent of the vendors respectively. Furthermore, average sales

Table 11.3
Firms Selling Goods or Services to Government, 1987 (Firms Formed
since 1979 Only)

	Black-owned	Asian-immigrant-owned	White-owned
Firm's traits			
Gross sales, 1987 (mean)	$121,493	$193,771	$255,265
Percent with sales			
under $100,000	82.1%	57.1%	67.4%
Business			
Retail	15.9%	42.0%	24.3%
Finance, insurance, and			
real estate	4.3%	1.2%	2.3%
All other services	47.0%	45.9%	44.5%
Construction	10.6%	1.5%	11.3%
Manufacturing	3.0%	3.1%	3.2%
Transportation	10.8%	1.4%	2.8%
Wholesaling	2.4%	2.0%	4.1%
Miscellaneous and unknown	6.1%	2.9%	7.5%
Share of government market (measured by numbers of firms)			
Percent of all small firms			
that sell to government	2.1%	1.9%	96.0%

Source: U.S. Bureau of the Census, Characteristics of Business Owners (CBO) database, 1992.

Note: Variables are defined in the appendix, "Databases and Variable Definitions," pp. 270–3.

per firm among the white-owned small businesses that sell to government are substantially larger than the government sales generated by black- and Asian-immigrant-owned firms.

Penetration of public procurement by minority businesses has been controversial, and journalists often portray minority-owned businesses as relying heavily on government contracts, which is quite inconsistent with the statistics in table 11.3. For example, Dinesh D'Souza, American Enterprise Institute fellow, asserts that "a large proportion of [black-owned business] receipts come from the government; many black businesses would collapse without government contracting preferences and set-asides" (1995, 33). Why are perceptions so out of touch with reality? Chapter 8's discussion of black mayors and their preferential procurement efforts targeting minority vendors provides a useful starting point for understanding this controversy. In fact, the minority-business share of public-sector procurement is extremely small nationwide, but substantial gains have been achieved in a few larger cities that have or have had black mayors.

Minority-owned firms operating in the nation's largest urban areas are much more likely to sell to state or local government than similar firms located elsewhere, and selling to government is most prevalent in cities with black mayors. Table 11.4 indicates that nearly 14 percent of the minority businesses in fifteen very large metropolitan areas sold goods or services to state or local governments in 1987. While minority-owned small businesses are overrepresented, nonminority-owned small businesses are underrepresented in the large urban areas described in table 11.4: they are less likely to sell to state or local governments than similar firms in the rest of the nation. Since the 1980s, controversy over preferential treatment of minority vendors has been intense in cities such as Atlanta and Philadelphia. In these metropolitan areas, minority-owned small businesses are more likely than nonminorities to be involved in selling to government, and average firm sales to state and local government are higher than among nonminority-owned firms (table 11.4). Preferential procurement policies were in force in 1987 in all but one of the cities described in table 11.4; New York City stood out as the sole exception (its preferential procurement program was initiated in 1992 by Mayor Dinkins). It was the only major urban area in which less than 10 percent of local minority firms sold goods or services to state or local government in 1987.

DO PREFERENTIAL PROCUREMENT PROGRAMS BENEFIT MINORITY-OWNED BUSINESSES?

Analyses presented in chapter 8 suggested that the black business community typically thrives in cities headed by black mayors. A presiding black mayor was associated with increased black business formation rates, larger black-owned firms, better-capitalized black-owned start-ups, and a higher proportion of black college graduates entering self-employment. Expanded access to public procurement clearly encourages creation and expansion of minority-owned businesses. It has opened up a multibillion dollar market: the minority construction sector, for example, derived over half of its revenues outside of the minority community in 1987 (Bates and Grown 1992). Employment in the

Table 11.4

Small Businesses Selling to State or Local Government by Area, 1987

	Percent of Firms Selling to State or Local Government	
	Minority firms	Nonminority firms
Metro area		
Atlanta	13.1%	8.9%
Baltimore	20.7%	9.0%
Detroit	17.4%	10.1%
Philadelphia	16.9%	12.4%
Washington, D.C.	19.7%	12.4%
Fifteen large metro areas[a]	13.9%	9.6%
	Mean Sales (in Dollars) to State and Local Government	
Atlanta	$75,336	$68,295
Baltimore	$33,448	$87,897
Detroit	$52,549	$17,410
Philadelphia	$72,120	$49,780
Washington, D.C.	$54,668	$29,057
Fifteen large metro areas[a]	$39,405	$71,196

Source: U.S. Bureau of the Census, Characteristics of Business Owners (CBO) database, 1992.

[a]The applicable areas are major centers of minority population, including the above five areas as well as Chicago, Cleveland, Dallas–Fort Worth, Houston, Los Angeles, Miami, New Orleans, New York, Oakland, and San Francisco.

affected minority business sectors has soared; most of the employees are minorities (Bates 1993b).

But there is another side to this success story. In many areas of the country, the facade of statistical success in preferential procurement rests on a foundation of misinformation and fraud. According to the Baltimore County Grand Jury, "a great number of certified minority businesses have traded the opportunity to gain a foothold in the construction industry for the quick profit available from selling the use of their name to nonminority firms" (1992, 4). Fraud in government procurement comes in many varieties, but one common type is renting out the company name. In such circumstances no legitimate minority business performs the commercially useful function of fulfilling the procurement contract; jobs are not created in the minority community, and the minority business community benefits, at best, from the fee—say 2 percent of the contract amount—that the minority front company collects for permitting another firm to use its name.

The findings of this chapter demonstrate that some minority firms benefit from their sales to government and some do not. Government procurement accrues naturally to minority firms that function in the broader, nonghetto economy, particularly in wholesale, construction, business services, and other skill-intensive services. Yet firms most reliant on government customers often suffer from their dependence. Preferential procurement programs are often designed and implemented with little thought to the broader environment that shapes small-business viability. Small, young firms, for example, are awarded large procurement contracts that they cannot handle. This encourages many small minority-owned businesses to overextend themselves, and the result may be business failure. Such circumstances encourage minority businesses to operate as fronts (Bates and Williams 1995).

The impact of preferential procurement depends quite heavily upon how government agencies administer their programs. Many cities and states make no serious effort to certify that the minority vendors benefiting from their programs are really minority-owned and -operated firms. Front companies are not even illegal in some jurisdictions.

An important finding of this chapter is that some minority vendors are sensitive to penalties for violating minority business certification and procurement program regulations. These firms flourish in the absence of fraud penalties. A group of minorities selling to government benefits from an environment in which minority business certification is comprehensive, bonding and working capital assistance are available, and assistance is delivered by a staff dedicated to helping potential and actual minority vendors. These types of assistance promote success and survival among minority vendors because they reduce the barriers that have traditionally minimized minority business participation in government procurement.

From the standpoint of the sponsoring governmental units, exactly what are minority-targeted preferential procurement programs designed to do? What is their purpose? This question was posed to administrators of preferential procurement programs in every state and every large city that had an active program in 1992 (JCPES 1994; COSCDA 1993). The most common response was that preferential procurement was a tool for generating growth and development of minority businesses. The purpose of Maryland's Minority Business Enterprise program typified many responses: the program's purpose is "to encourage and facilitate the growth and development of minority firms in Maryland through greater access to state contracts" (COSCDA 1993). Another frequent justification for preferential procurement is captured in the purpose of Detroit's Sheltered Market program: that program's goal is to remedy the present effects of past discrimination and disadvantage by giving MBEs a greater opportunity to participate in city contracts. How do these broad mandates actually translate into practice?

Motivated by chapter 8's finding that black-owned firms were thriving in cities that elected black mayors, I secured funding from the U.S. Department of Commerce to study preferential procurement programs operated by big cities. With the Joint Center for Political and Economic Studies (JCPES) of Washington, D.C., I collected detailed profiles of preferential procurement programs operated by over thirty large cities.[3] Useful data on program specifics were generated for twenty-eight large cities located in twenty-six metropolitan areas nationwide. In these twenty-six metropolitan areas, 1,085 MBEs described in the CBO database sold goods or services to state or local government. A detailed investigation of these 1,085 MBE vendors revealed that closure rates were highest among firms relying most heavily on sales to state or local government. Illustrative summary statistics are presented below:

	Sales to state and local government under 25 percent	Sales to state and local government 25 percent or more
Total sales, 1987 (mean)	$215,449	$121,498
Sales to state or local government, 1987 (mean)	$20,173	$70,814
Percent of firms shut down by late 1991	17.9%	29.3%

As I have pointed out above, the nation's most ambitious preferential procurement programs operate in cities with black mayors. If these cities are indeed more successful than others in aiding minority business vendors, how do they do it? Furthermore, why do the MBEs that rely most heavily on sales to state/local government fail disproportionately? Do these high firm closure rates typify MBE vendors in cities where black mayors preside? The analysis in the next section suggests that the nature of the preferential procurement program determines whether or not minority vendors benefit from their sales to government.

ANALYSIS OF PREFERENTIAL PROCUREMENT IN TWENTY-EIGHT LARGE CITIES

This section is innovative in that I introduce the actual characteristics of the minority business assistance programs operating in the central cities under study here. In light of the findings of greater vibrancy of black-owned businesses described in chapter 8, I paid particular attention to the types of assistance found in cities with presiding black mayors. Overwhelmingly, preferential procurement, packaged with complementary assistance, was how minority firms were helped in cities with black mayors. The specific policies likely to help minority vendors and the minority business community are spelled out below:

1. Procurement is handled by a staff whose specific responsibility is to assist potential and actual minority vendors.
2. Working capital is provided by local government to minority contract recipients, through short-term loans; quick-pay provisions (the minority vendor is guaranteed payment within thirty days); and/or direct payment of minority subcontractors (the government client does not rely on the project's prime contractor to pay the minority subcontractors).
3. On small- and medium-sized procurement contracts that have traditionally required that the vendor be bonded, bonding is waived or provided by a local government source for minority firms.
4. Large contracts are broken down to increase their accessibility to minority-owned businesses that are often smaller than their established competitors and, thus, unable to accept big jobs.
5. Since businesses are subjected to a rigorous certification process, assisted firms are likely to be genuine, functioning MBEs.

6. Significant penalties are imposed upon minority firms that circumvent program regulations; front firms are weeded out, leaving more work for genuine minority-owned small businesses.

7. Procurement departments attempt to see that contracts awarded to minorities result in significant value accruing to the minority community, for example, by not permitting agencies to meet their setaside goals by buying goods from minority brokers that carry no inventory and do not service the applicable products.

The seven variables created from JCPES survey data that correspond to these seven policies are formally defined below:

"Certification": equals one if the MBE certification process is comprehensive, including on-site inspections of firm operations; zero otherwise.

"Staff": equals one if the city employs a staff specifically to assist potential and actual MBE vendors; zero otherwise.

"Pay": equals one if the city provides working capital to minority vendors; zero otherwise.

"Bonding": equals one if the city provides bonding assistance to minority vendors; zero otherwise.

"Penalty": equals one if the city imposes significant penalties on minority vendors who violate certification or procurement program regulations; zero otherwise.

"Break": equals one if the city breaks down large procurement contracts to make them more accessible to minority vendors; zero otherwise.

"Broker": equals one if the city prohibits MBE brokers; zero otherwise.

For the seven variables describing operational aspects of preferential procurement programs, means are presented below for two groups of MBEs located in the twenty-six large metropolitan areas under consideration; the percentages represent proportions of all MBEs selling to government that were subject to the seven procurement policies.

	Sales to state and local government under 25 percent of firm revenues	Sales to state and local government of 25 percent or more of firm revenues
Certification	66.4%	56.9%
Staff	35.7%	42.4%
Pay	63.7%	63.6%
Bonding	30.2%	24.4%
Penalty	54.5%	47.2%
Break	95.1%	95.8%
Broker	36.3%	31.1%

It is noteworthy that the MBE vendor group with low mean sales and large contracts—those relying on state and local government for 25 percent or more of their total revenue—is overrepresented in the urban areas where MBE certification procedures are not rigorous.

A logistic regression analysis of MBE firm survival is presented in table 11.5 for the 1,085 vendors that sold goods or services to state or local governments in the twenty-six large metropolitan areas under consideration. This statistical analysis is broadly similar to logistic exercises in previous chapters that explained firm survival over the 1987–91 period by examining characteristics of owners and businesses (see, for example, table 7.3, p. 158). Governmental operational policies for assisting MBE vendors described above should contribute to the longevity of the minority firms that sell to state and local governments. (One of the seven policies—breaking down large contracts to make them more accessible to MBEs—could not be investigated econometrically because of insufficient sample variance.[4])

Table 11.5 presents two sets of logistic regressions: I analyzed MBE survival separately for vendors deriving under 25 percent of their sales from state or local government and vendors relying upon this source for 25 percent or more of their sales revenues. MBE vendors in the under-25-percent group make up 67 percent of the firms selling to state or local government in the twenty-six metropolitan areas under consideration. The analysis of MBE vendors with under 25 percent of revenues from government clients in table 11.5 identifies four practices of preferential procurement programs that promote the longevity of MBEs:

1. Working capital assistance is provided by the local government to contract recipients.

2. Bonding requirements are routinely waived for procurement contracts, or bonding is actually provided by the locality.
3. Rigorous certification processes are in place.
4. Staff is assigned to assist minority firms.

Why do these practices heighten the survival prospects of MBEs? Previous studies indicate that MBEs are much more likely than nonminority small businesses to suffer from undercapitalization and liquidity problems (Bates 1993b). Weak capitalization and limited access to sources of short-term debt such as commercial bank loans make it difficult for MBEs to finance current operations, much less substantial growth (Ando 1988; Bates 1993b). While government contracts are a potential source of growth, such business can also exacerbate illiquidity for MBEs. Government assistance that addresses this problem by providing working capital to MBE contract recipients alleviates one of the major barriers to expanded MBE involvement in government procurement and increases their survival prospects.

While bonding requirements were believed to constitute a major barrier to expanded MBE involvement in government procurement, quantitative evidence documenting this phenomenon was lacking. In the absence of hard data, the idea that bonding requirements serve as a barrier to potential MBE vendors—in private- as well as public-sector work—was only based on anecdotal evidence. The documentation in table 11.5 constitutes hard, quantitative evidence that bonding requirements are indeed a barrier to the development of the minority business community. Most often bonding is waived for MBE vendors, and this is disproportionately beneficial to construction firms, since construction is the area where bonding requirements are most widespread. Less frequently, localities actually write the bonds for MBE vendors, which circumvents the problem of surety businesses being unwilling to write bonds for MBEs.

When the logistic analysis in table 11.5 is replicated solely for MBEs deriving 25 percent or more of their revenues from sales to state or local governments, a troubling issue arises. The results indicate that no governmental assistance has the statistical power to delineate firm survivors from closures, suggesting that aid in such forms as working capital and bonding assistance do not benefit the MBEs that rely most heavily on government for their sales revenues. Other contrasts in the findings are noteworthy:

Table 11.5
Logistic Regression Explaining MBE Survival, for Firms Selling to State or Local Government, 1987–91

	MBEs deriving less than 25 percent of their sales from government		MBEs deriving 25 percent or more of their sales from government	
	Regression coefficient (standard error)	Variable mean	Regression coefficient (standard error)	Variable mean
Constant	3.145[a]	—	2.675	—
	(1.275)		(4.423)	
Education				
High school	2.346[a]	.152	.611	.256
	(.483)		(.725)	
College, 1–3 years	1.529[a]	.320	.474	.240
	(.376)		(.654)	
College graduate	2.730[a]	.155	.335	.258
	(.487)		(.699)	
Graduate school	3.050[a]	.217	1.078	.114
	(.499)		(.742)	
Managerial experience	.159	.304	−1.784[a]	.424
	(.239)		(.422)	
Married	−1.312[a]	.817	.409	.818
	(.392)		(.498)	
Asian	.202	.389	1.616	.323
	(.678)		(4.102)	
Black	.576	.240	−1.795	.329
	(.725)		(4.125)	
Hispanic	.082	.311	−1.827	.345
	(.685)		(4.112)	
Owner-labor input	.010	24.160	.042[a]	23.676
	(.011)		(.017)	
Capital	.212[a]	9.320	.163	9.095
	(.105)		(.166)	

Continued on next page

[a]Statistically significant at the 5-percent level.

Table 11.5—*Continued*

	MBEs deriving less than 25 percent of their sales from government		MBEs deriving 25 percent or more of their sales from government	
	Regression coefficient (standard error)	Variable mean	Regression coefficient (standard error)	Variable mean
Leverage	.025 (.027)	2.091	−.073[a] (.035)	3.781
Entered				
1984–1985	.339 (.382)	.170	3.161[a] (1.325)	.088
1986	−1.022[a] (.364)	.140	.473 (.569)	.216
1987	−1.082[a] (.323)	.212	−2.734[a] (.470)	.263
Retail[b]	.422 (.513)	.334		
Finance, insurance, real estate[b]	.883 (.802)	.028		
All other services[b]	.846 (.499)	.391		
Construction[b]	.667 (.816)	.040		
Manufacturing[b]	1.266 (.828)	.046		
Transportation[b]	.343 (.618)	.075		
Wholesaling[b]	1.688 (.941)	.033		
Certification	.531[a] (.285)	.664	.773 (.496)	.569
Staff	.638[a] (.285)	.357	−.443 (.500)	.424

Continued on next page

[a]Statistically significant at the 5-percent level.

[b]Business variables were dropped due to small sample size for MBEs deriving 25 percent or more of their sales from government.

Table 11.5 — *Continued*

	MBEs deriving less than 25 percent of their sales from government		MBEs deriving 25 percent or more of their sales from government	
	Regression coefficient (standard error)	Variable mean	Regression coefficient (standard error)	Variable mean
Pay	.795[a] (.277)	.637	−.129 (.446)	.636
Bonding	.956[a] (.347)	.302	−.382 (.547)	.244
Penalty	−.081 (.280)	.545	−.323 (.457)	.472
Broker	.115 (.312)	.363	−.526 (.494)	.311
N	744		311	
−2 Log L	518.2		256	
Chi-squared	170.2		170.8	

Sources: Procurement program information was compiled by the author; firm and owner traits were derived from the U.S. Bureau of the Census, Characteristics of Business Owners (CBO) database, 1992. Firms under consideration in table 11.5 are all located in twenty-six large metropolitan areas (Albuquerque, Atlanta, Austin, Baltimore, Boston, Charlotte, Chicago, Cincinnati, Cleveland, Dallas-Fort Worth, Denver, Indianapolis, Jacksonville, Kansas City, Los Angeles, Miami, Milwaukee, Minneapolis, New Orleans, Omaha, Philadelphia, San Antonio, San Diego, San Francisco-Oakland, Seattle, and Washington, D.C.).

[a]Statistically significant at the 5-percent level.

1. College-graduate owners were much more likely to see their firms remain in business in the under-25-percent group, but this relationship was weak and statistically insignificant among MBE vendors in the 25-percent-plus group.
2. Well-capitalized firms were more likely to survive among the under-25-percent MBEs, but not those in the 25-percent-plus vendor group.
3. Very young firms (1987 formations) were more likely to shut down than more established firms, but this relationship was over twice as strong for the MBEs most heavily reliant on government clients.

How is it that the owner's education, the firm's capitalization, and governmental assistance with bonding and working capital can have a very substantial impact on the survival of one MBE group and none on the other group? Consider the hypothesis that front firms are present in the 25-percent-plus MBE vendor group. For front firms:

1.   The MBE owner's human capital would have no relationship to firm survival, as the one running the firm would not be the MBE owner.
2.   MBE firm capitalization would have no relationship to firm survival, as the financial capital that is financing the production of goods and services for government clients belongs to another firm—the one that is actually filling the procurement contract.
3.   The MBE would have no obvious reason for remaining in business once the applicable contract was completed, as MBE front firms are often put together for the sole purpose of securing and completing a specific government contract. This would explain why the MBE vendors most reliant on government clients were 63.7 percent more likely to be out of business by 1991 than the other MBE vendors. It would also explain why young firms are overrepresented in the 25-percent-plus group. In fact, 47.9 percent of the MBEs having revenues from government of 25 percent or more had been in business for two or fewer years versus 35.2 percent of the other MBEs. Among the very youngest firms (1987 start-ups), finally, the 25-percent-plus firms were more than twice as likely as the MBEs less reliant on government to be out of business by 1991.

These facts, by themselves, do not demonstrate the presence of front firms, but they certainly suggest that front firms may be present. MBEs with certain levels of human and financial capital generally behave in predictable ways: stronger firms do better than weaker firms (Bates 1993b). When these predictable relationships do not characterize the behavior of an MBE subgroup, then some overriding force—such as the front-firm phenomenon—is likely to be suppressing normal operations. How can we measure the presence or absence of that overriding force? Table 11.6 addresses this issue. In this table, I used an OLS regression equation to estimate the log of 1987 total

Table 11.6

OLS Regression Explaining Firm Sales for MBEs Deriving 25 Percent
or More of Their Sales from Government, 1987

	Regression coefficient (standard error)	Variable mean
Constant	8.673[a] (1.155)	—
Education		
High school	.189 (.223)	.256
College, 1–3 years	.161 (.206)	.240
College graduate	.585[a] (.233)	.258
Graduate school	1.123[a] (.246)	.114
Managerial experience	−.078 (.144)	.424
Married	−.443[a] (.162)	.818
Asian	−.810 (.948)	.323
Black	−.635 (.949)	.329
Hispanic	−.851 (.947)	.345
Owner-labor input	.020[a] (.006)	23.676
Capital	.274[a] (.055)	9.095
Entered		
1984–1985	−.333 (.240)	.088
1986	−.061 (.195)	.216
1987	−.783[a] (.161)	.263

Continued on next page

[a]Statistically significant at the 5-percent level.

Table 11.6—*Continued*

	Regression coefficient (standard error)	Variable mean
Retail	.433 (.249)	.174
All other services	−.390 (.244)	.498
Finance, insurance, real estate	−1.423[a] (.342)	.049
Construction	.850[a] (.281)	.086
Manufacturing	.945 (.536)	.013
Transportation	−.146 (.315)	.083
Wholesaling	.916[a] (.433)	.022
Certification	−.133 (.159)	.569
Staff	−.104 (.153)	.424
Pay	−.007 (.137)	.636
Bonding	.407[a] (.185)	.244
Penalty	−.326[a] (.155)	.472
Broker	.150 (.169)	.311
N	311	
R^2	.388	
F	8.000	

Sources: Procurement program information was compiled by the author; firm and owner traits were derived from the U.S. Bureau of the Census, Characteristics of Business Owners (CBO) database, 1992.

[a]Statistically significant at the 5-percent level.

sales revenues for the MBEs deriving 25 percent or more of their sales revenues from state and local government. (The explanatory variables in table 11.6 are the same as those used in the logistic regression analysis in table 11.5.) The finding from table 11.6 that is particularly noteworthy concerns the impact of penalties; MBE sales are significantly lower in cities with stringent penalties for violations of preferential procurement program and certification regulations. In other words, the MBEs most heavily reliant on government achieve significantly higher average sales, other things being equal, in cities where front companies are not punished with financial penalties and the possibility of jail time for errant owners. These MBEs, indeed, behave collectively as though front companies are operating in their midst. When the OLS regression exercise in table 11.6 was replicated solely for MBEs deriving less than 25 percent of their revenues from state and local government, the penalty variable was not a significant determinant of sales. The policy implication of this finding is straightforward: the number of MBE front companies can be held down by penalizing such activity heavily.

CONCLUSIONS

Some MBEs benefit from their sales to government and some do not. Some MBEs are aided by the assistance offered by the large urban governments described above and some are not. On balance, the MBEs most reliant on sales to state and local government are often set back by this dependency. The fact that these firms behave in ways suggesting sensitivity to penalties for violating certification and procurement regulations is instructive. These MBEs—the small firms with the big contracts—appear disproportionately in areas lacking substantial fraud penalties; their sales are boosted by an absence of fraud penalties, other things being equal. Their behavior is consistent, in important ways, with that of MBE front firms. This is the bad news.

The goods news is that MBEs relying on state or local government for under 25 percent of their revenues often benefit from their relationship to their government customers. They benefit particularly from comprehensive MBE certification, availability of bonding and working capital, and government staffers whose job it is to help potential and actual MBE vendors.

The evidence presented here, in conjunction with evidence from other investigations, suggests that fraud in MBE preferential procurement programs is present in some—perhaps many—areas of the United States (Baltimore County Grand Jury 1992). Indianapolis, for example, conducted extensive field audits of MBEs holding city contracts in 1992: 30 percent of the city's certified minority vendors had their certifications revoked as a result (JCPES 1994). While the statistical success of some preferential procurement programs rests on a foundation of front companies, other governments have already demonstrated how preferential procurement can be used to help MBEs. First, they provide support for legitimate MBEs in areas such as bonding and working capital, which alleviates barriers to broader MBE participation in government procurement. Second, they check the proliferation of MBE front companies through on-site compliance reviews. "Only in the field will investigators discover the lengths to which unscrupulous companies will go to cover up the true nature of their operations" (Baltimore County Grand Jury 1992, 2). Third, their contracts with MBEs (including prime contractors dealing with MBE subcontractors where applicable) include written certifications that the MBE will actually perform the work on that contract, and they back up these certifications with penalties for noncompliance, including prosecution under the fraud provisions of the MBE statute. Finally, their penalties for fraud are substantial. In many areas of the country, MBE front companies are subject to nothing more than decertification if they are found to be in violation of the relevant MBE procurement statute. This is not enough.

Motivations for acting as front companies are diverse, and it is superficial to assume that this type of fraud reflects a firm's desire to make a quick buck rather than the minority owner's desire to build a substantial firm. MBEs can be pushed into becoming front companies because of structural deficiencies in preferential procurement programs. The all-too-common case of the very small MBE holding a very large contract illustrates this point clearly: in the absence of complementary assistance, some MBEs simply lack the capacity to handle large contracts. If the small MBE can be assured of prompt payment for services to government clients, then the issue of capacity to perform is much less likely to arise. If the small MBE, in contrast, buys the requisite materials and hires the additional workers necessary to produce a greatly expanded output for a government client, that firm runs the very real risk of being choked by a liquidity crisis if the client does not pay the MBE vendor for four or five months. In this case, selling the contract to a nonminority firm generates a quick profit, while actually fulfilling the contract means that the MBE risks going out of business. Such circumstances can make becoming a front company an intelligent choice for the aspiring MBE vendor.

The preferential procurement program can serve as either a valuable tool for fostering minority business development, or it can promote minority front companies that pass their procurement contracts onto nonminority firms. When governments contract with young, inexperienced minority vendors, pay their bills slowly, fail to penalize front companies, and the like, they are, in effect, encouraging the abuses that destroy the potential of their preferential procurement programs. In fact, they are promoting programmatic fraud.

NOTES

1. Systematic evidence about such assistance is available in the CBO database, which records firm involvement in various aid programs as well as the sales by small businesses of goods and services to government clients.

2. Weighted firm statistics are reported throughout this chapter, meaning that the numbers cited are representative of all small firms operating in 1987 in the United States. Mean overall MBE sales reported in this chapter are higher than those reported in applicable Census Bureau publications. The restrictive editing practices applied to the CBO database, which account for this result, are described in detail in the appendix, "Databases and Variable Definitions."

3. Detailed descriptions of all of the relevant MBE assistance programs appear in *Joint Center for Political and Economic Studies* (1994).

4. Because over 95 percent of the MBE vendors were located in areas practicing contract downsizing, fewer than ten MBEs that shut down their firms by 1991 were operating in urban areas where contract downsizing was not practiced.

CHAPTER TWELVE

The Meaning of Small-Business Success

A re firms owned by Asian immigrants lagging behind black-owned businesses? Depending on how success is defined, the viability of the Asian-immigrant small-business community can be portrayed in either a positive or a negative light. Asian immigrants living in the United States collectively report a higher incidence of self-employment than whites or blacks. If *success* is defined merely in terms of self-employment rates, then the Asian-immigrant-owned small-business community is clearly a great success. But self-employment rates should not be the measure of viability. People who own small businesses often must toil long hours, earning very little for their efforts; they may prefer to work as an employee. When small-business ownership means working poverty for owners hoping to escape to employee status, self-employment cannot be equated with success.

Firm profitability is another widely accepted measure of small-business success, and Asian-immigrant-owned firms collectively report higher average profits than black-owned businesses.[1] When profits are broken down into returns on the owner's financial- and human-capital investments and hours worked in the small business, however, the superior profitability of Asian-immigrant firms evaporates. Among owners who did not attend college, profits were under

$3.50 per hour among Asian immigrants versus $4.76 per hour among blacks.[2] (These figures apply to full-time owners only, and they are net of a 10 percent return attributed to the owner's equity-capital investment in the firm.) Corresponding profits for college-educated owners were under $6.00 per hour for Asian immigrants versus $6.41 for blacks.[3]

Per dollar of invested capital and per hour of work, black-owned businesses started between 1979 and 1987 were more profitable than Asian-immigrant-owned firms, when owners with and without a college education are examined separately. Being college educated is associated with increased profits, as are working longer hours and investing more of the owner's capital. Being Asian, per se, does not increase profits. College-educated Asian-immigrant owners earn slightly lower profits than similarly educated blacks; those without college credentials earn much less than similar black business owners. Both racially defined groups, in turn, lag behind nonminority firms in profitability. Regardless of the owner's race, full-time college-educated owners making large financial investments are the ones whose firms generate the highest profits.

Asian immigrants who have not attended college, nonetheless, do stand out for their very low returns for hours worked: the average Korean or Chinese owner generates $3.40 an hour, less than 60 percent of the corresponding $6.39 an hour produced by nonminorities. Most Asian-immigrant entrepreneurs, in fact, are college educated. The subminimum wage returns accruing to the less well educated undoubtedly hold down the number of firms owned by Asian immigrants who have not gone to college.

What about the picture drawn by social scientists of a supportive ethnic community that provides financing for business formation, a loyal, low-cost workforce, and a captive market of customers who want to do business with owners who speak their language and understand their preferences? Despite persistent evidence to the contrary, this appealing portrait of community-generated social capital incubating businesses continues to dominate the social science literature. What some see as the "naked social trust" attracting Asian immigrants to RCAs might more realistically be depicted as loan sharking. Even Ivan Light acknowledges that law enforcement types equate the standard practices of RCAs with usury and tax fraud (Light, Kwuon, and Zhong 1990, 41). Loan funds are attracted to RCAs, in part, by the knowledge that interest earnings need not be reported to the IRS; since RCAs commonly pay 30-percent-plus rates of return to their investors, tax-free interest income is potentially substantial (Light, Kwuon, and Zhong 1990, 41).

The loan-sharking side of RCA operation, of course, is what secures these high returns to investors. Faced with such social capital, it is not surprising that Asian-immigrant-owned firms prefer to borrow from banks (chapter 6). Undoubtedly, RCAs permit some firms to raise the capital needed for start-up, but how many marginal borrowers are destroyed trying to meet their usurious interest payments? Is the net effort an increase or a decrease in the profitability and survival rates of immigrant-owned small businesses? We do not know.

The role played by social capital in retarding immigrant business communities is broadly described by Portes and Sensenbrenner (1993). Strict compliance with group expectations may be a major source of social capital. It may promote repayment of loans from RCAs, and it may cut costs by reducing the number of lawyers required to enforce contracts among ethnic businesses. However, complying with group expectations can also lead to expensive demands. Portes and Sensenbrenner get to the crux of the problem: "Cozy intergroup relationships of the sort frequently found in solidarity communities can give rise to a gigantic free-riding problem" (1993, 1339). Less diligent group members enforce on successful members all kinds of demands "backed by the same normative structure that makes the existence of trust possible" (1993, 1339).

There is another downside to social capital rooted in enforceable trust. Conservative community values can discriminate against progressive entrepreneurs who may attempt, for example, to eliminate jobs via mechanization. Reaching beyond the ethnic community for clients can be similarly controversial. Nee and Nee, writing about traditional Chinatown, quoted an informant on the detrimental effects of community conservatism: "In old Chinatown, they didn't respect a scholarly person or an intelligent person. . . . They hold on to everything the way it was in China, in Kwangtung. Even though we're in a different society, a different era" (1973, 190). In this spirit, Portes and Sensenbrenner speculate, "The greater the social capital produced by bounded solidarity and community controls, then the greater the particularistic demands placed on successful entrepreneurs and the more extensive the restrictions on individual expression" (1993, 1341). Is it any wonder that the more successful Asian-immigrant-owned enterprises largely sell to nonminorities and borrow from banks?

Social capital notwithstanding, problems rooted in blocked mobility condemn many immigrant entrepreneurs to long hours of toil in businesses noted for their unpleasant working conditions and low financial returns. Low-profit fields, such as small-scale retailing and personal services, routinely attract college-educated Asian immigrants into small-business ownership, while similarly educated blacks and whites are much less likely to enter these lines of business.

ARE FIRMS OWNED BY BLACKS LAGGING BEHIND ASIAN-IMMIGRANT-OWNED BUSINESSES?

The average Asian-immigrant-owned firm is a larger, more profitable venture than its black counterpart. Obvious reasons for this disparity include the larger financial investments typifying Asian-immigrant business start-ups, the much higher percentage of Asian owners with college degrees, and the longer hours devoted to self-employment by the average Asian owner. The Asian advantage is not rooted in higher returns per dollar invested or per hour worked. The Asian advantage, instead, flows from the size of investments of human and financial capital into the small business.

Figures cited in chapter 5 indicated that the Asian-immigrant small-business community was dominated by four groups: Chinese own the largest percentage of firms (27.7 percent), followed by Koreans (21.7 percent), Asian Indians (19.7 percent), and Filipinos (10.1 percent). Immigrants from China, Korea, India, and the Philippines stand out as well-educated, urban, and predominantly employed in managerial and professional occupations relative to those who remain in their home countries (U.S. Commission on Civil Rights 1988).[4] Nearly 75 percent of the immigrant Asian Indian men living in the United States are college graduates; their self-employment experiences in the United States reflect their class backgrounds.

Popular perceptions of Asian immigrants bootstrapping their way out of poverty are rooted, in fact, in the experiences of West Coast Chinese and Japanese before World War II. In 1900, for example, Japanese Americans were overwhelmingly unskilled, working as farm laborers, miners, and domestic servants; only 2 percent were in middle-class occupations (Suzuki 1996). By 1990, Japanese Americans were better educated, earned a higher income on average, and were more likely to work as managers and professionals than white Americans. Was self-employment an important component of their upward mobility?

In the early twentieth century, the Japanese—particularly in western states—were segregated in the public schools, their businesses were boycotted, they were denied the right to buy farm land, and further Japanese immigration into the United States was completely cut off. Incarcerated en masse during World War II, Japanese Americans nonetheless emerged by the 1960s as model minorities who had overcome discrimination through their own efforts and without government aid (Daniels 1988). Some scholars see this achievement as a reflection of both cultural values and the workings of a competitive market economy (Sowell 1983). Daniels (1988) notes that the experiences of the Japanese and other Asian Americans were used as "intellectual brickbats" against the demands of African Americans and others for social and economic equality.

In fact, immigration and return migration, today as well as before World War II, largely account for the high economic status typifying Asian Americans. Borjas (1989) points out that the disproportionate return migration of lower-achieving immigrants increased the rate of economic improvement of immigrants who remained. Regarding Japanese Americans specifically, Suzuki's thorough empirical research (1994; 1995; 1996) demonstrates that "much of the measured economic achievement was due to selective return migration" (1995, 896).

After the Immigration Act of 1924 excluded Japanese from immigrating to the United States, there was a large return migration: "most of the net out-migration was by Japanese in the lowest occupational categories" (Suzuki 1995, 892). Table 12.1, adapted from Suzuki (1995), shows that nonfarm laborers and servants dominated Japanese return migration between 1921 and 1930. Suzuki concludes that "almost one-half of the increase in occupational status between 1920 and 1930 can be accounted for by selective return migration" (1995, 894) among Japanese Americans. Selective return migration may have had an even greater impact on the numbers in various occupations during the Great Depression. According to Suzuki, "During the 1930s the number of Japanese immigrants who were farmers, business people, and professionals fell by more than 15 percent, while the numbers of laborers, farm laborers, and servants fell by almost 50 percent" (1996, 17).

Entry and exit decisions among Japanese immigrants were shaped, in part, by marriage and family formation plans and aspirations. Until

Table 12.1

Japanese Aliens Entering and Leaving the United States by Occupation, 1921–30

	Entering	Departing	Net
Professionals, business people	19,540	18,667	873
Farmers and farm laborers	12,008	10,870	1,138
Skilled workers	4,169	4,017	152
Nonfarm laborers and servants	4,744	22,652	(17,908)
Other occupations	5,328	4,191	1,137
Total having occupations	45,789	60,397	(14,608)
Unemployed	25,156	26,050	(894)
Total	70,945	86,447	(15,502)

Source: Masao Suzuki, "Success Story? Japanese Immigrant Economic Achievement and Return Migration, 1920–1930," *Journal of Economic History* 55(4): table 2, 892.

1915, Japanese laborers immigrating to the United States were prohibited from bringing their wives. After 1915, Japanese men immigrating to the United States could bring their wives provided they had $800 or more in savings, quite a sum in those days (Ichioka 1988). Antimiscegenation laws prevented Japanese immigrants in California and other states from marrying whites. "This forced many to choose between returning to Japan and living out their lives without any family in the U.S." (Suzuki 1996, 16).

Tracing the effects of selective immigration, return migration, and restrictions on family formation on Asian Americans is not intended to detract from the record of economic achievement that has made them the best educated, best paid racially defined group in the United States. But Asian Americans achieved their success in historical conditions unique to them. The success experienced by Japanese Americans, or any other Asian group, does not imply that other racially defined groups, such as African Americans, can emulate the Japanese success story.

Historical circumstances have shaped the Asian-immigrant group so that those who are here and most actively involved in small business are better educated, on average, and capable of making larger financial investments in their firms than black Americans can. Self-employed Asian immigrants collectively generate lower returns on their labor and capital investments, on average, than black business owners because many are held back by ongoing constraints. Which group is more successful? Because the circumstances producing dominant self-employment patterns are so dissimilar, the question itself is not terribly meaningful.

UNANSWERED QUESTIONS

How should the success of Asian-immigrant small-business owners be judged? This study has stressed profit measures, such as financial returns per hour of work. Profit figures that examine a single year of a firm's performance, however, are very partial measures of a small business's success. Many immigrant entrepreneurs who own young firms are in the process of establishing themselves economically and socially in the United States. Transition to life in this country can be difficult, especially for those not fluent in English. Whether or not immigrating was wise is not a question that can be answered definitively during one's first year, or even first decade, of residence in the United States.

Self-employment is one option available to immigrants possessing managerial and professional skills, financial capital, and other resources. These individuals have the resources to transcend the barriers to creating a small business, particularly in small-scale retailing, where entry barriers are low. The possibility of running a small business expands one's options in the labor market. If suitable salaried employment is unavailable, the attractiveness of starting a small business increases.

As the years pass by, many people leave self-employment, often because salaried employment, a more attractive option, becomes available. Figures from chapter 4 indicated that 27.2 percent of the Asian Indian and Filipino immigrants running small businesses in 1987 were no longer owners of these firms in 1991. In 65 percent of those instances, the underlying firm was closed; for the other 35 percent, the firm continued to operate under new ownership. The exit rate from traditional businesses was much higher, due to more active sales of firms as well as more frequent closure. In retailing, owners left at a rate of nearly 10 percent annually among Asian Indian and Filipino immigrants.

Where did these departing owners go? Did they remain self-employed in a new business venture, accept salaried employment, or leave the labor force? We simply do not know. It is not really possible to judge whether small-business owners successfully adapted to life in America without follow-up information on their economic status. The initial disadvantages faced by immigrants arriving in the United States are often dealt with by accepting wage work or self-employment that underutilizes their skills, work experience, and educational background. After a decade or two in the United States, are those who opted for small-business ownership better off than demographically similar immigrants who worked as employees? Among the self-employed, are those who subsequently become salaried employees better off, as a group, than similar immigrants who chose to stick with small-business ownership? The whole process of adapting to economic opportunity in the United States needs to be studied using time-series data to judge whether bouts of self-employment help or hinder the adjustment process. Analysis of data on firm profitability in any given year is useful, but far from conclusive. If Asian immigrants earned higher self-employment returns than demographically similar nonimmigrants (controlling for financial investment), then a conclusion about success in small business would be tenable. But their self-employment returns, on average, are lower than those of nonimmigrants. We simply do not know if self-employment, in the aggregate, has accelerated or held back Asian immigrants' adaptation to life in the United States.

The highly educated immigrants studied in chapter 4 were certainly inclined to leave the small firms they owned in 1987. Analysis of Korean- and Chinese-immigrant owners running firms in traditional fields revealed a similar pattern: being a college graduate was negatively related to firm continuity, but the relationship was weak and not statistically significant. Among Asian-immigrant-owned firms in operation for ten or more years, findings from chapter 4 demonstrated lower firm concentrations in traditional fields, and a stronger orientation toward high-yielding small businesses. The evidence, on balance, indicates that involvement of college-educated Asian immigrants in traditional fields like small-scale retailing is part of a transitional process: as owners become fluent in English and familiar with options offered by the U.S. economy, they move on. Exactly where they move on to and whether small-business ownership helped to make them upwardly mobile are key questions to which we lack clear answers.

The issue of the effects of social capital on small-business formation and viability is far from resolved. The clear finding (chapters 3, 6, and 10) is that the smaller-scale, weaker Asian-immigrant-owned firms are the ones most likely to make use of social capital. While the weight of evidence has consistently caused me to emphasize the negative aspects of social capital, available data certainly do not provide definitive answers about how the various, diverse types of social capital shape small businesses.

Far from being autonomous units, small businesses find themselves embedded in social, political, and cultural contexts. Thus, perhaps we should focus "upon entrepreneurship as embedded in a social context, channeled and facilitated or constrained and inhibited by people's positions in social networks," (Aldrich and Zimmer 1986, 14). Building a business means that existing social relationships have to be activated and new ones created: it is "inherently a networking activity" (Dubini and Aldrich 1991, 306).

All of this not only sounds plausible but seems obvious. Concepts of social capital—particularly when they describe embeddedness and networking—are also so broad and so vague that their usefulness is quite unclear without concrete examples of how they affect small-business performance. Sophisticated empirical studies to date have generated little evidence that social capital is beneficial. Aldrich, Rosen, and Woodward (1987) could not find convincing evidence of six networking measures affecting business profitability. I have found that the use of social capital is associated with firm weakness because weak firms use social capital. But the chain of causation is difficult to pin down when weak firms consistently make greater use of social capital than do strong firms: trying to judge whether using social capital hinders or helps firms is tricky empirically in the face of this correlation. One obvious reason to rely heavily on social capital (or network support) is to compensate for shortfalls in human capital (Light and Karageorgis 1994). It can also compensate for a lack of financial capital: Yoon (1991a) found that RCA borrowing was motivated by firms' inability to get bank loans.

Investigations of the use of social capital and small-business performance are at an early stage in their intellectual life cycle. A consensus may develop that reliance on social capital helps some marginal firms come into existence that otherwise would not have made it, leading to an increase in the number of small-business start-ups. The evidence summarized in this book is broadly consistent with this notion. Whether reliance on such forms of social capital as protected markets and RCAs helps firms remain in business is less clear, and the evidence in this book weighs in on the negative side.

Every firm is embedded in a political and social context, and every firm is influenced by its participation in networks. No one denies this. The important task is to identify specific forms of social capital that have important effects on small-business viability. Pioneers like Ivan Light have done this by claiming that RCAs benefit Asian-immigrant-owned firms. Evidence in this book challenges Light's position. This does not mean that future researchers will be unable to link types of social capital positively to firm formation, growth, and survival. They probably will. To date, however, positive evidence that reliance on well-known forms of social capital benefits firm performance is fragmentary and qualitative. It is not convincing.

ANSWERED QUESTIONS

Creation of viable small businesses commonly entails skilled and capable entrepreneurs having access to financial capital to invest in the business ventures and access to viable markets for the products of their enterprises. Management, money, and markets are the essential building blocks: absence of one or more of these three elements of business viability often handicaps minority-owned firms.

Minority-owned businesses, more often than nonminority firms, exhibit mismatches between the owner's abilities and the type of market niche served. White pharmacists own pharmacies because this is the type of firm that best uses their work experience and skills. Korean immigrants educated in pharmacology who worked as pharmacists in Korea before immigration are much more likely than nonimmigrants to own businesses in the United States that have no connection to pharmacy. A mismatch exists, the causes of which lie in barriers unique to immigrants moving to a new country where business practices differ and a lack of language skills limits occupational choice. A mismatch exists when a preferential program lets an African American contractor be awarded a construction job without considering whether the contractor has the necessary financial liquidity and productive capacity to do the job. Mismatches can be found in nonminority small businesses, too, but more systematic mismatches of owner's managerial capacity, firm's financial capacity, and markets served typify black and Asian-immigrant small-business communities.

The range of markets served by minority-owned businesses has expanded greatly in recent decades. Forty years ago, the typical firm in the black business community was the mom-and-pop food store, the small restaurant, the beauty parlor, and the barbershop. Breaking into larger-scale lines of business and serving diverse clienteles has always been difficult for self-employed blacks due to barriers and constraints deeply rooted in American society. Although many of these constraints still linger, they have lessened, and since the 1970s, the black business community has increasingly entered the business mainstream.

Gains in human capital have been particularly important: a generation of college-educated black entrepreneurs is leading the way into emerging businesses serving racially diverse clienteles, including large corporations and government. Much of the uniqueness of the black business community today reflects the fact that financial-capital barriers have fallen much more slowly than other obstacles. Looking solely at young firms started by college-educated owners (table 8.2), 7.1 percent of business start-ups among nonminorities were in capital-intensive manufacturing and wholesaling; only 3.4 percent of black business start-ups, in contrast, were in these two fields. Black businesses are overrepresented in personal services, an area that stands out because it has the lowest capital requirements at start-up and the lowest mean profitability of any major small-business group in the United States. Financial-capital constraints depress the self-employment rate among black Americans, increase the small-business closure rate, and hold down the average size of firms in operation. The nature of the black business community, in turn, is skewed toward service businesses where capitalization requirements are low.

Forty years ago, the typical Asian American business was the restaurant, the food store, or the laundry. As constraints have declined, business diversity has flourished and clienteles have expanded into government and corporate realms. New-business creation was skewed in the 1980s by large-scale immigration of highly educated adults from countries such as South Korea, India, Hong Kong, and China. These immigrants accounted for nearly 70 percent of all Asian small-business start-ups in the United States during the 1980s. The Asian American small-business community stands out today because of its rapid growth in numbers—fueled by immigration—and its high incidence of owners with college degrees. While many of these highly educated and skilled business owners have been attracted to self-employment in professional services, another large group has concentrated in traditional lines—the restaurant, food store, and laundry dominant half a century ago—where profitability is low. Waldinger (1986) observed that the Asian-immigrant presence was particularly strong in small businesses requiring long hours in unpleasant conditions. Running a small retail store in a poor urban neighborhood has been a common choice. College graduates are typically overqualified for this type of self-employment. Their skills and experience would normally dictate managerial or professional salaried employment or perhaps self-employment in high-yielding fields offering incomes commensurate with those of white-collar employees. The college graduate running a retail store, quite simply, is underemployed.

Available evidence is far from comprehensive, but it suggests that overqualified, underemployed Asian-immigrant entrepreneurs are using small-business ownership as a transitional strategy (chapters 3–5). Faced with very limited occupational choices on arrival, many gravitate toward self-employment because they lack the specific skills (including English fluency) and contacts that might expand their options. As the barriers that skewed their occupational choices toward ownership of a marginal small business ease over time, Asian-immigrant entrepreneurs move up into positions commensurate with their education and skills. They escape from underemployment and work in jobs that are sufficiently attractive to justify the decision to leave their country of origin and migrate to the United States.

Future research will expand our understanding of Asian-immigrant involvement in small business by tracking through time the overqualified individuals who own the restaurants, the retail stores, and the laundries. What happens when they leave such firms? Do most become white-collar employees? Do some give up and return to their homelands? How many of them move into ownership of other small businesses? Answers to these questions will enable us to understand how successful self-employed immigrants seeking a new life for themselves and their families in the United States really are.

NOTES

1. Among young firms with owners working full-time in the business, for example, average 1987 before-tax profits were $19,296 for Asian-immigrant-owned firms, $17,014 for African American-owned firms, and $21,611 for nonminority-owned firms.

2. Among young firms with full-time owners who did not attend college, profits per hour were calculated by deducting a 10 percent return to equity from before-

tax profits. Thus, a firm started with a $20,000 equity investment that reported 1987 profits of $11,000 would have $2,000 in profits attributed to returns on capital and the remaining $9,000 attributed to returns to the owner's labor. If the owner worked 3,000 hours in the firm in 1987, profit per hour would be $3.00 ($9,000/3,000 hours). Actual profit-per-hour results were $3.59 for Asian Indians and Filipinos; $3.40 for Koreans and the Chinese; $3.32 for the Vietnamese; $4.76 for blacks; and $6.39 for nonminorities.

3. See profit calculations in chapters 4, 5, 7, and 8 for additional information on profitability.

4. Chinese immigrants, in fact, come to the United States from a variety of countries, including Hong Kong, Taiwan, the People's Republic, Vietnam, and so forth.

Appendix: Databases and Variable Definitions

DATABASES

I used the CBO database to describe small-business behavior in every chapter of this book. Most of my analyses using CBO data focus specifically on firms that generated gross revenues of $5,000 or more in 1987 and started business operations between 1979 and 1987. Studies of small business often fail to delineate groups of firms based on number of years of operation. Young firms are the primary focus of this book because the dynamics of firm behavior change greatly as firms age. Among firms in operation for ten or more years, for example, the owner's age is a major predictor of firm survival: old owners are more likely to shut down their firms than young owners. Among young firms, in contrast, the owner's age is much less important for predicting survival than the level of financial capital launching the firm. Old firms are survivors: the turmoil of sorting the viable from the nonviable is largely behind them. The firms that didn't make it are, of course, long gone. Because the struggle to achieve viability is a major focus in this study, looking at young firms makes sense.

Firms owned by Asian immigrants, furthermore, are a much younger group overall than nonminority-owned small businesses. Simple comparisons of white- and Asian-immigrant-owned firms, irrespective of the firm's age, run the risk of confusing age-related factors with differences between white and Asian-immigrant owners. The Asian small-business community itself differs sharply when younger and older firm groups are compared. Asian-owned firms in operation for ten or more years in 1987 were largely owned by Chinese and Japanese entrepreneurs. The younger group, in contrast, is much more skewed toward Asian Indian and Korean business owners. Analysis of firm groups, sorted by age, clarify the issues. Young firms, furthermore, tell us more than old firms about the future trajectory of small business. Personal services, for example, has long been the dominant niche for African American small-business owners. Yet comparisons of old and young firms reveal that personal services are fading, eclipsed by business services among black businesses started since 1979. The issues of interest in this study are usually addressed most effectively by limiting the analysis to younger firms only.

I used the SIPP database, compiled by the U.S. Bureau of the Census, in chapters 2 and 9 of this volume. The advantage of SIPP is its detailed data on household net worth and its components. No other database provides such a wealth of information on wealth. More than half of the young small firms represented in the CBO database that were started with some financial capital relied solely on the owner's equity capital: no debt was used. The source of this equity capital is almost entirely the household net worth of the small-business creator (Bates and Bradford 1992). Significant household wealth greatly enhances self-employment entry rates; a paucity of wealth greatly retards small-business formation.

The most popular large-scale databases used to date to investigate small-business behavior have been the Survey of Minority-Owned Business Enterprises (SMOBE) and the Public Use Microdata Sample (PUMS) databases; both are compiled by the U.S. Bureau of the Census. I will describe these databases briefly in this appendix to clarify why I have not used them in this book.

The CBO Database

GENERAL DESCRIPTION.   The data most widely used in this book were drawn from the CBO database compiled by the U.S. Bureau of the Census in 1992. These CBO data were generated by sampling all small-business income-tax returns for 1987 that reflected small-business or self-employment operations. The sampling base consisted of people who filed Schedule C, Form 1040 (sole proprietorships), Form 1065 (owners of partnerships), or Form 1120S (owners of subchapter S business corporations).

From this business tax-return base, the Census Bureau selected five samples of 25,000 each defined by gender and race or ethnicity: (1) white male owners, (2) white female owners, (3) black owners, (4) Hispanic owners, and (5) other minority owners (predominantly Asian). In cases where a business had more than one owner, all of the owners (up to ten) of the firm were included in the sample. If a firm had more than ten owners, the ten with the largest stakes were selected. These 125,000 owners were associated with 90,213 firms; 19,954 were corporations, 8,238 were partnerships, and 62,021 were sole proprietorships. Owners in these samples were sent questionnaires in 1991, asking detailed questions about the characteristics of firms and owners, the markets served, the assistance received, and other matters. Corporations responded at a rate of 79.8 percent, partnerships at a rate of 73.1 percent, and sole proprietorships at a rate of 70.0 percent. Among the respondents, item nonresponse rates were low. For the question identifying immigrant status, for example, usable responses were received from 95.8 percent of minorities who were neither black nor Hispanic (the lowest group response rate) and 96.5 percent of non-Hispanic white women (the highest group response rate).

The five samples of owners were not random: larger-scale firms using paid employees were systematically oversampled; tiny firms with no employees were undersampled. Responses from CBO questionnaires were combined with information from income-tax returns and social security records to generate the CBO database. Thus, sales figures are taken from income-tax returns, employment figures are taken from quarterly payroll returns filed with the IRS, selected gender and race information is taken from social security records, firm profitability information is taken from questionnaire responses, and so forth. All firms in the final CBO database were assigned weights to adjust for three types of biases that made the database nonrepresentative of small firms operating in 1987 nationwide. First, minority-owned firms and firms owned by women were heavily oversampled and weighted accordingly. Second, large-scale firms were oversampled and weighted accordingly. Third, nonrespondents were identified in terms of their 1987 sales, their line of business, and the state in which they were located. Using this detailed data on nonrespondents, respondent firms having the same sales, industry, and location were weighted more heavily, based on the assumption that nonrespondents resembled respondents. Note that while the unit of observation in the CBO database can be either the owner or the firm, throughout this book, firms (not owners) have been the unit of analysis.

STRONG POINTS.   This survey of 125,000 individual owners and 90,000 plus small firms is unlike any other small-business survey or database created to date. Other sources, such as the Public Use Microdata Samples (PUMS), which uses samples from the decennial census, describe self-employed people as individuals; periodic business census data describe individual business establishments as businesses. The CBO is the first very large, nationwide database that both describes self-employed people as individuals and describes the traits of the firms these people own—sales, employees, profits, financial-capital investment, and so forth. The CBO, furthermore, is designed to facilitate comparisons between minority and nonminority businesses. Additional detail on the CBO database appear in Nucci (1992).

WEAK POINTS.   One problem inherent in the design of the CBO database stems from the fact that self-employment and small-business ownership are not synonymous. The question "How did you acquire ownership of this business?" is likely to be confusing to a person who hosted a Tupperware party five years ago. Self-employment activities are supplemental for many people whose main labor status is "employee." Many are operating casual businesses, particularly those who file Schedule C income tax forms. Quite frequently, these casual business owners are full-time employees, and their revenues from self-employment are quite low. Over 30 percent of all small businesses operating in 1987, as defined in the CBO database, generated gross sales revenues of under $5,000. Indeed, anyone filing a Schedule C sole proprietorship return and generating gross revenues of at least $500 in 1987 is counted as a small business in the CBO database. This is misleading. By including such casual businesses, the Census Bureau's methodology seriously overstates the number of actual entities that most people would recognize as small businesses. Such casual businesses are minimized in the analyses using CBO data appearing in this book: only those that generated revenues of $5,000 or more in 1987 are included.

The summary statistics describing broad groups of minority businesses that appear throughout this book therefore are inconsistent with sales figures appearing in U.S. Bureau of the Census publications such as *Survey of Minority-Owned Business Enterprises: Summary* (1991, table 1). Mean sales figures describing the universe of minority businesses reported here are invariably higher because application of the $5,000 sales cutoff sharply reduces the size of the nation's minority business community.

Survey of Minority-Owned Business Enterprises (SMOBE)

GENERAL DESCRIPTION   SMOBE data, compiled by the U.S. Bureau of the Census, are more widely used in analyses of minority business than any other single data source. The SMOBE data are released at five-year intervals: the most recent data available, for 1992, were released in stages in 1996 and 1997. The U.S. Bureau of the Census compiles SMOBE data for three groups: blacks, Hispanics, and other minorities. It compiles data on firm characteristics from two sources: income-tax return tabulations and survey data. The SMOBE data are made public in aggregate forms; the firms are grouped by geographic location, business type, and employer status. Thus, for example, one can use the SMOBE date to calculate mean sales in 1992 for black-owned construction firms in Baltimore that used paid employees. In general, the SMOBE does not provide detailed data on firms unless the number in the area under consideration is quite large. In Minneapolis, for example, the SMOBE provides no information on mean sales by business group for businesses such as manufacturing and wholesaling because the number of black-owned firms in Minneapolis was too low to do so without violating prevailing standards on data confidentiality and disclosure. In geographic areas with fewer than 1,000 minority-owned firms, the SMOBE provides very little detailed information on business-specific groups of firms.

STRONG POINTS   Since the SMOBE data are published at five-year intervals, it is possible to calculate changes in the composition of minority business over time, by business group as well as by region (in regions with numerous minority firms). At substantial cost, it is possible to request special tabulations of the SMOBE data from the Census Bureau.

WEAK POINTS   The data on blacks are more accurate than the data on Hispanics and other minorities. The social security records used to identify blacks are less well suited to identifying other minorities such as Hispanics; prior to 1981, racial-group data were limited to whites, blacks, and others. The SMOBE conducts minority business surveys to try to rectify this problem. However, the data on specific regions are particularly suspect when they describe minority groups other than blacks. In addition, the SMOBE is constantly changing its methodology in ways that introduce multiple inconsistencies when comparing years. For example, in 1977, two firms owned by the same person would have been counted as one combined firm by the SMOBE; in 1982, they would have been counted as two separate firms. Finally, the SMOBE includes everyone who files a Schedule C income-tax return as a business owner, even those who are full-time employees and report very small amounts of self-employment income. Many of the supposed businesses are therefore the casual firms described above in the discussion of the CBO database's weaknesses. The SMOBE does not lend itself to deletion of these non-businesses, because it is not designed to be accessible to manipulation by scholarly researchers. Thus, the SMOBE overstates the number of minority-owned firms and understates the average sales per firm. The SMOBE, finally, is a business survey, revealing nothing about owners beyond race and gender. An example of research that is based on SMOBE data appears in Stevens (1984).

Public Use Microdata Samples (PUMS)

GENERAL DESCRIPTION   PUMS has been a popular data source among minority business researchers; see, for example, Fairlie and Meyer (1996), Borjas (1986), Boyd (1991a), and Light and Rosenstein (1995). Since 1980, when PUMS was expanded to include 5 percent of the household records covered by the decennial census, the data file has been enormous. The PUMS provides detailed data on self-employed individuals, including extensive demographic data, the individual's educational background, occupation, income by source, the geographic location of the home and workplace, and so forth.

STRONG POINTS   In contrast to the SMOBE, people are identified according to their primary labor-force attachment, which means that it is possible to sort recipients into groups for whom self-employment (as opposed to wage and salary work) is their primary activity in the labor market. The PUMS sample is large enough to permit area-specific analyses of minority firms in states where minorities are numerous and in individual large cities and metropolitan statistical areas (MSAs). Because the PUMS consists of data on self-employed individuals, it is easy for researchers to establish numerous business subsets to highlight such features as the business group and various demographic traits of owners. Because the data are available at ten-year intervals, one can trace the changing composition of minority business through time.

WEAK POINTS   The PUMS focuses on the traits of self-employed people, but it contains nothing directly about the traits of the businesses themselves, such as annual sales, number of employees, financial capital investment, and so forth. In addition, the PUMS has treated Hispanics inconsistently over the years; one must be very careful when comparing Hispanic self-employed groups in 1970 and 1980.

When researchers compare a self-employed group, such as Asian immigrants, to whites or blacks engaged in self-employment, absence of business traits greatly complicates interpretation of the findings. If, for example, self-employment earnings among Asian college graduates are observed to be lower than those of similar whites, this could mean that Asian immigrants really earn less or it could mean that Asians are disproportionately involved in young firms, which have lower average profits than older, established firms. Thus, the "Asian" trait is strongly correlated to the "age of firm" trait, but controlling for the firm's age, which could make the racial difference in self-employment earnings vanish, is impossible with PUMS. The real meaning of an observed racial difference in self-employment earnings therefore remains unknown.

Similarly, self-employment earnings for Asian immigrants may exceed those typifying blacks. The "Asian" trait, however, is strongly correlated to the amount of financial capital invested in the typical small-business venture: controlling for the owner's age, education, and other factors, "Asian" is, on average, associated with high financial capital, relative to the mean capitalization of black-owned firms. Higher earnings for Asians may reflect higher capitalization or some other business trait not recorded in the PUMS database. The meaning of a comparison between self-employment earnings of blacks and Asians is therefore quite unclear. The database was simply not designed to facilitate small-business analysis.

Survey of Income and Program Participation (SIPP)

GENERAL DESCRIPTION   SIPP panels originated by the U.S. Bureau of the Census in 1984 and 1988 are examined in this book. SIPP is a nationwide, longitudinal survey of households that provides detailed information on household net worth and adult self-employment activity. Households included in a SIPP panel are interviewed eight times, at four-month intervals. SIPP contains two main sections. The core interview covers basic demographic and social characteristics for each member of the household. Core questions, repeated at each interview, cover areas such as labor-force activity and types and amounts of income. Topical modules, known as "waves," covering governmental program recipiency, employment history, household net worth, and various other topics rotate among the various interviews.

STRONG POINTS   SIPP's large random sample provides an exceptional opportunity to investigate the wealth of average American households and to examine asset inequality among significant social and demographic groups. The major types of resources covered by SIPP's assets module include savings accounts, stocks, business equity, mutual funds, bonds, Keogh and IRA accounts, and equity in homes and vehicles. Liabilities covered in the survey include loans, credit card bills, medical bills, home mortgages, and personal debts. (The study did not cover pension funds or the cash value of insurance policies, jewelry, or household durables.) Thus SIPP provides an unusually comprehensive and rich source of information on assets and liabilities. Other surveys, by contrast, offer little information on household assets; they are also difficult to replicate.

SIPP's longitudinal structure is ideal for chapter 2's task of analyzing the impact of personal wealth on self-employment entry. By obtaining information on the extent to which initial wealth subsequently affected business entry, it is pos-sible to make inferences about the potential significance of financial barriers to business ownership. A cross-sectional analysis of factors underlying business ownership, in contrast, would not permit an unambiguous interpretation of wealth's impact because there is no simple relationship between household wealth and business ownership. Substantial wealth can be as much the result of business ownership as the cause. A cross-sectional analysis showing that wealth is positively related to business ownership could imply either that higher wealth facilitated new-business entry or that business ownership over time facilitated accumulation of wealth.

WEAK POINTS   Surveys of assets and wealth invariably underrepresent the upper levels, primarily because of the difficulty of obtaining the cooperation of enough very wealthy subjects. Thus, random field surveys conservatively understate the magnitude of wealth inequality. Random surveys also underestimate populations that are difficult to locate. Thus SIPP, like practically every other major social survey, tends to undersample such populations as unemployed young black males or other youthful populations.

SIPP is not a survey of small businesses, and it therefore suffers from deficiencies noted in the above discussion of the weak points of PUMS when used to study small-business behavior. Unlike PUMS, however, researchers to date have not pushed SIPP beyond its usefulness by basing analyses of self-employment earnings on SIPP data. Analyses to date have focused on the narrower objective of predicting self-employment entry; see, for example, Bates (1995c).

VARIABLE DEFINITIONS

SIPP Data

Definitions of the variables used in chapter 2's logistic regression analyses of self-employment entry (tables 2.1–2.5) are described below. The dependent variable "business entry" was defined to exclude people claiming self-employment status whose self-employment activities were trivial. To focus the analysis on noncasual business ownership, I defined self-employment entry as occurring if a business was formally incorporated or if business activity took place above a minimum scale. The two measures of "minimum scale" were, first, self-employment that generated annualized net profits or losses of at least $1,000 and, second, people working at least ten hours a week, on average, during one or more survey periods. Within the SIPP sample of all adults 21–60 years old who did not own a business in the first interview period, business entry took place if the individual reported business ownership, as defined above, during any of the subsequent seven interview periods (twenty-eight months). The dependent variable, "self-employment entry," is equal to one if business entry took place; for all others, it is equal to zero.

EXPLANATORY VARIABLES

Education: these variables equal one under the following conditions (and zero otherwise):
"Not high school": those who never graduated from high school.
"High school": those who are high-school graduates only.
"College, 1–3 years": those with some college education.
"College graduate": those who earned a college degree.
"Graduate school": those with at least some graduate education.

Household net worth ("wealth"): these variables equal one under the following conditions (and zero otherwise):
"Under $10,000": household net worth under $10,000.
"$10,000–25,000": household net worth of at least $10,000 and less than $25,000.
"$25,000–50,000": household net worth of at least $25,000 and less than $50,000.

"$50,000–100,000": household net worth of at least $50,000 and less than $100,000.
"$100,000 +": household net worth of at least $100,000.

Age: to account for possible nonlinearities, the individual's age ("Age") and the squared valued of the age ("Age^2") are both used as explanatory variables.

Gender: "Gender" is a dichotomous variable that equals one for men and zero for women.

Marital status: "Married" is a dichotomous variable that equals one if the individual is married, zero otherwise.

Work experience: "Work experience" is a continuous variable measuring the number of years of employment reported by the individual.

Race, ethnicity: these variables equal one under the following conditions (and zero otherwise):
"Black": if black, whether or not Hispanic.
"Hispanic": if Hispanic (of any race).
"Asian": if Asian or Pacific Islander.
"Minority": if black, Hispanic, Asian, Native American, Pacific Islander, or other minority.

Variables used in chapter 9's analysis of household net worth overlapped with the above list, but five new variables were introduced. The dependent variable in table 9.3's OLS regression analysis is the log of the dollar amount of household net worth reported in 1985. The population being analyzed resembles that of chapter 2 because it includes only adults aged 21 to 60; unlike chapter 2, however, the analysis of wealth includes people who were self-employed at the time of the initial SIPP interview. (Chapter 2 analyzed people not self-employed at the time of the initial interview.) Additional explanatory variables used to analyze wealth-holding patterns, which were not examined in chapter 2, are listed below.

EXPLANATORY VARIABLES

Home ownership: "Owns home" is a dichotomous variable that equals one for persons belonging to a homeowning household, zero otherwise.

Household income: the log of the dollar amount of household income from all sources is defined as "Household income."

Children: "Kids" is a dichotomous variable that equals one if children under the age of 18 are present in the household, zero otherwise.

Metropolitan area: "MSA" is a dichotomous variable that equals one if the household is located in a metropolitan area, zero otherwise.

CBO data

Variables from the CBO database are used in every chapter of this book. In chapters 1 and 2, I presented summary statistics and used logistic regression models to analyze firm survival patterns between 1987 and 1991. In all of chapter 2's logistic regression models, the dependent variable is whether or not the business that was operating in 1987 was still functioning in late 1991. Businesses that were still operating are considered active firms; those that had closed down are considered discontinued; active firms are represented by a dependent variable of one, while discontinued firms are zeros. When active and discontinued firms are represented in a table of summary statistics, this variable is "Percent of firms still operating, 1991" (see chapter 1). Variables appearing in tables of summary statistics or logistic regression equations in chapters 1 and 2 are formally defined below.

OWNER'S TRAITS

Education: these variables equal one under the following conditions (and zero otherwise):
"Not high school": those who never graduated from high school.
"High school": those who are high-school graduates only.
"College, 1–3 years": those with some college education.
"College graduate": those who earned a college degree.
"Graduate school": those with at least some graduate education.

Age: to account for possible nonlinearities, the individual's age ("Age") and the squared value of age ("Age^2") are both used as explanatory variables.

Gender: "Gender" is a dichotomous variable that equals one for men and zero for women.

Marital status: "Married" is a dichotomous variable that equals one if the individual is married and living with his or her spouse, zero otherwise.

Race, ethnicity: these variables equal one under the following conditions (and zero otherwise):
"Black": if black, whether or not Hispanic.
"Hispanic": if Hispanic (of any race).
"Asian immigrant": if Asian or Pacific Islander and not born in the United States.
"Asian American": if Asian or Pacific Islander and born in the United States.

"Other minority": if minority other than black, Hispanic, or Asian (largely Native Americans).

"Owner-labor input": number of hours during the 1987 calendar year spent by the owner working in the relevant small business, divided by 100.

"Managerial experience": equals one for those working in a managerial capacity prior to starting the business they owned in 1987, otherwise zero.

FIRM'S TRAITS

"Gross sales, 1987": the dollar amount of gross sales revenues generated by the firm during the 1987 calendar year.

"Net income, 1987": the dollar amount of firm net profits, before taxes, generated in 1987.

"Total financial capital": the dollar amount of debt plus equity capital used to start, or become the owner of, the business.

"Debt capital": the dollar amount of financial capital that was borrowed to enter or start the business.

"Equity capital": the dollar amount of financial capital that was not borrowed to enter or start the business.

"Capital": the log of the sum of debt and equity capital used to start or become the owner of the business.

"Leverage": the ratio of debt to equity capital invested in the firm at start-up.

"Number of employees": the average number of paid workers reported to the federal government on 1987 quarterly payroll forms.

"Bought ongoing firm" equals one if the owner entered a business that was already in operation, zero if the owner was the original founder of the business.

"Construction" equals one for firms operating in construction fields, otherwise zero.

"Skill-intensive" equals one for firms operating in professional services, business services, or finance, insurance, or real estate, otherwise zero.

"Capital-intensive" equals one for firms operating in manufacturing or wholesaling, otherwise zero.

"Entered: 1984–1985" equals one if the business was started or acquired during 1984 or 1985, otherwise zero.

"Entered: 1986" equals one if the business was started or acquired during 1986, otherwise zero.

"Entered: 1987" equals one if the business was started or acquired during 1987, otherwise zero.

In chapters 3 and 4, I used OLS regression models to analyze firm profitability and introduced additional CBO variables. In chapter 3's OLS regression exercises, the dependent variable is the log of the total dollar amount of firm profits, before taxes, generated in 1987. When this variable appears in tables of summary statistics, it is not in log form, and it is called "Net income, 1987." Independent variables appearing for the first time in chapters 3 and 4 are defined below.

OWNER'S CHARACTERISTICS

"Asian Indian" equals one for Asian Indian-immigrant owners, zero otherwise.
"Chinese" equals one for Chinese-immigrant owners, zero otherwise.
"Korean" equals one for Korean-immigrant owners, zero otherwise.
"Vietnamese" equals one for Vietnamese-immigrant owners, zero otherwise.

FIRM'S CHARACTERISTICS

"Minority clientele" equals one if 50 percent or more of the firm's customers were minorities, otherwise zero.

"Minority labor force": for firms having paid employees only in 1987, this variable measures the percentage of workers who were minorities; this continuous variable ranges in value from zero to one.

"Agglomeration" equals one for firms located in the New York City metropolitan area, Los Angeles County, Orange County, the San Francisco–Oakland metropolitan area, or the San Jose metropolitan area, otherwise zero.

"Traditional firm" equals one for firms operating in retailing or personal services, otherwise zero.

A variant of the logistic regression exercise analyzing firm survival is introduced in table 4.4: the dependent variable refers to the owner's perseverance in the firm instead of firm survival. If the owner of the firm in 1987 left this business by 1991, then the dependent variable in table 4.4 equals zero even if the firm remains in operation. If the owner of the firm in 1987 was still running the business in 1991, then the dependent variable equals one. This variant of the logistic regression model highlights the tendency of highly educated Asian Indians and Filipinos to leave self-employment by selling their firms rather than shutting them down.

Chapter 5 introduces no new dependent or explanatory variables, but chapter 6—with its focus on explaining the borrowing patterns of firms—does. "Debt capital" (defined above) is the dependent variable in the chapter 6 OLS regression models that analyze loan amounts received by borrowing firms. Four new explanatory variables are introduced in these OLS regressions, and all four measure firm traits:

"Loan source: family" equals one if firms used debt borrowed from family members such as parents to finance business start-up, otherwise zero.

"Loan source: friends" equals one if firms used debt borrowed from friends to finance business start-up, otherwise zero.

"Loan source: bank" equals one if firms used debt borrowed from financial institutions to finance business start-up, otherwise zero.

"Loan source: former owner" equals one if firms used debt borrowed from former owners of their small business to finance business entry, otherwise zero. Loans from this source arise from buyouts, and they are most common in retailing.

Chapter 7 introduces no variables that are entirely new, but a variant of the previously defined "minority clientele" is used in econometric models. Black firms are more likely than others to serve a predominantly minority clientele, particularly in traditional lines of business, where nearly all clients in fields like personal services are African Americans. The definition of "minority clientele" used in chapters 7 through 9 for analyzing black business is:

"Minority clientele" equals one if 75 percent or more of the firm's customers were minorities, otherwise zero.

Chapter 8 introduces new variables used only once, and they are defined fully within chapter 8's analysis of black business sales and numbers of firms.

Chapter 9 uses no new CBO variables, but chapter 10 introduces one explanatory variable that is a variant of previously defined variables:

"Family, friends loan source" equals one if loan source is family or friends, otherwise zero.

Chapter 11 introduces new variables that are unique to that chapter's analysis of government procurement policies; the new variables are therefore fully defined in that chapter.

References

Acs, Zolton, and David Audretsch. 1989. Small firm entry in manufacturing. *Economica* 56 (2): 255–65.

Aldrich, Howard, John Carter, Trevor Jones, David McEvoy, and Paul Vellemen. 1985. Ethnic residential segregation and the protected market hypothesis. *Social Forces* 63 (4): 996–1009.

Aldrich, Howard, and Albert Reiss. 1976. Continuities in the study of ecological succession: Changes in the race composition of neighborhoods and their businesses. *American Journal of Sociology* 81 (4): 846–66.

Aldrich, Howard, Ben Rosen, and William Woodward. 1987. The impact of social networks on business foundings and profit: A longitudinal study. In *Frontiers in entrepreneurial research*, edited by N. Churchill, J. Hornaday, O. Krasner, and K. Vesper. Wellesley, Mass.: Babson College.

Aldrich, Howard, and Roger Waldinger. 1990. Trends in ethnic businesses in the United States. In *Ethnic entrepreneurs: Immigrant business in industrial societies*, edited by Roger Waldinger, Howard Aldrich, and Robin Ward. Newbury Park, Calif.: Sage.

Aldrich, Howard, and Catherine Zimmer. 1986. Entrepreneurship in social networks. In *Population perspectives on organizations*, edited by Howard Aldrich. Uppsala: Acta Universitates Upsaliensis.

Alexis, Marcus. 1971. Some Negro-white differences in consumption. In *The black consumer*, edited by George Joyce and Norman Govoni. New York: Random House.

Ando, Faith. 1988. Capital issues and minority-owned business. *Review of Black Political Economy* 16 (4): 77–109.

Bailey, Thomas, and Roger Waldinger. 1991. Primary, secondary, and enclave labor markets: A training systems approach. *American Sociological Review* 56 (4): 432–45.

Baltimore County Grand Jury. 1992. Special report concerning the Maryland Minority Business Enterprise program. Unpublished.

Bates, Timothy. 1973. *Black capitalism: A quantitative analysis.* New York: Praeger.

———. 1978. Profitability in traditional and emerging lines of black business enterprise. *Journal of Urban Economics* 5 (2): 154–71.

———. 1984. Small Business Administration loan programs. In *Sources of financing for small business,* edited by Paul Horvitz and R. Richardson Pettit. Greenwich, Conn.: JAI Press.

———. 1985. Entrepreneur human capital endowments and minority business viability. *Journal of Human Resources* 20 (4): 540–54.

———. 1986. Characteristics of minorities who are entering self-employment. *Review of Black Political Economy* 15 (2): 31–49.

———. 1987. Self-employed minorities: Traits and trends. *Social Science Quarterly* 68 (3): 539–51.

———. 1989. Small business viability in the urban ghetto. *Journal of Regional Science* 29 (4): 625–43.

———. 1990a. The Characteristics of Business Owners data base. *Journal of Human Resources* 25 (4): 752–56.

———. 1990b. Entrepreneurial human capital inputs and small business longevity. *Review of Economics and Statistics* 72 (4): 551–59.

———. 1991. Commercial bank financing of white and black-owned small business startups. *Quarterly Review of Economics and Business* 31 (1): 64–80.

———. 1993a. Assessment of the New Jersey, New York City area small business construction sector. Report to the Port Authority of New York and New Jersey, and the Regional Alliance of Small Contractors.

———. 1993b. *Banking on black enterprise.* Washington, D.C.: Joint Center for Political and Economic Studies.

———. 1994a. An analysis of Korean immigrant-owned small business startups with comparisons to African American- and nonminority-owned firms. *Urban Affairs Quarterly* 30 (2): 227–48.

———. 1994b. Social resources generated by group support networks may not be beneficial to Asian immigrant-owned firms. *Social Forces* 72 (3): 671–89.

———. 1995a. An analysis of the SSBIC program: Problems and prospects. Final report to the U.S. Small Business Administration under grant SBIC-94-001-01.

———. 1995b. Explaining Asian immigrant self-employment patterns in the United States. Unpublished.

———. 1995c. Self-employment entry across industry groups. *Journal of Business Venturing* 10 (6): 143–56.

———. 1995d. Small businesses appear to benefit from state and local governments' economic development assistance. *Urban Affairs Review* 31 (2): 206–25.

————. 1997. The Minority Enterprise Small Business Investment Company program: Institutionalizing a nonviable minority business assistance infrastructure. *Urban Affairs Review* 32(5): 683–703.

Bates, Timothy, and William Bradford. 1979. *Financing black economic development.* New York: Academic Press.

————. 1992. Factors affecting new firm success and their use in venture capital financing. *Journal of Small Business Finance* 2 (1): 23–38.

Bates, Timothy, and Constance Dunham. 1993. Asian American success in self-employment. *Economic Development Quarterly* 7 (2): 199–214.

Bates, Timothy, and Caren Grown. 1992. Commercial bank lending practices and the development of black-owned construction companies. *Journal of Urban Affairs* 14 (1): 25–41.

Bates, Timothy, and David Howell. 1997. The declining status of African American men in the New York City construction industry. In *Race, markets, and social outcomes,* edited by Patrick Mason and Rhonda Williams. Boston: Kluwer.

Bates, Timothy, and Alfred Nucci. 1989. An analysis of small business size and rate of discontinuance. *Journal of Small Business Management* 27 (4): 1–7.

Bates, Timothy, and Lisa Servon. 1996. Why loans won't save the poor. *Inc.* 18: 27–28.

Bates, Timothy, and Darrell Williams. 1995. Preferential procurement programs and minority-owned businesses. *Journal of Urban Affairs* 17 (1): 1–17.

Blau, Francine, and John Graham. 1990. Black-white differences in wealth and asset composition. *Quarterly Journal of Economics* 105 (2): 321–39.

Bonacich, Edna, and Ivan Light. 1988. *Immigrant entrepreneurs: Koreans in Los Angeles 1965–1982* Berkeley: University of California Press.

Bonacich, Edna, and John Modell. 1981. *The economic basis of ethnic solidarity.* Berkeley: University of California Press.

Borjas, George, 1986. The self-employment experience of immigrants. *Journal of Human Resources* 21 (4): 485–506.

————. 1989. Economic theory and international migration. *International Migration Review* 23 (3): 457–85.

————. 1990. *Friends or strangers: The impact of immigrants on the U.S. economy.* New York: Basic Books.

————. 1994. The economics of immigration. *Journal of Economic Literature* 32 (4): 1667–1717.

Boston, Thomas. 1992. Are Atlanta's MBE programs socially beneficial? Unpublished paper delivered at Association for Public Policy and Management annual conference, Denver, Colo., October 30, 1992.

————. 1997. *Strict scrutiny: Minority setasides and African American entrepreneurship.* New York: Routledge.

Boyd, Robert. 1990a. Black and Asian self-employment in large metropolitan areas: A comparative analysis. *Social Problems* 37 (2): 258–74.

———. 1990b. Black business transformation, black well-being, and public policy. *Population Research and Policy Review* 9: 117–32.

———. 1991a. A contextual analysis of black self-employment in large metropolitan areas, 1970–1980. *Social Forces* 70 (2): 409–29.

———. 1991b. Inequality in the earnings of self-employed African and Asian Americans. *Sociological Perspectives* 34 (4): 447–72.

Brimmer, Andrew. 1966. The Negro in the national economy. In *American Negro reference book*, edited by John David. Englewood Cliffs, N.J.: Prentice Hall.

———. 1968. Desegregation and Negro leadership. In *Business leadership and the Negro crisis*, edited by Eli Ginsberg. New York: McGraw-Hill.

Brimmer, Andrew, and Henry Terrell. 1971. The economic potential of black capitalism. *Public Policy* 14 (2): 289–308.

Bruderl, Josef, Peter Preisendorfer, and Rolf Ziegler. 1992. Survival chances of newly founded business organizations. *American Sociological Review* 57 (2): 227–41.

Butler, John. 1991. *Entrepreneurship and self-help among black Americans.* Albany: State University of New York.

Caplovitz, David. 1967. *The poor pay more.* New York: Free Press.

Carsrud, A. L., K. W. Olm, and G. G. Eddy. 1986. Entrepreneurship: Research in quest of a paradigm. *The Art and science of entrepreneurship*, edited by D. L. Sexton and R. W. Smilor. Cambridge, Mass.: Ballinger.

Carter, D., and R. Wilson. 1992. *Minorities in higher education.* Washington, D.C.: American Council on Higher Education.

———. 1995. *Minorities in higher education.* Washington, D.C.: American Council on Higher Education.

Chan, Janet, and Yuet-Wah Cheung. 1985. Ethnic resources and business enterprise: A study of Chinese businesses in Toronto. *Human Organization* 44 (2): 142–54.

Clark, P., and T. Huston. 1993. *Assisting the smallest businesses.* Washington, D.C.: The Aspen Institute.

Cooper, A. C., and William Dunkelberg. 1982. Entrepreneurial typologies: An empirical study. *Frontiers of entrepreneurship research*, edited by K. Vesper. Boston: Babson College.

Cooper, A. C., C. Y. Woo, and William Dunkelberg. 1989. Entrepreneurship and the initial size of firms. *Journal of Business Venturing* 4 (5): 317–32.

COSCDA. 1993. *National directory of state minority business enterprise programs.* Report to the U.S. Department of Commerce, Minority Business Development Agency.

Daniels, Roger. 1988. *Asian America.* Seattle: University of Washington Press.

Desantis, Victor. 1990. Profiles of individual cities and counties. In *The municipal yearbook*. Washington, D.C.: International City Management Association.

Development Associates, Inc. 1987. *Attitudes and inclinations of minority youth toward business ownership.* Washington, D.C.: U.S. Department of Commerce, Minority Business Development Agency.

Devine, Theresa, and Joyce Mlaker. 1992. Inter-industry variation in the determinants of self-employment. Unpublished.

Drake, St. Clair, and Horace Cayton. 1962. *Black metropolis.* New York: Harper and Row.

D'Souza, Dinesh. 1995. Work and the African American. *American Enterprise* 6 (5): 33–34.

Dubini, Paola, and Howard Aldrich. 1991. Personal and extended networks are central to the entrepreneurial process. *Journal of Business Venturing* 6 (4): 305–13.

Du Bois, W. E. B. 1899. *The Philadelphia Negro: A social study.* Reprint, New York: Schocken Books, 1967.

Eisinger, Peter. 1984. Black mayors and the politics of racial advancement. In *Readings in urban politics: Past, present, and future,* edited by Harlan Hahn and Charles Levine. New York: Longmans.

Evans, David. 1987. The relationship between firm size, growth, and age: Estimates for 100 manufacturing industries. *Journal of Industrial Economics* 35 (4): 567–81.

Evans, David, and Boyan Jovanovic. 1989. An estimated model of entrepreneurial choice under liquidity constraints. *Journal of Political Economy* 97 (4): 808–27.

Evans, David, and Linda Leighton. 1989. Some empirical aspects of entrepreneurship. *American Economic Review.* 79 (3): 519–35.

Evans, M. D. R. 1989. Immigrant entrepreneurship: Effects of ethnic market size and isolated labor pool. *American Sociological Review* 54 (6): 950–62.

Fairlie, Robert. 1994. The absence of the African-American owned business: An analysis of the dynamics of self-employment. Unpublished.

Fairlie, Robert, and Bruce Meyer. 1996. Ethnic and racial self-employment differences and possible explanations. *Journal of Human Resources* 31 (4): 757–93.

Fleming, G., and Bernice Sheldon. 1938. Fine food for Philadelphia. *Crisis* 45 (4): 107–114.

Foley, E. 1966. The Negro businessman: In search of a tradition. In *The Negro American,* edited by Talcott Parsons and Kenneth Clark. Boston: Houghton Mifflin.

Fratoe, Frank. 1986. A sociological analysis of minority business. *Review of Black Political Economy.* 15 (2): 5–29.

———. 1988. Social capital of small business owners. *Review of Black Political Economy* 16 (4): 33–50.

Fratoe, Frank, and Ronald Meeks. 1988. *Business participation rates and self-employment incomes: An analysis of the 50 largest ancestry groups.* Los Angeles: UCLA Center for Afro-American Studies.

Fusfeld, Daniel, and Timothy Bates. 1984. *Political economy of the urban ghetto.* Carbondale: Southern Illinois University Press.

Galenson, Marjorie. 1972. Do blacks save more? *American Economic Review* 62 (1): 211–16.

Hamermesh, Daniel. 1982. Social insurance and consumption. *American Economic Review* 72 (1): 101–13.

Harmon, J. H., Arnett Lindsay, and Carter Woodson. 1929. *The Negro as a businessman.* College Park, Md.: McGrath.

Harris, Abram. 1936. *The Negro as capitalist.* Philadelphia: American Academy of Political and Social Science.

Holsey, Albon. 1938. Seventy-five years of Negro business. *Crisis* 45 (7): 241–42.

Holtz-Eakin, D., D. Joulfaian, and H. Rosen. 1994. Sticking it out: Entrepreneurial survival and liquidity constraints. *Journal of Political Economy* 102 (1): 53–75.

Houghton, Mary, 1995. Lessons about economic development interventions. Unpublished paper delivered at Association of Collegiate Schools of Planning annual meeting, Detroit, Mich., October 1995.

Ichioka, Yuji. 1988. *The Issei.* New York: The Free Press.

Jaynes, Gerald, and Robin Williams. 1989. *A common destiny: Blacks in American society.* Washington, D.C.: National Academy Press.

Johnson, James H., Jr. 1995. The competitive advantage of the inner city: Comment. *Harvard Business Review* 73: 152.

Joint Center for Political and Economic Studies (JCPES). 1987. *Black elected officials: A national roster.* Washington, D.C.: Joint Center for Political and Economic Studies.

———. 1994. *Assessment of minority business development programs.* Report to the U.S. Department of Commerce, Minority Business Development Agency.

Jovanovic, Boyan. 1982. Selection and the evolution of industry. *Econometrica* 50 (3): 649–70.

Kassoudji, Sherrie. 1988. English language abilities and the labor market opportunities of Hispanic and East Asian men. *Journal of Labor Economics* 6 (2): 205–28.

Kihlstrom, Richard, and Jean Laffont. 1979. A general equilibrium theory of firm formation based on risk-aversion. *Journal of Political Economy* 87 (4): 719–48.

Kim, Illsoo. 1981. *The new urban immigrants: The Korean community in New York.* Princeton, N.J.: Princeton University Press.

Kim, Kwang, Won Hurh, and Marilyn Fernandez. 1989. Intragroup differences in business participation: Three Asian immigrant groups. *International Migration Review* 23 (1): 73–95.

Kotkin, J. 1986. The reluctant entrepreneurs. *Inc.* 8 (9): 81–86.

Kusmer, K. 1976. *A ghetto takes shape: Black Cleveland, 1870–1930.* Chicago: University of Chicago Press.

Kutter, Robert. 1994. Only connect. *American Prospect.* 17: 6–10.

Kwong, Peter. 1987. *The new Chinatown.* New York: Hill and Wang.

Lee, Dong. 1992. Commodification of ethnicity: The sociospatial reproduction of immigrant entrepreneurs. *Urban Affairs Quarterly* 28 (2): 258–75.

Leiberson, Stanley. 1980. *A piece of the pie: Blacks and white immigrants since 1880.* Berkeley: University of California Press.

Levitan, S., and R. Belous. 1979. *More than subsistence: Minimum wages for the working poor.* Baltimore: Johns Hopkins University Press.

Light, Ivan. 1972. *Ethnic enterprise in America.* Berkeley: University of California Press.

————. 1980. Asian enterprise in America: Chinese, Japanese, and Koreans in small business. In *Self-help in urban America: Patterns of minority business enterprise*, edited by Scott Cummings. Port Washington, N.Y.: Kennibat Press.

Light, Ivan, and Stavros Karageorgis. 1994. Ethnic economy. In *The handbook of economic sociology*, edited by Neil Swelser and Richard Swedborg. New York: Princeton University Press.

Light, Ivan, Im Jung Kwuon, and Deng Zhong. 1990. Korean rotating credit associations in Los Angeles. *Amerasia Journal* 16 (2): 35–54.

Light, Ivan, and Carolyn Rosenstein. 1995. *Race, ethnicity, and entrepreneurship in urban America*. New York: Aldine De Gruyter.

Logan, John, Richard Alba, and Thomas McNulty. 1994. Ethnic economics in metropolitan regions. *Social Forces* 72 (3): 691–724.

Lucas, Robert. 1978. On the size distribution of business firms. *Bell Journal of Economics* 9 (2): 508–23.

Meyer, Bruce. 1990. Why are there so few black entrepreneurs? National Bureau of Economic Research, Working Paper No. 3537.

Min, Pyong. 1984a. From white collar occupations to small business: Korean immigrants' occupational adjustment. *Sociological Quarterly* 25 (3): 333–452.

————. 1984b. A structural analysis of Korean business in the United States. *Ethnic Groups* 6 (1): 1–25.

————. 1986–87. Filipino and Korean immigrants in small business: A comparative analysis. *Amerasia Journal* 13 (1): 53–71.

————. 1988. Ethnic business enterprise: Korean small business in Atlanta. Discussion paper. New York: Center for Migration Studies.

————. 1993. Korean immigrants in Los Angeles. In *Immigration and entrepreneurship: Culture, capital, and ethnic networks*, edited by Ivan Light and Parminder Bhachu. New Brunswick, N.J: Transaction Publishers.

Moore, Robert. 1983. Employer discrimination: Evidence from self-employed workers. *Review of Economics and Statistics* 65 (3): 496–500.

Moulder, Evelina. 1987. Profiles of individual cities and counties. In *The municipal yearbook*. Washington, D.C.: International City Management Association.

Nee, Victor, and Brett Nee. 1973. *Longtime California: A documentary study of an American Chinatown*. New York: Pantheon.

Nucci, Alfred. 1992. The Characteristics of Business Owners data base. Discussion paper. U.S. Bureau of the Census, Center for Economic Studies.

O'Hare, W., R. Yu-Li, R. Chatterjee, and P. Shuker. 1982. *Blacks on the move: A decade of demographic change*. Washington, D.C.: Joint Center for Political Studies.

Oliver, Melvin L., and Thomas M. Shapiro. 1995. *Black wealth/white wealth: A new perspective on racial inequality*. New York: Routledge.

Park, In-Sook. 1990. Koreans immigrating to the United States: A pre-departure analysis. Discussion paper. University of Hawaii, East-West Center Population Institute.

Pierce, Joseph. 1947. *Negro business and business education*. New York: Harper and Brothers.

Portes, Alejandro, and Julia Sensenbrenner. 1993. Embeddedness and immigration: Notes on the social determinants of economic action. *American Journal of Sociology* 98 (6): 1320–50.

Portes, Alejandro, and Min Zhou. 1996. Self-employment and the earnings of immigrants. *American Sociological Review* 61 (2): 219–30.

Raheim, Salome. 1996. Micro enterprise as an approach for promoting economic development in social work. *International Social Work* 39 (1): 69–82.

Raheim, Salome, and Catherine Foster. 1995. *Self-employment demonstration final evaluation report.* Washington, D.C.: Corporation for Enterprise Development.

Regional Alliance for Small Contractors and the New York Building Conference. 1993. *Creating growth opportunities for minority and women-owned construction firms.* Unpublished.

Reimers, Cordelia. 1996. Methodological commentary. In *Immigrants and immigration policy: Individual skills, family ties, and group identities,* edited by Harriet Duleep and Phanindra Wunnova. Greenwich, Conn.: JAI Press.

Reynolds, P., and B. Miller. 1992. New firm gestation: Conception, birth, and implications for research. *Journal of Business Venturing* 7 (5): 405–17.

Sassen-Koob, Saskia. 1989. New York City's informal economy. In *The informal economy: Studies in advanced and less developed countries,* edited by A. Portes, M. Castells, and L. Benton. Baltimore: John Hopkins University Press.

Sowell, Thomas. 1983. *The economics and politics of race.* New York: Morrow.

Stein, Judith. 1986. *The world of Marcus Garvey.* Baton Rouge: LSU Press.

Stevens, Richard. 1984. Measuring minority business formation and failure. *Review of Black Political Economy* 12 (4): 71–84.

Suzuki, Masao. 1994. Japanese American economic achievement, 1900–1942. Ph.D. diss., Stanford University.

———. 1995. Success story? Japanese immigrant economic achievement and return migration, 1920–1930. *Journal of Economic History* 55 (4): 889–901.

———. 1996. Selective immigration, return migration, and family formation. Unpublished.

U.S. Bureau of the Census. 1985. *City government finances in 1982–1983.* Washington, D.C.: U.S. Department of Commerce.

———. 1990. *City government finances in 1987–1988.* Washington, D.C.: U.S. Department of Commerce.

———. 1991. *Survey of minority-owned business enterprises: Summary.* Washington, D.C.: Government Printing Office.

———. 1996. *Survey of minority-owned business enterprises: Summary.* Washington, D.C.: Government Printing Office.

U.S. Bureau of Economic Analysis. 1989. *Local area personal income: 1982–1987.* Washington, D.C.: U.S. Department of Commerce.

———. 1990. *Local area personal income: 1983–1988.* Washington, D.C.: U.S. Department of Commerce.

U.S. Bureau of Labor Statistics. 1982. *Employment and earnings*. Washington, D.C.: U.S. Department of Labor. April.

———. 1987. *Employment and earnings*. Washington, D.C.: U.S. Department of Labor. April.

U.S. Commission on Civil Rights. 1988. *The economic status of Americans of Asian descent*. Clearinghouse Publication 95. October.

U.S. Commission on Minority Business Development. 1992. *Final report*. Washington, D.C.: Government Printing Office.

Waldinger, Roger. 1986. *Through the eye of the needle*. New York: NYU Press.

———. 1994. The making of an immigrant niche. *International Migration Review* 28 (1): 3–30.

———. 1996. Who makes the beds? Who washes the dishes? Black/immigrant competition reassessed. In *Immigrants and immigration policy: Individual skills, family ties, and group identities*, edited by Harriet Duleep and Phanindra Wunnava. Greenwich, Conn.: JAI Press.

Waldinger, Roger, Howard Aldrich, and Robin Ward. 1990. *Ethnic entrepreneurs*. Newbury Park, Calif.: Sage.

Waldinger, Roger, and Thomas Bailey. 1991. The continuing significance of race: Racial conflict and racial discrimination in construction. *Politics and Society* 19 (3): 291–323.

Weaver, Robert. 1948. *The Negro ghetto*. New York: Russell and Russell.

Yoon, In Jin. 1991a. The changing significance of ethnic and class resources in immigrant business. *International Migration Review* 25 (2): 303–31.

———. 1991b. *Self-help in business: Chinese-, Japanese-, Korean-Americans, blacks, and whites*. Ph. D. diss., University of Chicago.

Index

African American self-employment, 4, 5, 8–9, 11, 17–19, 21–2, 142–62, 163–88, 191. *See also self-employment headings*

age of business owner, 28, 34–9, 43–4, 47, 59–61, 64, 71–2, 197

Alien Land Laws, 7

Asian American self-employment, 2, 6, 12–13, 21, 27–8, 40–1, 97–121, 248. *See also self-employment headings*

Asian Indian self-employment, 67, 74, 78–9, 84–93. *See also self-employment headings*

Black Belt, of Chicago, 149

black capitalism, 19

Black Enterprise, 11

Black Star Line, 148

blocked mobility, 16–18, 20–1, 84–5, 94–5, 118; and Asian Americans, 70, 120; and class resources, 99; connection to traditional lines of business, 89; definition of, 16; and immigrant workers, 251; impact on self-employment, 101–14

blocked opportunities. *See* blocked mobility

borrowing for business startup: African

Americans, 191–2, 203–5; Asian Americans, 203–5; nonminorities, 192–3, 203–5

borrowing, by business owners, 125–39, 215–16

Brimmer, Andrew, 142–4

business capitalization: and equity, 4; African Americans, 191, 192, 194, 204; Asian Americans, 200–4; nonminorities, 192, 194

business services industry, 168–9

"buy black" campaign, 147–9

capital, debt: of firm, 4

capital, financial: and African American-owned businesses, 149, 189–91; and Asian-owned businesses, 104–5, 113, 189–90, 251; and Hispanic-owned businesses, 208; impacting business longevity, 64–9, 86–9, 208–9; impacting small business entry, 26–40, 104–6, 189–90; invested by small business owners, 1–3, 12, 20, 86–7, 91–2

capital, human: and African American-owned businesses, 163–88, 258; and Asian-immigrant-owned businesses, 104–5, 113, 133–4; and blocked oppor-

capital, human *(continued)*:
    tunities, 16–17; and firm longevity,
    86–7; constraints on self-employment
    entry, 26–40; impact on self-employ-
    ment, 4, 14, 190, 193–5; interaction
    with financial capital, 91–3
capital, social, 55–6, 64–9, 250; as deter-
    minants of small business longevity,
    64–9, 255–7
Characteristics of Business Owners
    (CBO) database: applicability to this
    study, 3–4; description and definition of
    terms, 262–4
child labor, in small business, 63
Chinatown, 24, 52, 56, 63, 250
Chinese self-employment, 121–41. *See
    also self-employment headings*
class resources, impact on self-employ-
    ment, 14–16, 20–1, 25
clienteles, business, 21; of African
    Americans, 142, 146, 151–2, 159,
    160–2; co-ethnic, 54, 66–8; and firm
    age, 41; and firm survival, 87–9; and
    profitability, 71–2; and protected mar-
    kets, 56–62; race-based, 6, 7, 8, 11; of
    Vietnamese, 74
Coca Cola Bottling Company, of
    Philadelphia, 11
Community Reinvestment Act, 8
construction industry, 27, 33–40, 45–9,
    160, 168–9, 173–4, 210
costs of self-employment, 105–6
Cuban Miami, 24

databases of businesses, 3; of U.S. Census
    Bureau, 25, 175, 177–80
debt, small business: of African
    Americans, 191, 193–5, 198, 205; of
    Asian Americans, 122–3, 205; of busi-
    ness owners, 126–34, 137; financing
    patterns, 216. *See also* capital, debt
Detroit's Sheltered Market program, 234
discrimination. *See* racial discrimina-
    tion
diversification, of minority businesses,
    8–13, 151–61
D'Souza, Dinesh, 230
Du Bois, W.E.B., 145

econometric models of firm survival, 45–9
Economic Opportunity Loan (EOL) pro-
    gram, 143–4, 170–1, 172

educational levels, and skilled services
    business entry, 33–6
educational patterns of small business
    owners: of African Americans, 4, 9–11,
    21–2, 25, 151, 157–8, 164–8, 258; of
    Asian Americans, 10–13, 20, 55, 58, 92,
    95–6, 211, 223, 248–9, 251, 253, 255;
    of Asian Indians, 99–101, 106–13, 251;
    of Chinese, 7, 99–101, 106–13, 223; of
    Filipinos, 99–101, 106–13; of Japanese,
    252–3; of Koreans, 99–101, 106–13,
    223; of nonminorities, 164–5; of
    Vietnamese, 99–101
emerging firms, 151–61, 185–6
enterprise zones, 18
ethnic economies, 51–3; and employee
    loyalty, 62–3; and family labor, 63–4
ethnicity: clientele, 7; entrepreneurs,
    15–16; in business formation, 250; soli-
    darity, 118–20; workforce, 16, 249
ethnic stratification, 145

family members: involvement in self-
    employment, 52, 83, 89; loans to busi-
    ness owners, 127–41, 153, 198, 205,
    216–19
farming, 7
Filipino self-employment, 79, 84–93. *See
    also self-employment headings*
financing self-employment, 121–3; in
    retailing, 215–20; loan size/source,
    128–37; social capital, 123–8. *See also*
    family members; loans
firm distribution by industry, 166

Garvey, Marcus, 148
geographic concentration of small busi-
    nesses, 51–2, 57, 62, 65, 78; in immi-
    grant ethnic communities, 51–2
ghetto economic development, 19,
    168–70, 172
government policies and self-employment
    patterns, 18–20
government preferential procurement
    practices, 20, 225, 230–9, 246–7; and
    African Americans, 230; and Asian
    Americans, 230; and nonminorities,
    229–31; and set-aside legislation, 174–5
government small business assistance, 22,
    225–9, 235–47; to African Americans,
    227–9; to Asian Americans, 227; char-
    acteristics of assisted firms, 226–31

Great Depression, 148, 150, 252
grocery stores, 2, 5, 12

Hayti district of Durham, North
  Carolina, 148, 150
Hispanic self-employment, 19, 63. *See also*
  self-employment headings
Houghton, Mary, 172–3

immigrant ethnic communities, geographic concentration of, 51–2
immigrants, 10–11, 254; as entrepreneurs,
  52, 56–7, 207; illegal workers, 18–19;
  self-employment, 2, 12, 13, 21, 210–11;
  and upward mobility, 207–15
Immigration Act of 1924, 252
industry types. *See individual industry*
  headings

Japanese self-employment, 7. *See also self-*
  employment headings
Jim Crow, 146

King, Rodney, 170
Korean self-employment, 16–17, 18–19,
  78, 121–41. *See also self-employment*
  headings

labor, sources of, 62–4
language barriers impacting entrepreneurship, 17, 80–1, 84: of Asian
  Americans, 102–3, 106–16, 133; of
  Asian Indians, 102–3, 106–13, 251; of
  Chinese, 102–3, 106–18; of Filipinos
  102–3, 106–13; of Koreans, 1–3,
  106–18; of Vietnamese, 102–3; rates,
  43–8
laundries, 6, 7, 12, 20, 54
life cycle, of Asian-owned businesses,
  91–4
life insurance industry, 146–8, 150
Light, Ivan, 1, 2, 3, 6, 7, 16–19, 50–3, 56,
  66, 73–4, 78, 121–4, 207, 210–11, 215,
  249–50, 256–7; theory of overcoming
  financial capital barriers, 199–203
loans, availability of for small business: to
  African Americans, 148–9, 151, 173–4,
  217; to Asian Americans, 217; to
  Chinese, 217; to Koreans, 16–17,
  19–20, 215
loans, government: to minority borrowers, 8–9, 19–20, 235–6; to nonminority

borrowers, 228. *See also* government
  preferential procurement practices
loans, small business, 8–9, 19–20, 121–37,
  148, 170–4, 215, 250; for college-educated owners, 129–34, 135–9
longevity, firm. *See* self-employment
  longevity; survival, firm

manufacturing industry, 84–5, 166–7, 169,
  192
marital status of business owners, 27,
  31–5, 43, 47, 63–4, 69, 71–2, 87, 89
market accessibility: of African
  Americans, 163–88, 257–8; of Asian
  Americans, 110–13, 254, 257–8
Maryland's Minority Business Enterprise
  program, 234
mayors, African American: impact on
  black entrepreneurship, 174–88, 230–2,
  234–5
minorities: and business, 4–5, 7–8, 12,
  18–20, 27, 39, 41, 52; business aid to,
  172–4; employment opportunities,
  17–18, 25, 175–6; receiving government loans, 5–9, 19–20, 235–6
minority business enterprise (MBE), 152,
  234–47
Minority Enterprise Small Business
  Investment Company (MESBIC), 19

net wealth: of African Americans versus
  whites, 196–9; of Asian Americans, 100;
  and holdings of business owners,
  27–40, 81–3, 87, 152–3, 189–90, 194–9,
  212–15
net worth, household, 20
newspapers, African American community, 146
Nixon, Richard, 19
nonminority self-employment, 3, 4, 20,
  27. *See also self-employment headings*
North Carolina Mutual Insurance
  Company, 146

personal services industry, 53–4, 166–7,
  168–9
personal wealth, and likelihood of self-
  employment entry, 29–33
Philadelphia Negro, The, 145
printing industry, African American, 146
procurement. *See* government preferential
  procurement practices

product markets, protected, 56–7, 62
professional services industry, 53–5, 168–9
profitability of small businesses, 21, 69–73, 79–84; of Asian Americans, 107, 109, 114–18
push and pull factors impacting self-employment, 16, 77–84, 106–7, 113–18; high- and low-yielding businesses, 84–6

race riots, 145–7, 170
Race Traits and Tendencies of the American Negro, 146
racial discrimination: impact on African American-owned businesses, 163; in education of minorities, 6; in the labor market, 1, 6, 17, 24, 62, 144, 163, 252; and racial caste system, 6, 8
racial segregation: in black-owned businesses, 142–44, 148; in Japanese-owned businesses, 252–3
Reagan administration, 18
rehab industry (building), 173–4
resources, social, 15–18, 20–1
restaurants, 6, 7, 12, 53–4
retail industry, 6, 11–12, 53–4, 81–2, 168–9, 211–12, 212–24
rotating credit associations (RCAs), 15, 122–4, 126–8, 140, 202–3, 256–7

sales of firms, gross, 4
Self-Employment Investment Demonstration (SEID) project, 171
self-employment longevity: exit, 25; opportunity structures, 14, 25; theories of entry, 25, 40, 55, 77, 84–91, 190
self-employment rates, 5–6, 21, 27–8, 77–8, 84–91; of African Americans, 24–5, 248–9; of Asian Americans, 12, 95–8, 103–6, 248, 251, 259; of Asian Indians, 97–101, 103–6, 113, 251, 254; of Chinese, 97–101, 103–6, 251; disparities between races, 38–40; of English, 13; of Filipinos, 13, 97–101, 103–6, 251, 254; of Hispanics, 50–2; of Koreans, 13, 24, 78, 83, 97–101, 103–6, 251; of Lebanese, 13; of males, 27–8, 31–8, 88; of Mexicans, 13; of Norwegians, 13; of Puerto Ricans, 13, 24; of United States, 97–101; of Vietnamese, 99–101, 103–6, 113

self-employment success, 213–14; of African Americans, 1, 6–12, 24, 143–4, 148–51, 175–7, 185, 190–1; of African Americans versus Asian Americans, 145; of Asian Americans, 77–9, 97, 248, 253–4; of Chinese, 218–19; in cities with black mayors, 175–6; definition of, 248; of Japanese, 6, 151–3, 252–3; of Koreans, 67, 217–19
skill-intensive service fields, 27–8, 33–8, 45–9, 81, 84–5, 87, 89, 190–1
Small Business Administration, 19, 143, 156, 170, 173
small business characteristics: of entrants, 24–7; of firms, 4, 125, 165, 168; of owners, 4, 6, 26–34, 39–40, 44, 156–7, 192, 208, 210–11, 251, 257, 259
South Shore Bank of Chicago, 172–4
Survey of Income and Program Participation (SIPP) database, 20, 28–9, 196–7, 198
survival, firm, 41–2, 44, 45–9, 59–61, 86–91, 215, 218–19; and education of owner, 44–5, 69–73

traditional business communities: African American, 120–1, 144–61, 173–5, 186; Chinese, 6–7, 57, 62; Japanese, 6–7; versus emerging lines of business, 5–13
transportation industry, 160, 166

upward mobility and self-employment: and capital invested, 208–11; and education of owner, 211–15
U.S. Commission on Minority Business Development, 171

Vietnamese self-employment, 67, 140. *See also self-employment headings*

wealth. *See* net wealth; personal wealth
welfare recipients, 171
wholesaling industry, 84, 167
work experience and self-employment, 10, 27, 29–30, 36, 38, 40, 48, 59–61, 65, 87–8, 159–61; of immigrants, 17, 27, 83–4
World War I, 145–7, 163
World War II, 252